New Directions in Crochet

A Studio Book
The Viking Press~
New York

New Directions in Crochet

A Diagrammed Course to Easier Crocheting, with More Than 200 Designs and Patterns

Anne Rabun Ough

To the "Cs" in my life

Copyright © 1981 by Anne Rabun Ough
All rights reserved

First published in 1981 by The Viking Press (A Studio Book)
625 Madison Avenue, New York, N.Y. 10022

Published simultaneously in Canada by
Penguin Books Canada Limited

Library of Congress Cataloging in Publication Data
Ough, Anne Rabun.
  New directions in crochet.
  (A Studio book)
  Includes index.
  1. Crocheting. 2. Crocheting—Patterns.
  I. Title. TT820.093   746.43′4   80-52646
ISBN 0-670-40008-4

Printed in the United States of America
Color printed in Japan by
Dai Nippon Printing Company Ltd., Tokyo

Set in Times Roman

Contents

I wish to express my thanks to my associate, Charlotte Rabun, and to the photographers Doug Fong and Spectrographics of Davis, California.

—A.R.O.

Introduction

All the basic instructions in this book are given in both American and British terms. Directions for making the pattern stitches are given in written crochet abbreviations and in diagrams which employ a system of symbols, a graphic shorthand form of notation which is used extensively in Japan and to an increasing degree in Europe. This system has been adapted and expanded here to include all the symbols necessary to make all the stitches and patterns presented in this book. A complete glossary of the symbols is given in the first chapter of the book. Once you have learned these symbols, you will be able to follow crochet patterns much more quickly than ever before. I also include written instructions for the benefit of those skilled crocheters who are accustomed to them and may prefer to use this familiar method, but even these have been improved to make following them easier.

The large percentage of crocheters who usually need a finished piece of crochet or the help of a friend to guide them in learning a new stitch will find that these easily mastered basic symbols provide an immediately recognizable picture of the pattern as a whole and of each stitch to be made—one that can be followed with much greater clarity than a photographed sample alone. The method condenses the most intricate designs into easily followed diagrams. I have also attempted to provide symbols that suggest the action to be taken as well as the stitch to be made. With these symbol diagrams, checking the progress of your crocheting becomes simpler, and the tedium of trying to keep your place in lengthy written directions is eliminated. The uniformity of your crocheting also should be enormously improved, because the symbols in the diagram and the crocheted stitches have the same dimensional relationships.

Because no one crochet guide can really contain all the variations possible, a complete selection of basic stitches and patterns is given here, but I include only a limited number of examples of the use of symbol crochet in such areas as Jacquard, filet, and the making of motifs. The imaginative reader, however, may use these basic stitches and patterns to create an infinite number of new patterns.

The section on Fisherman crochet adds new dimensions to the craft. There I have included my own new "cable" stitch and adapted other crochet stitches to create patterns that look like Aran Island or Fisherman knits. For the reader who has been hesitant to undertake Fisherman knits because of their difficulty, Fisherman crochet offers an opportunity to accomplish similar effects while using simpler techniques.

Jacquard crochet allows the crocheter to follow knitting or other needlework color graphs to create multicolor woven effects. The Extended Single Crochet stitch (introduced here as a "basic" stitch) will work a gauge of approximately the same number of stitches per inch as rows per inch and adds an ideal means of achieving exciting Jacquard designs and patterns.

Chapter 8 on Crochet Embroidery (also known as tambour work) includes patterns that offer the reader a modern application of this quick, simple method of embroidery, and still another way to use the skills and materials of crochet.

To inspire the reader to start using some of these easy-to-follow patterns, I have selected a few elegant but simple projects. The crocheted garments, including a poncho and a coat pattern, which may be shortened to make a sweater, can be made in any stitch pattern desired, using the basic measurements given for each piece in the garment.

That the book includes both "new" stitches and old stitches adapted for new use has been noted. Although many of these are stitches that I have never seen in print and consider original, some crocheters at some time or other may have experimented with all of them. The combination of a hand, a hook, and a piece of thread is probably the most creative craft situation known.

"A picture is worth a thousand words" may be a slight exaggeration and an old cliché, but with a little effort you may decide that it does apply to Symbol Crochet diagrams.

Chapter 1

How to Crochet ▮▮▮▮▮▮▮▮▮▮▮▮▮▮▮▮▮▮▮▮▮▮▮▮▮▮

Directions for making the Basic Stitches of crochet are given in the following pages in both American and British terms. Terms used in the United Kingdom are enclosed in brackets with the initials UK following the name of the stitch. However, once you have learned the system of international crochet symbols in the Glossary in this chapter, you will be able to work all the patterns without the aid of these conventional terms—the symbol diagrams will show you quickly and easily just what to do.

In the pattern directions, abbreviations appear in both capital and small letters. Capital letters represent verbs—a stitch to be made or an action to be taken. Small letters represent a noun—a stitch that is to be worked *into*. For example, "Work a DC in each of next 4 sc" or "Skip 1 st, SC in last ch, Ch 4, Turn." All abbreviations and symbols used in the pattern sections are explained in the Glossary.

A new basic stitch ▮▮▮

A newcomer to the list of Basic Stitches is the Extended Single Crochet (ExSC). (You may have experimentally encountered this stitch in the past but here it is given a formal name—and you will find that it forms the basis of some interesting new stitch patterns given in later chapters.) This is a very versatile stitch which creates a softer fabric than one worked in single, half-double, or double crochet, and yet it is solid. It is an excellent stitch for making such things as sweaters, baby afghans, or mittens. As noted in the Introduction, it is a useful stitch for following color graphs, for it works out to approximately the same number of stitches per inch as rows per inch.

Measurements are given in both inches and centimeters, and yarn quantities are specified as grams as well as ounces. Centimeter equivalents are rounded off to the nearest inch. Yarn quantities are rounded off to multiples of the number of ounces in an average skein of the recommended yarn.

BASIC STITCHES

To start

1. Make a loop.

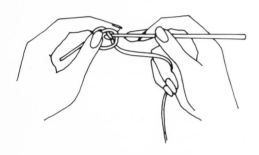

2. Insert hook and pull bottom thread up through loop.

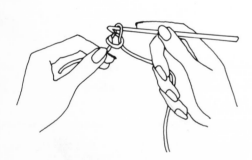

3. Tighten loop.

Chain Stitches (Ch)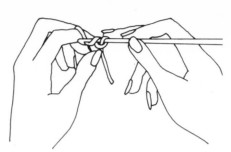

1. Yarn over (YO—wrap yarn around hook).

2. Pull yarn through loop on hook, forming a new loop. Repeat steps 1 and 2, forming a chain of loops.

Slip Stitch (Sl St) [UK Single Crochet]

1. Skip last chain stitch made and insert hook under two threads of second stitch from hook.

2. Pull yarn through chain and on through loop on hook.

3. Insert hook under two threads of next chain. Repeat 2.

Single Crochet (SC) [UK Double Crochet] ✝

3. Bring yarn over hook and through both loops.

4. Insert hook under two threads of next chain and yarn over. Repeat 2 and 3 to end of row. Chain 1 to turn. (The turning chain forms the first stitch of the next row.)

Extended Single Crochet (ExSC) [UK Extended Double Crochet] ✝

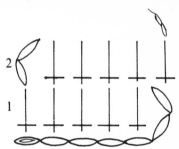

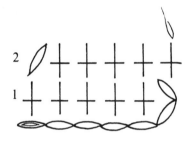

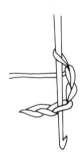

1. Skip two chains. Insert hook under two threads of next chain.

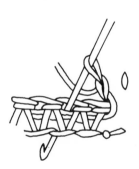

5. To start first stitch of Row 2, insert hook in second stitch of previous row.

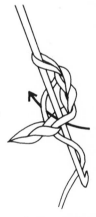

1. Skip two chain stitches. Insert hook under two threads of next chain and yarn over.

2. Pull yarn through chain. You now have two loops on hook. Bring yarn over hook and *through one loop only,* leaving two loops on hook.

2. Pull up yarn. You now have two loops on hook.

6. In last stitch of Row 2, chain 1 to turn.

11

3. Bring yarn over hook and take it through *both* loops.

4. Start second stitch in next chain. Insert hook, yarn over, and repeat 2 and 3 to end of row. Chain 2 to turn. The turning chain forms the first stitch of the next row.

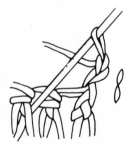

5. Start Row 2 in second stitch of previous row. Work to end of row.

6. Last stitch of Row 2. Chain 2 to turn and continue as above.

Half Double Crochet (HDC) [UK Half Treble Crochet]

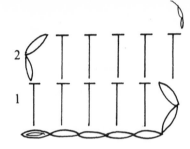

1. Bring yarn over hook.

2. Insert hook under two threads of third chain from hook, yarn over again, and pull yarn through chain. You will have three loops on hook.

3. Bring yarn over hook and through all three loops.

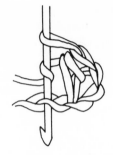

4. Yarn over hook and insert hook under two threads of next chain. Repeat 2 and 3. Work to end of row. Chain 2. Turn. The turning chain forms the first stitch of the next row.

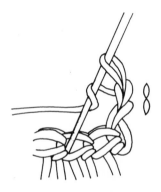

5. Start Row 2 in second stitch of previous row. Work as above to end of row.

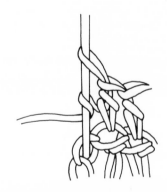

6. Last stitch of Row 2. Continue working rows in this manner.

Double Crochet (DC) [UK Treble Crochet]

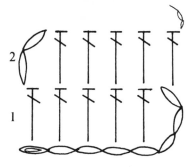

1. Yarn over hook.

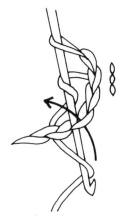

2. Skip three chains and insert hook under two threads of next chain. Pull yarn through stitch. There will be three loops on hook.

3. Yarn over hook and draw the thread through two loops. Two loops remain on hook.

4. Yarn over hook and draw thread through two remaining loops.

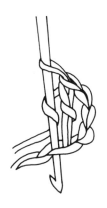

5. To start next stitch, yarn over hook and insert hook under two threads of next chain. Repeat 3 and 4. Continue to end of row. Chain (Ch) 2 to turn. The turning chain forms the first stitch of the next row.

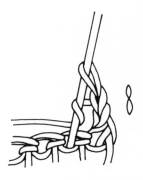

6. Start Row 2 in second stitch of previous row. Work to end of row.

7. Last stitch of row. Complete stitch and Chain 2 to turn. Continue working rows in this manner.

Triple Crochet (TC) [UK Double Treble]

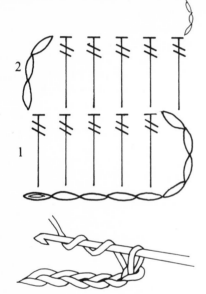

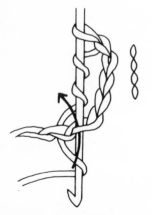

1. Yarn over hook two times.

2. Skip four chains. Insert hook under two threads of next chain. Pull yarn up through chain. You will have four loops on hook.

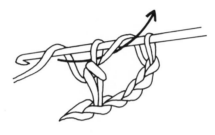

3. Yarn over and through two loops. (Three loops remain on hook.)

4. Yarn over and through two loops. (Two loops remain.)

5. Yarn over and through two loops.

6. To start next stitch, yarn over 2 times. Insert hook under two threads of next chain. Pull yarn up through chain. Repeat 2, 3, and 4. Continue to end of row. Chain 3, turn.

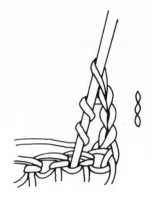

7. Start Row 2 in second stitch of previous row. Work to end of row.

8. Last stitch of Row 2. Chain 3 to turn and continue working rows in this manner.

Double Triple Crochet (DTC) [UK Treble Treble]

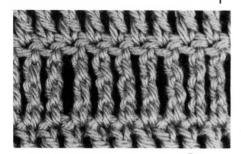

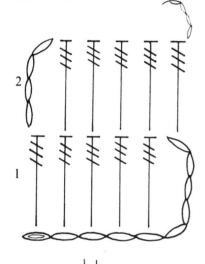

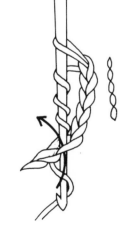

1. Yarn over hook three times. Skip five chains. Insert hook under two threads of next chain. Pull thread up through chain, making five loops on hook. Yarn over and through two loops 4 times. Chain four to turn at end of row.

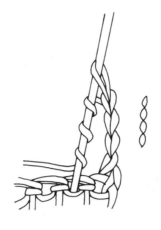

2. Start Row 2 in second stitch of previous row. Work to end of row.

3. Last stitch of Row 2. Chain 4 to turn and continue to work rows in this manner.

Triple Triple Crochet (TTC) [UK Double Treble Treble]

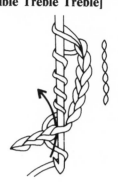

1. Yarn over hook four times. Skip six chains. Insert hook under two threads of next chain. Pull yarn up through chain (six loops on hook). Yarn over and through two loops 5 times. Chain 5 to turn at end of row.

2. Start Row 2. Work to end.

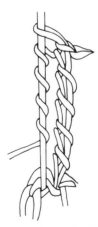

3. Last stitch of Row 2. Chain 5 to turn and continue to work rows in this manner.

Compound stitches

Such names as ball, puff, popcorn, cluster, and the like are given to those stitches that are made by working many stitches into another stitch. These have been divided into three groups—Puff, Popcorn, and Cluster—according to the manner in which they are worked. Each of these compound stitches is represented by a symbol which indicates the number and type of basic stitches to be worked and is explained in the Glossary.

Foundation chains

All crochet projects start with a foundation chain. One of the most common problems of crocheting is that the beginning of the work tends to "pull in" because the foundation chain is too tight. If you are unable to make a loose, even chain by releasing tension on the thread, either use a hook a size larger than the one you will use for the project, or use two strands of yarn and the hook designated for the project. Drop the second strand as you make the turning chain, leaving it out of the work from that point onward.

Turning

To bring the work into position for starting a new row, it is necessary to make a *turning chain* at the end of each row. Because the depth of the different stitches varies, the length of the turning chains also varies, as noted in the instructions for the Basic Stitches.

In the instructions for most of the stitches and stitch patterns in this book there is one more chain in the first turning chain than in the second and subsequent turning chains. The extra chain at the beginning of the first row is necessary to form the base or foot of the stitch, while in the second and subsequent rows the last stitch in the row becomes the base. *The pattern diagrams show where to insert your hook for the first and last stitch of the second row. By making sure that your stitches conform to these diagrams you will always achieve square and even edges along the borders of your work.*

Tension

The tension (the tautness or "drag") of the thread as it is worked is important both to the quality of the stitch and to the ease of crocheting. When the thread is held too loosely the stitches are too open and "stringy" and when it is held too tightly the stitches are difficult to work and are hard to the touch. In crocheting the hand should be relaxed and the muscles used should be only those necessary to hold the hook in one hand and the work in the other. Your grip should be only tight enough so that the hook or the work does not fall out of your hands. The working thread may be looped over the first finger, under the middle finger, and over the little finger. Some crocheters find that just letting the thread fall under the first finger provides enough tension. The degree of tension you use will affect the gauge of the pattern you are following and thus the dimensions of the article you are making.

GLOSSARY OF INTERNATIONAL SYMBOLS

		UNITED STATES	UNITED KINGDOM
1	⬯	Chain (Ch)	Chain
2	⬯	First chain	First chain
3	⬮	Slip Stitch (Sl St)	Single Crochet or Slip Stitch
4	†	Single Crochet (SC)	Double Crochet
5	⊥	Extended Single Crochet (ExSC)	Extended Double Crochet
6	T	Half Double Crochet (HDC)	Half Treble Crochet
7	⊤	Double Crochet (DC)	Treble Crochet
8	⧧	Triple Crochet (TC)	Long or Double Treble Crochet
9	⧣	Double Triple Crochet (DTC)	Treble Treble Crochet
10	⧣	Triple Triple Crochet (TTC)	Double Treble Treble Crochet
11	⊥	Work stitch in front loop only.	Work stitch in front loop only.

	UNITED STATES	UNITED KINGDOM

12 ⊥ Work stitch in back loop only.

Work stitch in back loop only.

13 ⊥ Work under 2 strands of stitch.

Work under 2 strands of stitch.

14 ⊥ Work under chain.

Work under chain.

15 Working from the *Front,* work *around* the stitch.

Working from the *Front,* work *around* the stitch.

16 Working from the *Back,* work *around* the stitch.

Working from the *Back,* work *around* the stitch.

17 Work stitch from back. (Any stitch shown with dotted lines is a stitch to be worked *in back* of another or *from the back.*)

Work stitch from back. (Any stitch shown with dotted lines is a stitch to be worked *in back* of another or *from the back.*)

18 Make stitch longer than normal; make it as long as the number of chains shown at the right of the symbol.

Make stitch longer than normal; make it as long as the number of chains shown at the right of the symbol.

19 Start a single crochet: hold the 2 loops on the hook.

Start a double crochet: hold the 2 loops on the hook.

20 Start a double crochet: hold 3 loops on the hook.

Start a treble crochet: hold 3 loops on the hook.

	UNITED STATES	UNITED KINGDOM
21	Start a triple crochet: hold 4 loops on the hook.	Start a double treble: hold 4 loops on the hook.
22	Start a double triple crochet: hold 5 loops on the hook.	Start a treble treble: hold 5 loops on the hook.
23	Yarn over and through 1 loop.	Yarn over and through 1 loop.
24	Yarn over and through 2 loops.	Yarn over and through 2 loops.
25	Yarn over and through 3 loops, etc.	Yarn over and through 3 loops, etc.
26	Small Popcorn: Work 3 single crochets in same stitch. Remove hook from loop and insert it under 2 threads of first single crochet. Pull dropped loop through.	Small Popcorn: Work 3 double crochets in same stitch. Remove hook from loop and insert it under 2 threads of first double crochet. Pull dropped loop through.
27	Medium Popcorn: Work 4 double crochets in same stitch. Remove hook from loop and insert it under 2 threads of first double crochet. Pull dropped loop through.	Medium Popcorn: Work 4 treble crochets in same stitch. Remove hook from loop and insert it under 2 threads of first treble crochet. Pull dropped loop through.
28	Large Popcorn: Work 5 triple crochets in same stitch. Remove hook from loop and insert it under 2 strands of first triple crochet. Pull dropped loop through.	Large Popcorn: Work 5 double treble crochets in same stitch. Remove hook from loop and insert it under 2 strands of first double treble crochet. Pull dropped loop through.
29	Medium Puff (Bobble or Ball): (Yarn over, insert hook and pull up thread) 4 times in same stitch. Yarn over and through all loops on hook.	Medium Puff (Bobble or Ball): (Yarn over, insert hook and pull up thread) 4 times in same stitch. Yarn over and through all loops on hook.

30

Large Puff (Bobble or Ball):
(Yarn over 2 times, insert hook and
pull up thread) 5 times in same stitch.
Yarn over and through all loops on
hook.

Large Puff (Bobble or Ball):
(Yarn over 2 times, insert hook and
pull up thread) 5 times in same stitch.
Yarn over and through all loops on
hook.

31

Small Cluster Stitch: (Insert hook,
pull up thread, yarn over and through
1 loop) 3 times in same stitch. Yarn
over and through all loops on hook.

Small Cluster Stitch: (Insert hook,
pull up thread, yarn over and through
1 loop) 3 times in same stitch. Yarn
over and through all loops on hook.

32

Medium Cluster Stitch: (Yarn over,
insert hook, pull up thread, yarn over
and through 2 loops) 4 times in same
stitch. Yarn over and through all
loops on hook.

Medium Cluster Stitch: (Yarn over,
insert hook, pull up thread, yarn over
and through 2 loops) 4 times in same
stitch. Yarn over and through all
loops on hook.

33

Large Cluster Stitch: (Yarn over 2
times, insert hook and pull up thread.
Yarn over and through 2 loops twice)
5 times in same stitch. Yarn over and
through all loops on hook.

Large Cluster Stitch: (Yarn over 2
times, insert hook and pull up thread.
Yarn over and through 2 loops twice)
5 times in same stitch. Yarn over and
through all loops on hook.

34

Do not turn.

Do not turn.

35

Follow to next stitch.

Follow to next stitch.

36

Indicates color to use.

Indicates color to use.

37

Repeat these stitches as needed for
pattern repeat; complete row by working the remainder of the stitches in
the row.

Repeat these stitches as needed for
pattern repeat; complete row by working the remainder of the stitches in
the row.

Determining stitch gauge

The stitch gauge is a measurement of the number of stitches horizontally, and the number of rows vertically, per inch (or in a given number of centimeters), in a sample square of a given pattern. In most cases the gauge depends on the size of the thread or yarn and the hook used, but it is affected by the tension with which you hold the yarn. Standard patterns for items which must be made to a specific size, such as coats or sweaters, usually indicate what the gauge is to be. Always make a sample swatch for any specific project. Using the size hook and the yarn suggested in the chosen pattern, work a 4″ × 4″ (10cm × 10cm) swatch, lay it flat, and measure the height and width to see if the number of stitches per inch conforms to that given in the pattern. If you have too many stitches per inch, try a larger hook. If there are too few, the next smaller hook may solve the problem. Some crocheters have to use hooks several sizes different from those suggested in a pattern to obtain the proper gauge.

Later in this book, you will find an outline diagram giving measurements for making a coat or sweater in three different sizes. A Check stitch pattern is suggested, but by using the method given above for determining the gauge, you might make the same garment with any one of a number of attractive stitch patterns given in this book. Whenever you are adapting patterns for garments or combining pattern stitches to make patchwork afghans, working the sample swatch to determine gauge is the first step in making sure that all the pieces fit together.

Remember also that lacy patterns tend to be smaller in area than solid patterns with the same number of stitches. To be sure that two patterns will match for joining, you may have to switch to a larger hook to work the lacy parts.

To make any flat article, choose your yarn and hook and make a sample of 4″ × 4″ swatch. Count the number of stitches per inch in the width of the article to be made. This will tell you how many stitches are required for your foundation chain. Be sure to allow for the requirements of the multiple of the pattern stitch you have chosen as described below.

Multiples

To determine the length of the foundation chain for an article made in a pattern stitch, the multiple of that stitch must be taken into consideration. The multiple is given at the beginning of each stitch pattern in this book, immediately below the name of the stitch. The multiple indicates how many stitches there are in each pattern repeat and (in some cases) how many stitches are needed for beginning or ending the row, plus the number of chain stitches needed to turn at the beginning of the first row to start the pattern. For example, "multiple of 5 + 1 plus 3 chs" means that in order to make a foundation chain of sufficient length to make four repeats of the pattern, you must multiply 4 times 5, then add 1 (making a total of 21 stitches) *plus* 3 more chain stitches. The final three stitches form the turning chain needed to begin Row 1 and become the first stitch.

If you wish to combine different pattern stitches in a single article (such as an afghan) remember that both must have multiples that work out to the same number of stitches per row or else you must increase (or decrease) the number of stitches at the *beginning of the final* row of Pattern A so that it will equal the number of stitches required by the multiple of Pattern B. In figuring the total number of stitches per row, include only the number of stitches in the multiple itself (i.e., the 5 + 1) and not the *plus* figure given for the turning chain.

Attaching thread

To attach thread at any point along a row of crocheting:

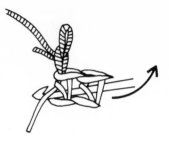

1. Insert the hook under both threads of the stitch. Pull up the new thread, leaving a tail about 1 or 2″ long.

2. Hold the doubled ends together and continue working. In this illustration, the new yarn is being added in a row of Double Crochet stitches.

3. Insert the hook in the old stitches and pull the tail of the thread in the old color inside the stitches.

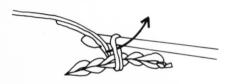

2. Make one or more chains (depending on the stitch being used) with the doubled thread.

Changing colors at the end of a row

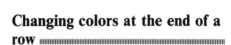

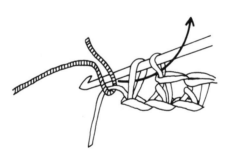

1. On the last yarn-over before the color change, overlap 1″ of the new color with 1″ of the old color.

Tying off

To tie off completed work, make an extra chain stitch. Cut the thread a few inches away from the work. Bring the cut end through the loop of the chain stitch and pull it up tightly, thus making a knot. Work the loose end into the back of the work with a crochet hook or darning needle.

Adding new yarn

When you come to the end of a ball of yarn and must work in a new one:

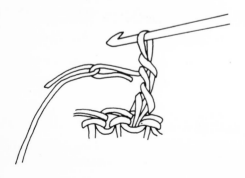

1. Overlap the ends of the old and new strands about 1 or 2″.

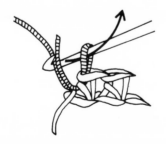

2. Pull up the doubled new color and make a chain with this doubled strand.

Shaping

Designs for sweaters, jackets, skirts, and other garments frequently involve shaping them to suit the needs of size or fashion. Shaping is accomplished by increasing or decreasing the length of the rows, either at the end or beginning of the row, or within the row.

To increase

A

To increase 1 stitch at the beginning of a row: Work a stitch in the first stitch (the one at the base of the turning chain that is normally skipped).

B

To increase 1 stitch in the middle or at the end of a row: Work 2 stitches in the same stitch. To increase many stitches in one row, distribute the increases evenly throughout the row.

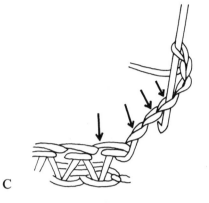

C

To increase more than 1 stitch at the beginning of a row: Chain the number of stitches to be added plus the number needed for a normal turning chain. Skip the number of chains you would skip if you were working the first row of the pattern (1 more than the normal turning chain) and work back across the chain. The drawing shows an increase of 4 stitches in a row of single crochet.

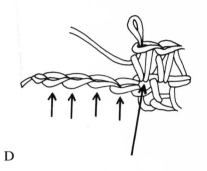

D

To increase at the beginning and the end of the same row: Increase at the beginning as above. At the end of the row attach a new thread in the turning chain, chain 1 more than the number of stitches to be increased, cut the thread and pull up the last chain tightly to form a tie-off. Continue working the row across the added chain. Here an increase of 4 stitches is being added to a row of single crochet.

Increasing

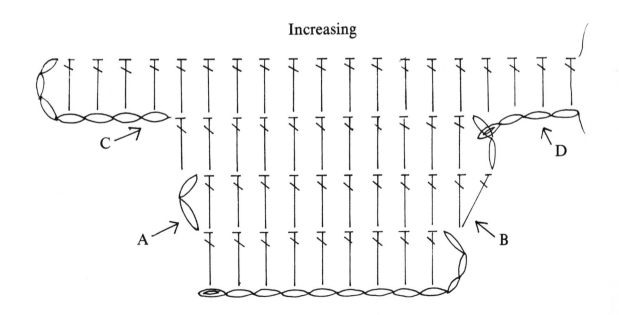

To decrease

A

To decrease 1 stitch in single crochet, extended single crochet or half-double crochet: Pull up the thread in the next 2 stitches, bring the yarn over the hook and draw it through 3 loops.

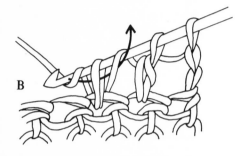

B

To decrease 1 stitch in double crochet: (Yarn over, insert hook, pull up thread, yarn over and through 2 loops) in each of the next two stitches.

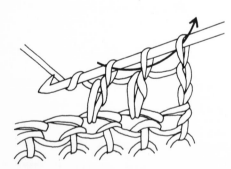

Yarn over and through the 3 loops on the hook. Work triple crochet, double triple, etc. in the same manner, holding the last loop of the stitch on the hook for 2 stitches, then work them off together.

To decrease many stitches in one row: Work as above, being sure to distribute the decreases evenly throughout the row.

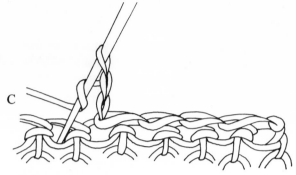

C

To decrease more than 1 stitch at the beginning of a row: Do not make a turning chain at the end of the row. Instead, turn and slip stitch across the number of stitches to be decreased. Make the number of turning chains required for the stitch in use and continue across the row in the usual manner. Here 4 stitches are being decreased in a row of double crochet.

Or you may cut the thread at the end of the row, skip the number of stitches to be decreased, and attach the thread in next stitch. (Be sure to count turning chain as one of the stitches to be skipped.)

D

To decrease many stitches at end of row: Do not work number of stitches to be decreased; work across the row to that point, then turn the work, remembering to count the turning chain of the previous row among the stitches to be left unworked.

Decreasing

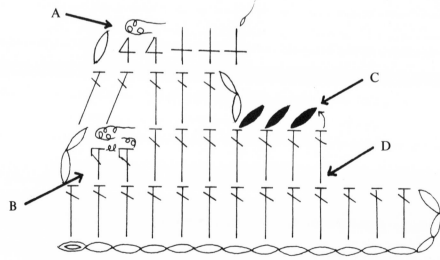

Joining

Crocheted articles may be joined
either by sewing them together with
an overcasting stitch, or slip-stitching
them together with a crochet hook.
Articles meant to lie flat should be
sewn. Those that are meant to show a
visible seam, such as sweaters or
jackets, should be crocheted together.

Overcasting

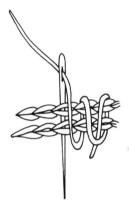

Use a large blunt needle and the same
thread as that used in the crocheting.
Take the needle under both strands of
the stitches on either side of the seam
and overcast them together as you
would in ordinary sewing. Be careful
not to pull the yarn too tight or it will
make the seam appear corded.

Slip-stitching

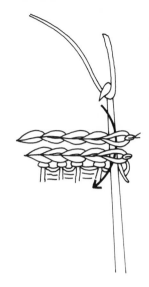

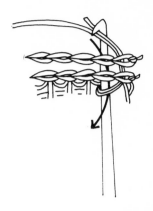

1. Holding right sides together, insert
   the hook under both strands of the
   stitches on either side of the seam.
   Draw the yarn through the stitches,
   leaving a loop on the hook.

2. With the loop on the hook, insert
   the hook under the next adjoining
   stitches and pull the yarn through
   the stitches and the loop, leaving a
   new loop on the hook. Repeat until
   the seam is closed, and tie off.

Edgings and borders

Many of the pattern stitches in this book can be used as decorative edgings for shawls, afghans, and other articles. Directions for adapting them as edgings are noted in brackets following the instructions for many of the patterns given in Chapters 2, 3, and 4. To add an edging, a base is needed. A border of one or two rows of Single or Double Crochet makes a firm foundation for this purpose, or will serve as a finishing touch by itself.

Side borders

To make a border along the *sides* of an article worked in a pattern stitch, lay the work flat and mark it with safety pins every 3″ (7.5cm). Between the pins, work three times the number of stitches as there are in your stitch gauge for the article. (If your stitch gauge is 3 stitches per inch, there should be 9 stitches between each pair of pins.)

If the article has been worked in one of the Basic Stitches, the following chart will serve as a guide to working the side borders:

Single Crochet	1 stitch per row
Extended Single Crochet	4 stitches for every 3 rows
Half Double Crochet	4 stitches for every 3 rows
Double Crochet	3 stitches for every 2 rows
Triple Crochet	2 stitches per row
Double Triple Crochet	3 stitches per row

Border corners

Extra stitches are needed to carry a crocheted border around a corner or it will curl up instead of lying flat. Directions for working the corners of plain borders done in each of the Basic Stitches are as follows:

Single Crochet (SC)

Method A (solid corners): Work 3 SC at each corner. On 2nd and subsequent rows, work 3 SC in middle sc of previous row. When working more than 7 rows, work only 1 SC at corner of every 8th row.

Method B (open corners): Work SC, Ch 1, SC at each corner. On 2nd and subsequent rows, work SC, Ch 1, SC under ch of previous row. When working more than 7 rows, do not increase at corners on every 8th row. However, if you skipped working under the ch, you would have a large opening, so work as follows: In last st before corner, Pull Up thread, Pull Up thread under ch, YO and through 3 loops. Ch 1, Pull Up thread under ch, Pull Up thread in next st, YO and through 3 loops. (This is the same as working a decrease.)

Extended Single Crochet (ExSC)

Method A (*solid corners*): Work 3 ExSC at each corner. On 2nd and subsequent rows, work 3 ExSC in middle st of previous row. When working more than 10 rows, work 5 ExSC at each corner every 11th row.

Method B (*open corners*): Work ExSC, Ch 1, ExSC at each corner. On 2nd and subsequent rows work ExSC, Ch 1, ExSC under ch of previous row. When working more than 10 rows, work 2 ExSC, Ch 1, 2 ExSC every 11th row.

Half Double Crochet (HDC)

Method A (*solid corners*): Work 3 HDC at each corner. On 2nd and subsequent rows, work 3 HDC in middle hdc of previous row. When working more than 4 rows, work 5 HDC at each corner every 5th row.

Method B (*open corners*): Work HDC, Ch 1, HDC at each corner. On 2nd and subsequent rows work HDC, Ch 1, HDC under ch of previous row. When working more than 4 rows, work 2 HDC, Ch 1, 2 HDC under ch at corner every 5th row.

Double Crochet (DC)

Method A (*solid corners*): Row 1: Work 5 DC at each corner. Row 2: Work 5 DC in middle dc of previous row. Row 3: Work 3 DC in middle st of previous row. Repeat these 3 rows.

Method B (*open corners*): Row 1: Work 2 DC, Ch 1, 2 DC at each corner. Row 2: Work 2 DC, Ch 1, 2 DC under ch of previous row. Row 3: Work DC, Ch 1, DC under ch of previous row. Repeat these 3 rows.

Triple Crochet (TC)

Method A (*solid corners*): Row 1: Work 7 TC at each corner. Row 2: Work 7 TC in middle tc of previous row. Row 3: Work 5 TC in middle stitch of previous row. Repeat these 3 rows.
Method B (*open corners*): Row 1: Work 3 TC, Ch 1, 3 TC at each corner. Row 2: Work 3 TC, Ch 1, 3 TC under ch of previous row. Row 3: Work 2 TC, Ch 1, 2 TC under ch of previous row. Repeat these 3 rows.

Double Triple Crochet (DTC)

Method A (*solid corners*): Work 7 DTC at each corner. On 2nd and subsequent rows work 7 DTC in middle dtc of previous row.
Method B (*open corners*): Work 3 DTC, Ch 1, 3 DTC at each corner. On 2nd and subsequent rows work 3 DTC, Ch 1, 3 DTC under ch of previous row.

Working corners of pattern stitch edgings

There are no easy formulas for working the corners of elaborate pattern stitch borders. The advanced crocheter will be able to work out individual solutions. The less experienced would be wise to choose patterns that have only 3 or 4 stitches in the pattern repeat for edgings that must be taken around corners. To turn corners with such patterns, work the number of stitches for the stitch used as given above.

Working corners of shell stitch borders

Shell patterns are favorites for borders. The following directions will enable you to work the corners of edgings adapted from Pattern Stitches 25, 26, 27, 28, 32, and 33 in Chapter 3.

As a base for the edging, work one or more rows of single crochet around the square or rectangle, working 3 single crochets at each corner. Tie off yarn.

Row 1: Counting the center stitch of the 3 single crochets at the corner as the first stitch, skip the number of stitches required for the pattern repeat (see Multiples, page 22) and attach the yarn in the next stitch. Chain the number of stitches indicated for the turning chain at the end of Row 1 of the pattern. Work as for the first row of the pattern. (There should be a shell in the center single crochet at each corner, so if necessary adjust the pattern along the sides by skipping either one more or one less stitch than specified in the pattern. If it is necessary to make several of these adjustments, distribute them evenly along the sides.) At the end of the row, work a Shell (counting the beginning chain as one stitch) in the same stitch where the yarn was attached. Slip Stitch to the last chain of the beginning chain, make the turning chain, and turn.

Row 2: Work in the pattern up to the corner. At the corner, work a Shell in the 2nd stitch of the corner shell, Ch 1 and work a Shell in the 4th stitch of corner shell. Continue around the rectangle following the pattern and making the corners as above. Finish the row with the last stitches of the pattern in the same stitch as first stitch of the row, Slip Stitch in the last chain of the turning chain, make the turning chain and turn.

Row 3: Work in pattern. At the corners, work a Shell in the chain between the 2 shells of the previous row. Complete the row as above.

Repeat Rows 2 and 3 for pattern.

Adding borders to woven fabric ‖‖

To add crocheted borders to woven fabric, make a sample swatch of the pattern to be used in order to determine the gauge. Hem the fabric by machine or by hand, or baste the hem and let a border of single crochet serve to hold the hem in place. Borders may be worked directly onto the fabric if it is loose-woven, otherwise a base of blanket stitch will be needed.

Blanket stitch ▌▌▌▌▌▌▌▌▌▌▌▌▌▌▌▌▌▌▌▌

Crocheted borders on woven fabric ▌▌▌▌▌▌▌▌▌▌▌▌▌▌▌▌▌▌

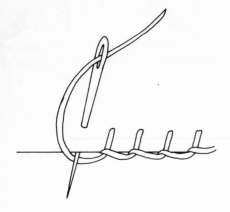

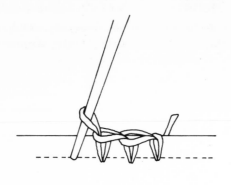

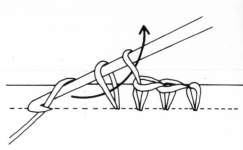

Work the blanket stitch along the hem with a tapestry needle. Make the same number of single crochet or blanket stitches per inch as there are stitches per inch in the gauge of your sample swatch of the edging pattern. Before starting a pattern stitch, you may want to add a row of single crochet stitches to the blanket stitch to make a firmer base.

To crochet directly into a woven fabric, use a steel hook. Insert the hook between the threads of the fabric and draw up a loop. Make a single crochet stitch. Continue across the hem, inserting the hook in the fabric between each crochet stitch. Make the same number of stitches per inch as there are stitches in your pattern gauge sample. Work three single crochet stitches at corners.

Making fringe ▌▌▌▌▌▌▌▌▌▌▌▌▌▌▌▌▌▌▌▌▌▌

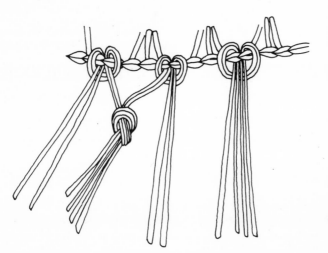

Decide on the length of the fringe desired. Cut the yarn double this length plus 2″ more if it is to be a plain fringe. For a double or triple tied fringe, add 2″ more for each tying. Fold the strands in the middle and bring them through the edge of the work, then bring the ends through the loop made by the folded strand. (In macramé, this is known as a reverse double half-hitch, or lark's head knot.) If the pattern stitch used to make the article does not have a firm edge, it is wise to add a border of single or double crochet to make a solid base for the fringe.

2

3

5

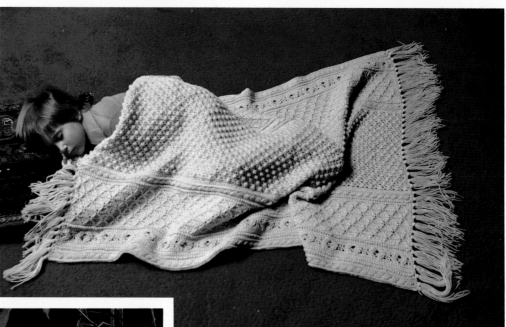

6

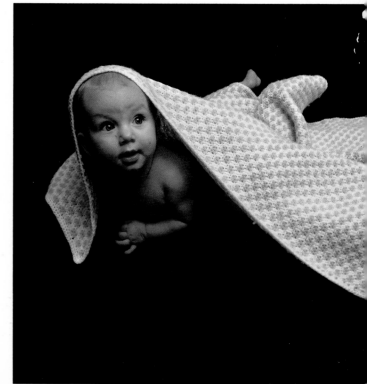

7

9

10

12

13

COMPARATIVE CROCHET HOOK SIZES

	ALUMINUM OR PLASTIC			STEEL	
U.S.	U.K.	Int'l (mm)	U.S.	U.K.	Int'l (mm)
	14	2	14	6	.6
	13		13	5½	
B	12	2.5	12	5	.75
C	11	3	11	4½	
D	10		10	4	1
E	9	3.5	9	3½	
F	8	4	8	3	1.25
G	7	4.5	7	2½	1.5
H	6	5	6	2	1.75
I	5	5.5	5	1½	
J	4	6	4	1	2
K	2	7	3	1/0	
			2	2/0	2.5
			1	3/0	3
			0		
			00		3.5

(small)

↑

(large)

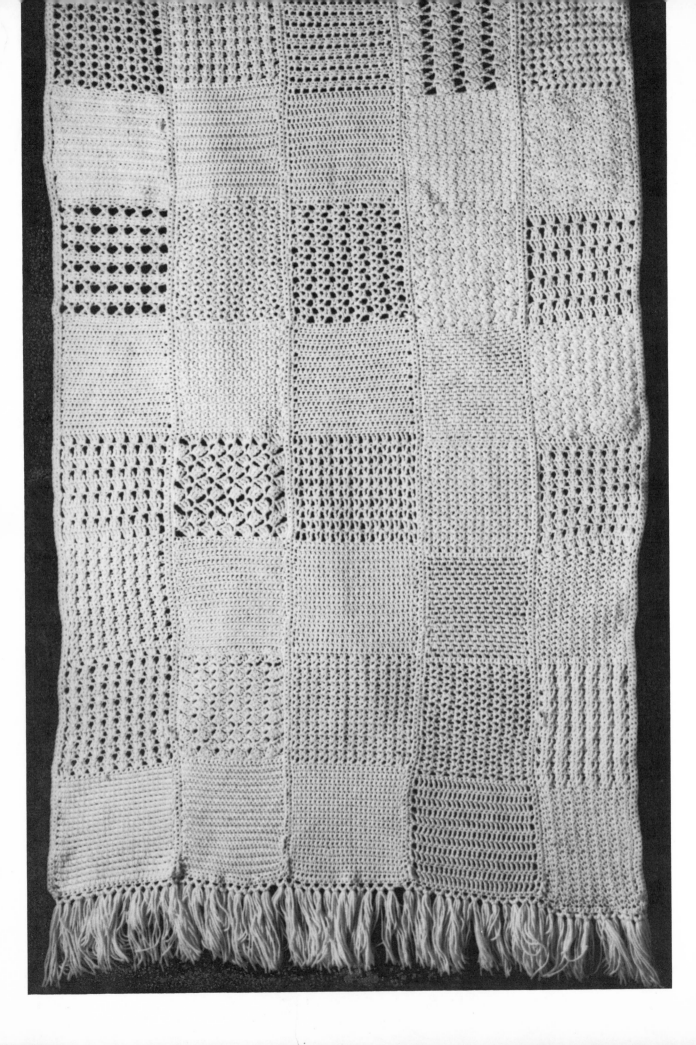

Chapter 2

Simple One and Two Row Pattern Stitches ▉▉▉▉▉▉▉▉▉▉▉▉▉▉▉▉▉▉

The pattern stitches in this chapter are relatively simple. They produce a variety of attractive close fabrics and openwork effects. By making trials of these stitches in sample panels, you can make a beautiful pillow or afghan as you learn. It's an excellent way for beginners to practice crochet and for experienced crocheters to find out how easy it is to follow the diagrams of symbol crochet. Many combinations of stitches are possible, but two suggested projects, one for an afghan and the other for a pillow top, follow the general instructions given here.

Before starting a sampler pillow or afghan, it is important to practice on some of the basic stitches, for you will find that your stitch gauge gradually alters as you learn to make even stitches. Using four-ply yarn (knitting worsted) and an I hook (UK 5, Int'l 5.5), work a piece about 4″ (10cm) long by 4″ wide of each of the basic stitches. If you do not get three stitches per inch (2.5cm) change to a larger or smaller hook before starting your sampler panels. While you are making the panels, check the stitch gauge often and adjust the hook size if necessary. Stitch for stitch, lacy patterns produce a smaller area than solid ones.

In working some of the pattern stitches, you may find that they come out wider or narrower than previous patterns. To correct this, pull out that part of the work and change to a smaller or larger hook.

Samplers may be worked in panels or squares of any size, but the ones given in the projects which follow are made in continuous panels 6″ (15cm) wide by 18″ (45cm) long for pillows and 8″ (20cm) by 64″ (160cm) long for afghans. As the rows are worked, the pattern stitch used is changed every 6″ for pillows, and every 8″ for afghans. When the panels are finished, they are joined together. As the depth of the rows for the different pattern stitches (and therefore the number of rows needed) will vary, the length of the panels as well as of each pattern unit should be measured as you go along.

It is very easy to gain or lose a stitch in crochet, so count the number of stitches in the final row of each pattern unit to make sure you have the requisite number of stitches for beginning the next pattern. If you don't, increase or decrease accordingly.

Finishing the sampler

To finish the sampler, lay the individual panels flat. Mark every 3″ (7.5cm) along the sides with a safety pin. Attach yarn at one end of the strip and Ch 2. Work 9 single crochets between each pin. Tie off the yarn. Work along the sides of all the panels in this manner, then sew them together with an overcast stitch as explained in Chapter 1.

When the panels are sewn together, attach yarn at one corner and work one row of single crochet all around the entire pillow or afghan, working 3 single crochets at the corners. If a fringe is desired, work Row 1 of Chain 2 Lace (Pattern #25, this chapter) along the ends of the afghan and attach the fringe as shown in Chapter 1.

Block the piece by holding a steam iron about 1″ above it, allowing the steam to penetrate the yarn. Lay the finished article flat and allow it to dry overnight.

Sampler Pillow 18″ × 18″ (45cm × 45cm)

Material: 4 ounces (100 grams) of four-ply knitting worsted
Hook size: I (UK 5, Int'l 5.5)
Gauge: 3 SC equals 1″ (2.5cm)

For the foundation chain to start the first pattern stitch of each panel, Ch 17 and add the number of chains given as the "plus" figure which follows the multiple for that stitch. (For example, for Pattern Stitch #1, Madrid Stitch, Ch 17 plus 3 chs.) When working the turning chain to begin the next and subsequent patterns, ch 1 less than the specified plus figure.

When the pattern unit changes to one of the Basic Stitches (such as Single or Double Crochet) work them as described in Chapter 1. That is, to start the first row of the Basic Stitch, make the number of turning chains ordinarily required to start the first stitch of the second row of the designated Basic Stitch. You will have 18 stitches, including the turning chain.

The pillow is made in three panels 6″ (15cm) wide by 18″ (45cm) long. Each panel includes three different pattern stitches. Work enough rows of each stitch to make a pattern unit 6″ long, then change to the next stitch. Measure the panels as you go along, making sure that after each unit is completed, the panels measure first 6″, then 12″, and finally 18″. All of the stitches are from this chapter.

Panel 1
#11 Madrid Stitch
Single Crochet (On the first row, do
   not work under ch 1 between dcs.)
#14 Rug Stitch

Panel 2
Extended Single Crochet
#29 Duchess Stitch (Begin the pattern
   with Row 3.)
Half Double Crochet (Increase 1
   stitch at the beginning of the first
   row.)

Panel 3
#36 Judith Stitch #2
Double Crochet
#40 Alternating Stitch
Join the panels as described above,
   then block the completed cover.

Material: 40 ounces (1200 grams) of four-ply knitting worsted
Hook size: I (UK 5, Int'l 5.5)
Gauge: 3 SC equals 1″ (2.5cm)
The afghan is made in five panels. Each panel is 8″ (20cm) wide and 64″ (160cm) long. Eight pattern stitches are used in each panel. Work each pattern for 8″, measuring as you go along. The panel should measure progressively 8″, 16″, 24″, 32″, 40″, 48″ 56″, and 64″ (or 20cm, 40cm, 60cm, 80cm, 100cm, 120cm, 140cm, 160cm) long as you finish each pattern.

To make the foundation chain for the first pattern of each panel, Ch 25 and add the number of chains given in the plus figure specified after the multiple of the designated pattern. (You should have 26 stitches, including the turning chain.) To work the turning chain for the subsequent patterns in the panel, chain one less than the plus figure specified in the multiple for the new pattern. Work Basic Stitches as explained in Chapter 1. To introduce a pattern unit of one of the Basic Stitches, make the number of turning chains required to start the second row of that stitch. All the other stitches used are from this chapter.

The panels are worked in numerical order but are joined in the following order:

Panel 4	Panel 2	Panel 1	Panel 3	Panel 5

Panel 1
Chain 25 to start. Work each pattern for 8″.

- Single Crochet (Basic Stitch)
- #9 V's in Double Crochet
- Extended Single Crochet (Basic Stitch)
- #10 V's in Triple Crochet
- Half Double Crochet (Basic Stitch)
- #11 Madrid Stitch
- Double Crochet (Basic Stitch) (On the first row of dc, do not work in the chain between the dcs.)
- #14 Rug Stitch

Panel 2
Work 8″ of each pattern. Between each pattern square, work 1 row of Single Crochet (SC) as noted. In measuring panels 2 through 5 as you work, the row of SC is included as part of the succeeding 8″ pattern block.

- Triple Crochet (Basic Stitch)
  - SC 1 row
- #16 Open V's in Double Crochet
  - SC 1 row
- #1 Double Grain
  - SC 1 row
- #20 Triangles in Double Crochet
  - SC 1 row. Work only 1 SC under ch 2.
- #2 Granite Stitch
  - SC 1 row
- #26 Star Stitch
  - SC 1 row
- #3 Seed Stitch
  - SC 1 row
- #27 Vertical Scallop Stitch

Panel 3
Work 8″ of each pattern. Include 1 row of SC between each pattern as in Panel 2.

#4 Ridge Stitch
  SC 1 row
#31 Small Crazy Stitch
  SC 1 row. Work 2 SC in first dc, SC in all other dc, 1 SC under ch 3, and *do not* work in sc.
#5 Albania Stitch
  SC 1 row
#32 Large Crazy Stitch
  SC 1 row. Work 2 SC in first tc, SC in all other tcs, and 1 SC under ch 3 and *do not* work in dc.
#6 Bouclé Stitch
  SC 1 row.
#34 Forget-Me-Knot Stitch
  SC 1 row
#7 Shadow Stitch
  SC 1 row
#35 Judith Stitch #1

Panel 4

Work 8″ of each pattern. Include 1 row of SC between each pattern as in Panels 2 and 3.
  #15 Open V's in Single Crochet
    SC 1 row
  #36 Judith Stitch #2
    SC 1 row
  #19 Triangles in Single Crochet
    SC 1 row. Work only 1 SC under ch 2.
  #43 Medium Lozenge Stitch
    SC 1 row
  #26 Star Stitch
    SC 1 row
  #44 Large Lozenge Stitch
    SC 1 row
  #29 Duchess Stitch
    SC 1 row
  #47 Crossed Triple Crochet #1

Panel 5

Work 8″ of each pattern. Include 1 row of SC between each pattern.
  #38 Padded Single Crochet
    SC 1 row. Work first SC in st at base of turning chain.
  #43 Medium Lozenge Stitch
    SC 1 row

#35 Judith Stitch #1
  SC 1 row
#44 Large Lozenge Stitch
  SC 1 row
Half Double Crochet (Basic Stitch)
  SC 1 row

#48 Crossed Triple Crochet #2
  SC 1 row
#54 Piqué Double Stitch
  SC 1 row
#51 Teepee Stitch

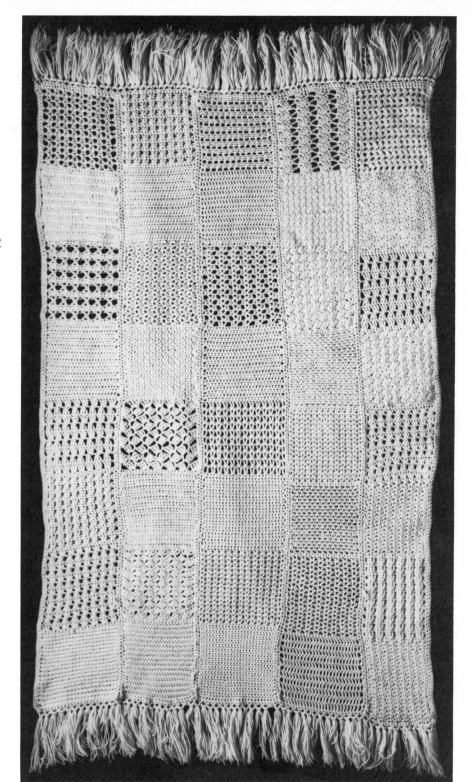

Designing your own projects ▐▌▌▌▌▌▌▌▌▌▌▌▌▌▌▌▌▌▌▌▌▌▌

Any stitch may be used to make pillow tops, afghans, shawls, mufflers, and other articles. To start, make a chain longer than the width given in the standard sizes given below and work the first row as long as the specified width, being careful not to stretch the piece when measuring.

Pillows ▐▌▌▌

Pillow tops can be any size, but ready-made pillow forms are available in the following approximate sizes:

> 12″ × 12″ (30cm × 30cm)
> 14″ × 14″ (33cm × 33cm)
> 15″ × 15″ (38cm × 38cm)
> 16″ × 16″ (40cm × 40cm)
> 18″ × 18″ (45cm × 45cm)

If you are planning to add a single crochet edge, make the pillow top 1″ less than the size given. (See page 28 for instructions for working borders and corners.) If the finished square is larger than the size given, use the next larger size pillow form for a snug fitting cover. If you are making your own pillow insert always make it 1″ larger than the pillow cover.

The way in which a pillow is finished should always show the work to its best advantage. There are many ways to make a back and finish the edges of a pillow. Here are some suggestions.

Pillow backs: You can duplicate the front design to make a reversible pillow or work a plain back panel in one of the Basic Stitches. Avoid patterns and colors that will compete with the design of the front. Woven fabric pillow backs add a little stiffness and this may be desirable if a soft crocheted piece forms the front.

A fabric back should have a zipper so that the cover can be easily removed for dry cleaning or washing. Zippers are not recommended for crocheted backs as they tend to get caught on the thread. Round the corners of a fabric back slightly (a half-dollar coin makes a good guide).

Pillow edges: Many people prefer to "frame" their pillows with a corded edging. Cable cording may be covered with bias-cut fabric and inserted between the front and the back. Always sew the cording to the front first, slashing the cording to the stitching line for ease at the corners. Use the first stitching line as a guide when sewing the two sides together to be sure you are sewing close to the edge. (Use the cording foot for both stitchings.)

There are many choices for interesting edgings for crocheted pillows. Make a row of Single Crochet around the piece, working stitches along the sides and around the corners as described on page 28. Add another row of Single Crochet, a row of Slip Stitch, a row of Padded Single Crochet (#38, this chapter) or a row of Knurl Stitch (Chapter 3, #92), working under both strands of yarn. Done in this way, the Knurl Stitch is really a Single Crochet worked backwards (from left to right).

Another method of trimming the edges is to form a cord from a hank of yarn. Measure off six or more strands of yarn that are 6″ (15cm) longer than the distance around the pillow. Hold all the strands together and smooth them by pulling them through your hand. Work one row of Single Crochet around the pillow, Slip Stitch the last stitch to the first, and turn the work (do not chain). Hold the strands along the top of the stitches, leaving a 3″ (7.5cm) "tail" at the beginning. The crochet hook with its loop should be on one side of the strands and the yarn from the ball on the other side. * Chain 1, Slip stitch into next stitch. (Only the chain covers the cord.) Repeat from * around. Tie off. Cut the ends at an angle so that they are all different lengths and pull them inside pillow. (Instead of crocheting over the bundled yarn you could overcast over it, working into each of the stitches, and finish the ends as above.)

Afghans

The most common sizes for afghans are:
> **Baby afghan** 30″ × 45″ (75cm × 115cm), not including fringe.
> **Regular afghans** 45″ × 65″ (115cm × 165cm), not including fringe.

To add a border or fringe, see instructions in Chapter 1. Or choose a suitable stitch from Chapter 3 or 4 and add a lace edging to the border.

Mufflers

Average sizes for mufflers are:
> **Children** 7″ × 36″ (18cm × 90cm)
> **Women** 9″ × 42″ (23cm × 100cm)
> **Men** 10″ × 48″ (25cm × 120cm)

Purses

To make a purse, crochet a panel approximately 10″ × 20″ (25cm × 50cm). Fold it in the middle and complete it by following the instructions given for making purses in the projects at the end of Chapter 6.

41

Coats

A pattern for making coats of various dimensions is given in Chapter 6. The example shown is done in a Check stitch but the same plan could be used with many other pattern stitches.

Placemats and runners

A good size for placemats is 11½″ × 15½″ (29cm × 38cm).

Runners can be 11½ × 3″ (29cm × 7.5cm) but the advantage of designing your own is that they can be made to fit the place where they will be used. For articles such as these, choose closely crocheted, flat patterns. Popcorn, puff, or other heavily textured stitches will make dishes, glassware, and decorative objects tip dangerously. A very open lace stitch would defeat the purpose of the placemat.

Stoles

The average stole is a rectangle 20″ (50cm) wide by 80″ (200cm) long. Open patterns require about 12 ounces (300 grams) of yarn. For more solid patterns, about 20 ounces (500 grams) is needed.

To start, make a chain more than 20″ long. Work the first row of the pattern until the piece measures 20″ without stretching. Turn the work and continue to work rows in pattern until the desired length of the stole is reached. Add fringe if desired.

Triangular shawls

The instructions given below produce a shawl that is slightly rounded, with more width over the arms for added warmth. *Material:* Sport yarn, baby yarn, or four-ply knitting worsted. The quantities listed are approximately the same for all three types of yarn. They will vary slightly with the pattern stitch selected.

Small 40″ × 20″ (100cm × 50cm), 8 ounces (200 grams)
Medium 65″ × 30″ (165cm × 75cm), 12 ounces (300 grams)
Large 90″ × 40″ (225cm × 100cm), 16 ounces (400 grams)

Make a chain a little longer than the width of the shawl (the larger dimension given for the size selected). Work row of the chosen pattern and measure the piece *without stretching it* to make sure it is the right length. Work four rows of the pattern.

Check the number of stitches in the pattern repeat and proceed accordingly:

For pattern repeats of 2 to 4 stitches: Do not work the last pattern repeat on the next 2 rows. Work 2 rows without decreases. Repeat the last 4 rows two more times. Leave off the last pattern repeat of every row until only one or two patterns remain. Tie off the yarn.

For pattern repeats of 6 to 8 stitches: Start by making a foundation chain and working 4 rows of the pattern. Do not work the last pattern on the next two rows. Work 4 rows even. Repeat the last 6 rows one time more. Do not work the last pattern on the next 2 rows. Work 2 rows even. Repeat the last 4 rows until only one or two pattern repeats remain.

To add fringe, see instructions in Chapter 1.

Quechquemitl (*Plate 1*)

A poncho made in two rectangles done in Ridge Stitch (#4, this chapter.)

Material: Four-ply yarn (knitting worsted) in two colors, in quantity for size as listed below.

Hook size: H (UK 6, Int'l 5)

Gauge: 4 SC equals 1″ (2.5cm)

Children

Small 12″ × 20″ (30cm × 50cm): 6 ounces (160 grams) each of Color A and Color B. For each piece, make a foundation chain of 82 stitches.

Medium 16″ × 24″ (40cm × 60cm): 10 ounces (280 grams) of each color. Ch 98 to start.

Large 18″ × 28″ (45cm × 70cm): 12 ounces (320 grams) of each color. Ch 114 to start.

Women

Small 20″ × 34″ (50cm × 85cm): 14 ounces (360 grams) of each color. Ch 138 to start.

Large 22″ × 38″ (55cm × 95cm): 16 ounces (440 grams) of each color. CH 154 to start.

Men

Small Same as Women's Large. Ch 154 to start.

Large 26″ × 40″ (65cm × 100cm): 20 ounces (560 grams) of each color. Ch 162 to start.

With Color A, make a foundation chain of the required length for the size selected. Work the first row in this color, then change to Color B for Row 2, working it in as shown in Figures 1 and 2. On every row, leave "tails" of both yarns approximately 5″ long (for a child's poncho) or 7″ long (for an adult).

Alternate colors at the beginning of each new row. Repeat until you have enough rows to provide the rectangle width required for the poncho size. Tie the loose "tails" of yarn together to form fringe (Figure 3). Make a second section in the same way. Sew the two sections together at right angles as shown in Figure 4.

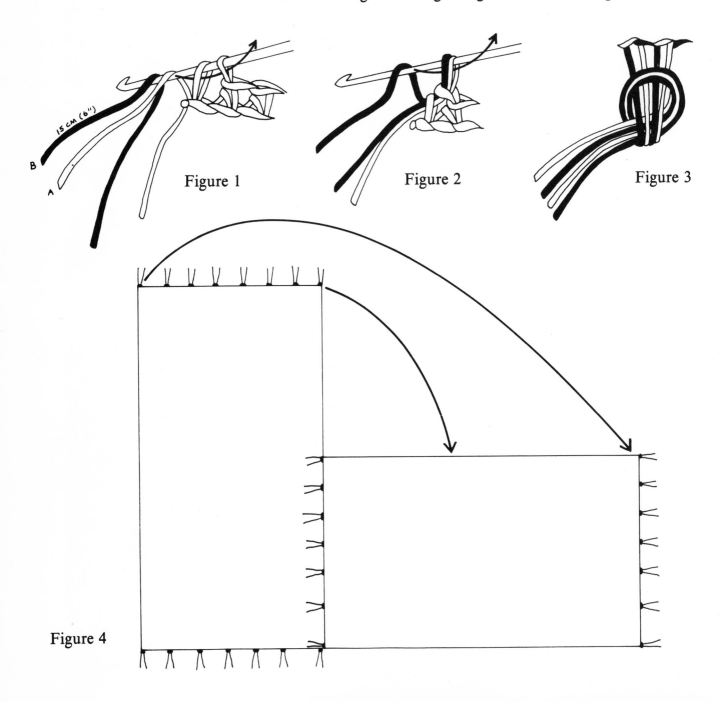

Figure 1

Figure 2

Figure 3

Figure 4

Note: In working these pattern stitches, remember that capitalized words and abbreviations (SC, DC, ExSC, YO, Skip, etc.) indicate a stitch that is to be *worked* or an action to be taken. Abbreviations in small letters (sc, dc, tc) indicate a stitch that is to be *worked into*.

1 / Double Grain Stitch
(multiple of 2 + 1 plus 3 chs)

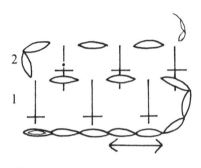

Row 1: Working on a chain foundation, work ExSC in 4th ch from hook, * Ch 1, Skip 1 st, ExSC in next st. Repeat from * across, Ch 2, Turn.

Row 2: * Work ExSC under the ch 1 of previous row, Ch 1. Repeat from * across, ending with ExSC under turning chain, Ch 2, Turn.

Repeat Row 2 for pattern.

2 / Granite Stitch
(multiple of 2 + 1 plus 3 chs)

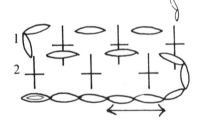

Row 1: Working on a chain foundation, work SC in 4th ch from hook, * Ch 1, Skip 1 ch, SC in next ch. Repeat from * across, Ch 2, Turn.

Row 2: SC under first ch of previous row. * Ch 1, SC under next ch. Repeat from * across, ending with last SC under turning ch, Ch 2, Turn.

Repeat Row 2 for pattern.

3 / Seed Stitch
(multiple of 2 + 1 plus 3 chs)

Row 1: Working on a chain foundation, SC in 4th ch from hook, * DC in next ch, SC in next ch. Repeat from * across, Ch 2, Turn.
Row 2: * Work SC in dc, DC in sc. Repeat from * across, ending with SC in 3rd ch of turning ch, Ch 2, Turn.
Repeat Row 2 for pattern, ending rows with SC in 2nd ch of turning ch, Ch 2, Turn.

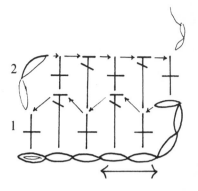

4 / Ridge Stitch
(any number of stitches)

Row 1: Working on a chain foundation, SC in 3rd ch from hook and in each ch across, Ch 1, Turn.
Row 2: Inserting hook under *back* thread only, SC in each st across, ending with SC in 2nd ch of turning ch, Ch 1, Turn.
Repeat Row 2 for pattern.

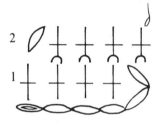

5 / Albania Stitch
(any number of stitches)

Row 1: Working on a chain foundation, SC in 3rd ch from hook and in each ch across, Ch 1, Turn.
Row 2: Inserting hook in *front* thread only, SC in each st across, SC in 2nd ch of turning ch at end of row, Ch 1, Turn.
Repeat Row 2 for pattern.

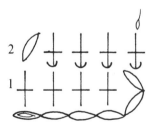

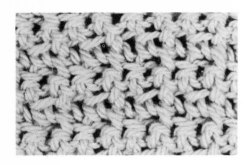

6 / Bouclé Stitch
(multiple of 2 plus 1 ch)

Row 1: Working on a chain foundation, SC in 3rd ch from hook
and in each ch across, Ch 1,
Turn.

Row 2: * SC in *front loop* of next st,
SC in *back loop* of next st.
Repeat from * across ending
with SC in *front loop* of 2nd
ch of turning ch. Ch 1, Turn.

Repeat Row 2 for pattern, ending
with SC in turning ch.

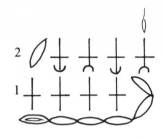

7 / Shadow Stitch
(any number of stitches)

Row 1: Working on a chain foundation, work SC in 3rd ch from
hook and each st across, Ch
2, Turn.

Row 2: Inserting hook in *back* thread
of st, work DC in each st
across, working last DC in
back loop of turning ch, Ch 1,
Turn.

Row 3: Inserting hook in *back* thread
of st, work SC in next st and
in each st across, ending with
SC in turning ch, Ch 2, Turn.

Repeat Rows 2 and 3 for pattern.

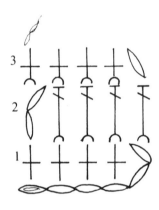

8 / V's in Extended Single Crochet
(multiple of 2 + 1 plus 3 chs)

Row 1: Working on a chain foundation
work ExSC in 4th chain
from hook. * Skip 1 ch, work
2 ExSC in next ch. Repeat
from * across. Ch 2, Turn.

Row 2: Work 1 ExSC between first 2
exsc. * 2 ExSC between next
2 exsc. Repeat from * across,
ending with 2 ExSC under
turning ch, Ch 2, Turn.

Repeat Row 2 for pattern.

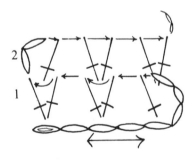

9 / V's in Double Crochet (Lattice)
(multiple of 2 + 1 plus 3 chs)

Row 1: Working on a chain foundation, work DC in 4th ch from hook. * Skip 1 ch, 2 DC in next st. Repeat from * across, Ch 2, Turn.

Row 2: Work DC between the first 2 dc, * 2 DC between each 2 dc of previous row. Repeat from * across, ending with 2 DC under turning chain, Ch 2, Turn.

Repeat Row 2 for pattern.

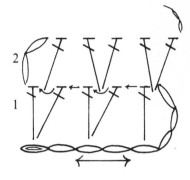

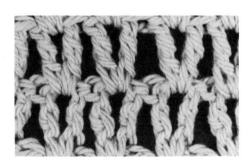

10 / V's in Triple Crochet
(multiple of 2 + 1 plus 4 chs)

Row 1: Working on a chain foundation, TC in 5th ch from hook. * Skip 1 st, 2 TC in next ch. Repeat from * across, Ch 3, Turn.

Row 2: Work TC between the first 2 tc. * 2 TC between tc of previous row. Repeat from * across, ending with last 2 TC under the turning ch, Ch 3, Turn.

Repeat Row 2 for pattern.

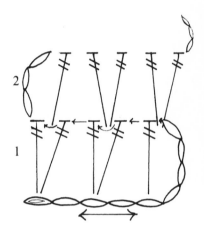

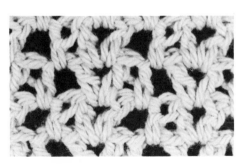

11 / Madrid Stitch
(multiple of 4 + 1 plus 3 chs)

Row 1: Working on a chain foundation, HDC in 4th ch from hook. * Work (DC, Ch 1, DC) in next st, Ch 1, Skip 2 sts, HDC in next st. Repeat from * across, Ch 2, Turn.

Row 2: * HDC under first ch 1, work (DC, Ch 1, DC) under next ch 1, Ch 1. Repeat from * across ending with HDC under turning ch, Ch 2, Turn.

Repeat Row 2 for pattern.

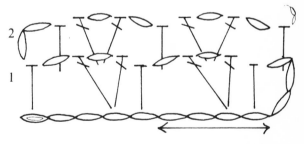

12 / Contrary Stitch
(multiple 2 + 1 plus 2 chs)

Row 1: Working on a chain foundation, work (SC, Ch 1, SC) in 3rd ch from hook, Skip 1 ch. * (SC, Ch 1, SC) into next ch. Skip 1 ch. Repeat from * across, ending with SC in last ch, Ch 2, Turn.

Row 2: * (SC, Ch 1, SC) under ch. Repeat from * across, ending with SC in turning ch, Ch 2, Turn.

Repeat Row 2 for pattern.

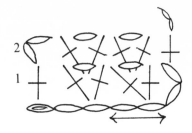

13 / Bush Stitch
(multiple of 2 + 1 plus 3 chs)

Row 1: Working on a chain foundation, Skip 3 chs, * Work 2 SC in next ch, Skip 1 ch. Repeat from * across, ending with 2 SC in last ch, Ch 1, Turn.

Row 2: Work 2 SC *between* each 2 sc group of previous row, working last 2 SC under turning ch, Ch 1, Turn.

Repeat Row 2 for pattern.

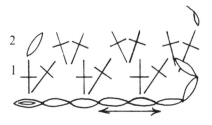

14 / Rug Stitch
(multiple of 2 + 1 plus 3 chs)

Row 1: Working on a chain foundation, work HDC in 4th ch from hook. YO, Insert hook from left to right, horizontally around previous hdc, Pull Up thread, YO and through 3 loops (a hdc). * Skip 1 st, HDC in next st. Work a HDC *around* st in the same manner as the first st. Repeat from * across, ending with Skip 1 st, HDC in last st, Ch 1, Turn.

Row 2: SC in next hdc and in each hdc across, ending with last SC in 3rd ch of turning ch, Ch 2, Turn.

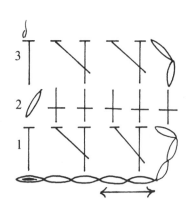

Row 3: * HDC in next sc, work HDC *around* completed hdc, skip 1 sc, Repeat from * across, ending with HDC in turning ch, Ch 1, Turn.

Repeat Rows 2 and 3 for pattern.

15 / Open V's in Single Crochet
(*multiple of 3 + 1 plus 2 chs*)

Row 1: Working on a chain foundation, Skip 3 chs, * work (SC, Ch 1, SC) in next ch, Skip 2 chs. Repeat from * across, ending with Skipping only 1 ch, SC in next ch, Ch 1, Turn.

Row 2: * Work (SC, Ch 1, SC) under next ch. Repeat from * across, ending with SC in turning ch, Ch 1, Turn.

Repeat Row 2 for pattern.

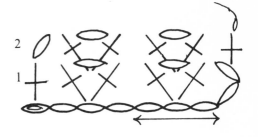

16 / Open V's in Double Crochet
(*multiple of 3 + 1 plus 3 chs*)

Row 1: Working on a chain foundation, Skip 4 chs, * work (DC, Ch 1, DC) in next ch, Skip 2 chs. Repeat from * across ending with Skipping only 1 ch, DC in last ch, Ch 2, Turn.

Row 2: * Work (DC, Ch 1, DC) under next ch. Repeat from * across, ending with DC in turning ch, Ch 2, Turn.

Repeat Row 2 for pattern.

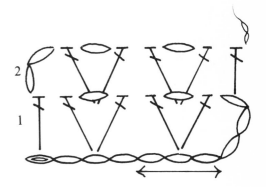

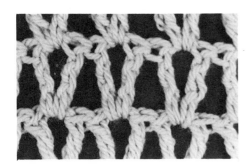

17 / Open V's in Triple Crochet (Lattice) #1
(*multiple of 3 + 2 plus 4 chs*)

Row 1: Working on a chain foundation, work (TC, Ch 1, TC) in 7th ch from hook, * Skip 2 sts, work (TC, Ch 1, TC) in next st. Repeat from * across, ending with Skip 1 ch, TC in last st, Ch 3, Turn.

Row 2: Work (TC, Ch 1, TC) under each ch 1 across, TC in 6th ch of turning ch, Ch 3, Turn.

Repeat Row 2 for pattern.

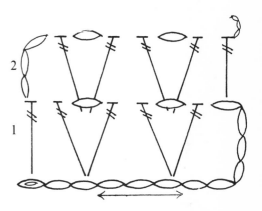

18 / Open V's in Triple Crochet (Lattice) #2
(*multiple of 3 + 2 plus 4 chs*)

Row 1: Working on a chain foundation, work as for Row 1 in Pattern 17 above, Ch 1, Turn.
Row 2: SC in each tc and ch across, ending with SC in 6th ch of turning ch, Ch 3, Turn.
Row 3: Skip 1 st, * work (TC, Ch 1, TC) in next st, Skip 2 sts. Repeat from * across, ending Skip only 1 st, TC in turning ch, Ch 1, Turn.
Repeat Rows 2 and 3 for pattern.

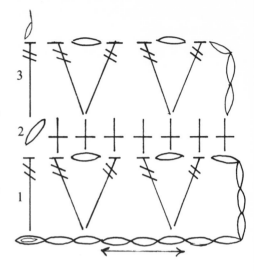

19 / Triangles in Single Crochet
(*multiple of 3 + 1 plus 2 chs*)

Row 1: Working on a chain foundation, Skip 3 chs, * work (SC, Ch 2, SC) in next ch, Skip 2 chs. Repeat from * across, ending with Skipping only 1 ch, SC in last ch, Ch 1, Turn.
Row 2: * Work (SC, Ch 2, SC) under next ch 2. Repeat from * across, ending with SC in turning ch, Ch 1, Turn.
Repeat Row 2 for pattern.

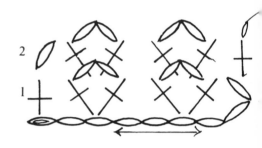

20 / Triangles in Double Crochet
(*multiple of 3 + 1 plus 3 chs*)

Row 1: Working on a chain foundation, Skip 4 chs, * work (DC, Ch 2, DC) in next ch, Skip 2 chs. Repeat from * across, ending with Skipping only 1 ch, DC in last ch, Ch 2, Turn.
Row 2: * Work (DC, Ch 2, DC) under ch 2. Repeat from * across, ending with DC in turning ch, Ch 2, Turn.
Repeat Row 2 for pattern.

[**EDGING:** Work Row 1 only. An edging of Triangles in Double Crochet is a good base for attaching fringe.]

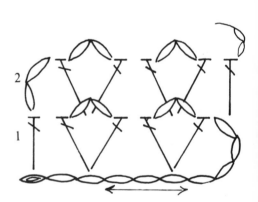

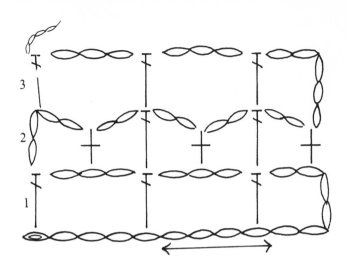

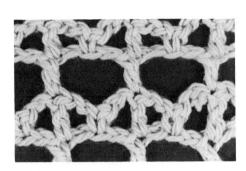

21 / Fancy Grill
(multiple of 4 + 3 plus 4 chs)

Row 1: Working on a chain foundation, DC in 7th ch from hook. * Ch 3, Skip 3 chs, DC in next st. Repeat from * across, Ch 4, Turn.

Row 2: * SC in 2nd ch of ch 3 of previous row, Ch 2, DC in next dc, Ch 2. Repeat from * across, ending with SC in 5th ch of turning ch, Ch 5, Turn.

Row 3: * DC in next dc, Ch 3, Repeat from * across ending with DC in 3rd ch of turning ch, Ch 4, Turn.

Repeat Rows 2 and 3 for pattern.

[EDGING: Work Rows 1 and 2.]

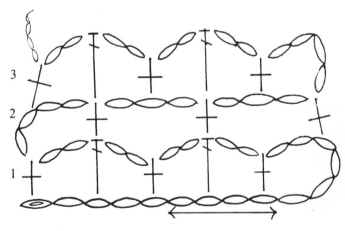

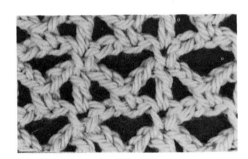

22 / Zig-Zag Mesh Stitch
(multiple of 4 + 3 plus 4 chs)

Row 1: Working on a chain foundation, SC in 7th ch from hook, * Ch 2, Skip 1 st, DC in next st, Ch 2, Skip 1 st, SC in next st. Repeat from * across, Ch 4, Turn.

Row 2: * SC in dc, Ch 3. Repeat from * across, ending with SC in 4th ch of turning ch, Ch 4, Turn.

Row 3: * SC in 2nd ch, Ch 2, DC in sc, Ch 2, Repeat from * across, ending with SC in 2nd ch of turning ch, Ch 4, Turn.

Repeat Rows 2 and 3 for pattern.

[EDGING: Work Rows 1 through 3.]

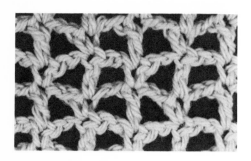

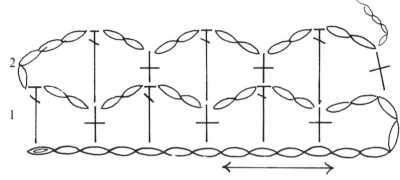

23 / Arch Mesh Stitch
(multiple of 4 + 1 plus 4 chs)

Row 1: Working on a *loose* chain foundation, SC in 7th ch from hook. * Ch 2, Skip 1 st, DC in next st, Ch 2, Skip 1 st, SC in next st. Repeat from * across ending with Ch 2, Skip 1 ch, DC in last st, Ch 4, Turn.

Row 2: * DC in sc, Ch 2, SC in dc, Ch 2. Repeat from * across, ending with last SC in 4th ch of turning ch, Ch 4, Turn.

Repeat Row 2 for pattern.

[EDGING: Work Row 1. For a wider lace border, work Rows 1 and 2 for several rows.]

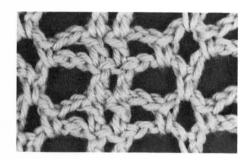

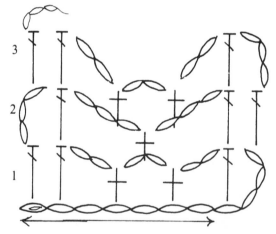

24 / Lace Bridges
(multiple of 7 + 1 plus 3 chs)

Row 1: Working on a chain foundation, DC in 4th ch from hook. * (Ch 2, Skip 1 ch, SC in next ch) twice, Ch 2, Skip 1 ch, DC in each of next 2 chs. Repeat from * across, Ch 3, Turn.

Row 2: DC in next st, * Ch 3, SC under ch 2 between 2 sc, Ch 3, DC in each of next 2 dc. Repeat from * across, ending with last DC in 3rd ch of turning ch, Ch 3, Turn.

Row 3: DC in next dc, * Ch 2, SC under next ch 3, Ch 2, SC under next ch 3, Ch 2, DC in each of next 2 dc. Repeat from * across, ending with last DC in 3rd ch of turning ch, Ch 3, Turn.

Repeat Rows 2 and 3 for pattern.

[EDGING: Work Rows 1 through 3.]

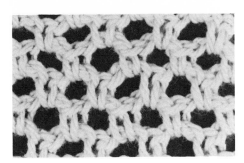

25 / Chain 2 Lace
(multiple of 3 + 1 plus 3 chs)

Row 1: Working on a chain foundation, SC in 4th ch from hook. * Ch 2, Skip 2 chs, SC in next ch. Repeat from * across, Ch 2, Turn.
Row 2: * SC under ch 2, Ch 2. Repeat from * across, ending with last SC under turning ch, Ch 2, Turn.
Repeat Row 2 for pattern.

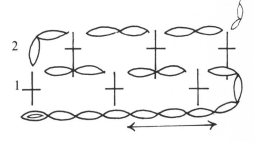

[EDGING: Work Row 1. Chain 2 Lace makes an open edging convenient for attaching fringe.]

26 / Star Stitch
(multiple of 3 + 1 plus 2 chs)

Row 1: Working on a chain foundation, work 2 DC in 3rd ch from hook. * Skip 2 sts, (SC, 2 DC) into next st. Repeat from * across, ending with SC in last ch, Ch 1, Turn.
Row 2: 2 DC in st at base of turning ch. * (SC, 2 DC) in sc. Repeat from * across, ending with SC in turning ch, Ch 1, Turn.

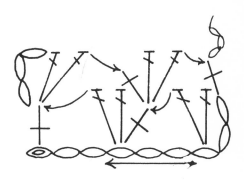

Repeat Row 2 for pattern.

[EDGING: Work Row 1.]

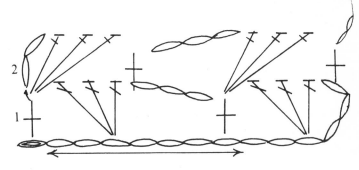

27 / Vertical Scallop Stitch
(multiple of 7 + 4 plus 3 chs)

Row 1: Working on a chain foundation, work 3 DC in 4th ch from hook. Skip 2 sts, SC in next st. * Ch 3, Skip 3 sts, 3 DC in next st, Skip 2 sts, SC in next st. Repeat from * across, ending with SC in last ch, Ch 3, Turn.

Row 2: 3 DC in base of turning ch, * SC under ch 3, Ch 3, 3 DC in next sc. Repeat from * across, ending with SC in turning ch, Ch 2, Turn.
Repeat Row 2 for pattern.

[Vertical Scallop is a popular stitch for making afghans.]

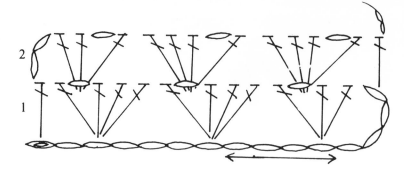

28 / Changing Double Crochets
(*multiple of 4 plus 3 chs*)

Row 1: Working on a chain foundation, work (2 DC, Ch 1, DC) in 5th ch from hook. * Skip 3 sts, work (3 DC, Ch 1, DC) in next st. Repeat from * across, ending with Skip 1 st, DC in last st, Ch 2, Turn.

Row 2: (2 DC, Ch 1, DC) under ch 1. * (3 DC, Ch 1, DC) under next ch 1. Repeat from * across, ending with DC in last ch of turning ch, Ch 2, Turn.
Repeat Row 2 for pattern.

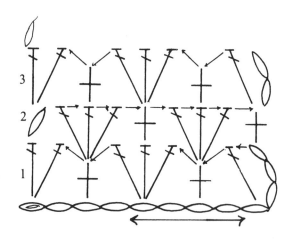

29 / Duchess Stitch
(*multiple of 4 + 1 plus 3 chs*)

Row 1: Working on a chain foundation, DC in 4th ch from hook. * Skip 1 ch, SC in next st, Skip 1 st, work 3 DC in next st. Repeat from * across, ending with 2 DC (instead of 3) in last ch, Ch 1, Turn.

Row 2: * Work 3 DC in sc, SC in middle st of 3 dc. Repeat from * across, ending with last SC in 3rd ch of turning ch. Ch 2, Turn.

Row 3: DC in sc at base of ch, * SC in middle st of 3 dc group, 3 DC in next sc. Repeat from * across, ending with 2 DC (instead of 3) in turning ch, Ch 1, Turn.
Repeat Rows 2 and 3 for pattern.

[EDGING: Work Row 1.]

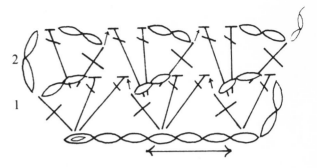

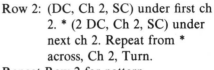

30 / Hoosier Stitch
(multiple of 3 + 1 plus 2 chs)

Row 1: Working on a chain foundation, DC in 3rd ch from hook, Ch 2, SC in same st as dc. * Skip 2 sts, (2 DC, Ch 2, SC) in next st, Repeat from * across, Ch 2, Turn.

Row 2: (DC, Ch 2, SC) under first ch 2. * (2 DC, Ch 2, SC) under next ch 2. Repeat from * across, Ch 2, Turn.
Repeat Row 2 for pattern.

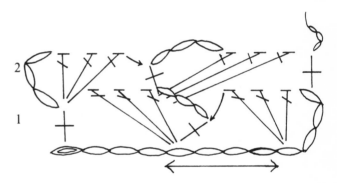

31 / Small Crazy Stitch
(multiple of 4 + 1 plus 3 chs)

Row 1: Working on a chain foundation, work 3 DC in 4th ch from hook, * Skip 3 sts, (SC, Ch 3, 3 DC) in next st. Repeat from * across, ending with SC only in last ch, Ch 3, Turn.

Row 2: Work 3 DC in st at base of ch, * SC under ch 3, Ch 3, 3 DC under same ch 3. Repeat from * across, ending with SC in turning ch, Ch 2, Turn.
Repeat Row 2 for pattern.

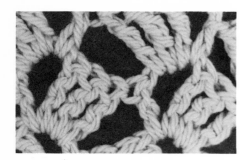

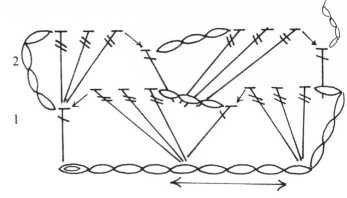

32 / Large Crazy Stitch
(*multiple of 4 + 1 plus 4 chs*)

Row 1: Working on a chain foundation, work 3 TC in 5th ch from hook, Skip 3 chs, * Work (DC, Ch 3, 3 TC) in next ch, Skip 3 chs. Repeat from * across, ending with DC in last ch, Ch 4, Turn.

Row 2: Work 3 TC in dc at base of ch, * Work (DC, Ch 3, 3 TC) under next ch 3. Repeat from * across, ending with DC under turning ch, Ch 4, Turn.
Repeat Row 2 for pattern.

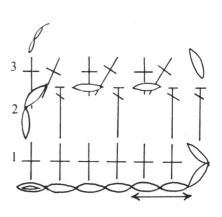

33 / Open-Work Rib Stitch
(*multiple of 2 plus 2 chs*)

Row 1: Working on a chain foundation, SC in 3rd ch from hook and in each ch across, Ch 2, Turn.

Row 2: * DC in next sc, Ch 1, Skip 1 sc. Repeat from * across, ending with DC in last sc and DC in 2nd ch of turning ch, Ch 1, Turn.

Row 3: Work 2 SC under each ch 1 across, ending with 2 SC under turning ch, Ch 2, Turn.
Repeat Rows 2 and 3 for pattern.

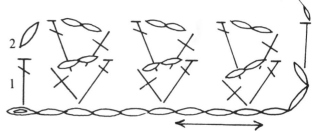

34 / Forget-Me-Knot Stitch
(*multiple of 3 + 1 plus 2 chs*)

Row 1: Working on a chain foundation, (DC, Ch 2, SC) in 4th ch from hook, * Skip 2 sts, work (DC, Ch 2, SC) in next st. Repeat from * across, ending with Skip 1 st, DC in last ch, Ch 1, Turn.

Row 2: * Work (DC, Ch 2, SC) under ch 2. Repeat from * across, ending with HDC in turning ch, Ch 1, Turn.
Repeat Row 2 for pattern.

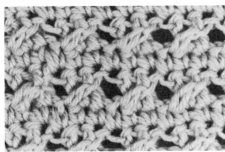

35 / Judith Stitch #1
(*multiple of 3 + 1 plus 2 chs*)

Row 1: Working on a chain foundation, SC in 3rd ch from hook and in each ch across, Ch 2, Turn.
Row 2: * Skip 1 st, DC in each of next 2 sc, then *working from the back,* work a DC in skipped st. Repeat from * across, ending with DC in 2nd ch of turning ch. Ch 1, Turn.
Row 3: SC in each st across, ending with SC in turning ch, Ch 2, Turn.

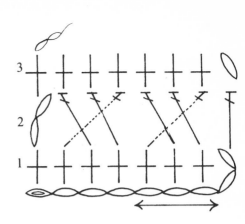

Repeat Rows 2 and 3 for pattern.

36 / Judith Stitch #2
(*multiple of 4 + 1 plus 1 ch*)

Row 1: Working on a chain foundation, SC in 3rd ch from hook and in each st across, Ch 2, Turn.

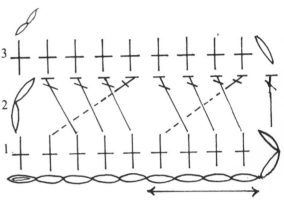

Row 2: * Skip 1 st, DC in next 3 sts. *Working from the front,* Insert hook in skipped st and draw up a long loop, (YO and through 2 loops) 2 times (long DC). Repeat from * across ending with DC in turning ch, Ch 1, Turn.

Row 3: SC in each st across ending with SC in 2nd ch of turning ch, Ch 2, Turn.

Repeat Rows 2 and 3 for pattern.

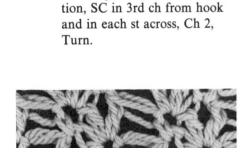

37 / Acacia Stitch
(*multiple of 5 + 3 plus 3 chs*)

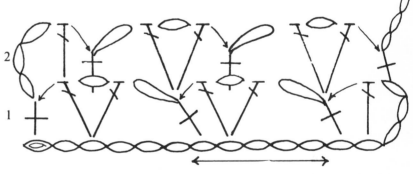

Row 1: Working on a chain foundation, DC in 4th ch from hook. * SC in next st, Draw Up a long loop as long as 3 chs of foundation ch, Skip 3 sts, (DC, Ch 1, DC) in next st. Repeat from * across, Skip 1 st, SC in last st, Ch 3, Turn.

Row 2: DC in first dc, * Make SC under ch 1, Pull Up long loop, (DC, Ch 1, DC) in next sc. Repeat from * across, ending with SC under turning ch, Ch 3, Turn.

Repeat Row 2 for pattern.

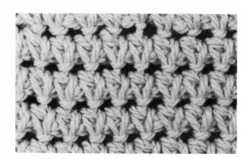

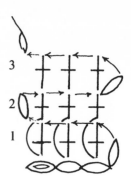

Row 1: On a chain foundation work 1 row SC, Ch 1, Turn.

Row 2: Inserting the hook in the same place as it was inserted in Row 1 make SC in each st across, Ch 1, Turn.

Row 3: SC across in normal manner making first SC in st at base of ch, Ch 1, Turn.

Repeat Rows 2 and 3 for pattern.

38 / Padded Single Crochet
(any number of stitches)

[Padded Single Crochet is good for hat brims and other items which need a firm, thick fabric.]

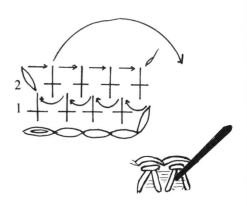

Row 1: On a chain foundation, SC in 2nd ch from hook and SC in each st to end of row, Ch 1, Turn.

Row 2: Inserting hook between vertical threads of the stitch, SC across working last st in turning chain, Ch 1, Turn.

Repeat Row 2 for pattern.

[Afghan stitch provides a close, firm fabric for purses, rugs, and other articles.]

39 / Afghan or Knit Stitch
(any number of stitches)

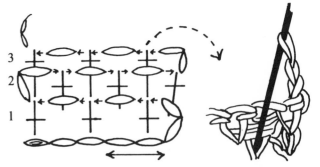

40 / Alternating Stitch
(multiple of 2 + 1 plus 2 chs)

Row 1: Working on a foundation chain, work SC in 3rd ch from hook. * Ch 1, Skip 1 st, SC in next st. Repeat from * across, Ch 2, Turn.

Row 2: * SC under ch 1, Ch 1. Repeat from * across, SC under turning ch, Ch 2, Turn.

Row 3: * Working into Row 1 (skip Row 2), work SC *between* 2 vertical threads, Ch 1. Repeat from * across, ending with SC around turning ch and into Row 1. Ch 2, Turn.

Repeat Row 3 for pattern, always skipping last row worked as shown in the drawing.

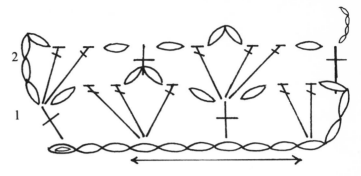

41 / Lozenge Triple Stitch
(*multiple of 6 + 4 plus 3 chs*)

Row 1: Working on a chain foundation, work 2 DC in 4th ch from hook, * Ch 1, Skip 2 sts, SC in next st, Ch 1, Skip 2 sts, (DC, Ch 2, 2 DC) in next st. Repeat from * across, ending with: Ch 1, Skip 2 sts, SC in last st, Ch 4, Turn.

Row 2: 2 DC in st at base of ch, * Ch 1, SC under ch 2, Ch 1, (DC, Ch 2, 2 DC) into next sc. Repeat from * across, ending with Ch 1, SC under turning ch, Ch 4, Turn.
Repeat Row 2 for pattern.

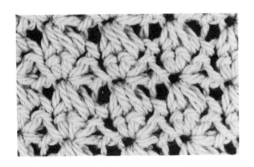

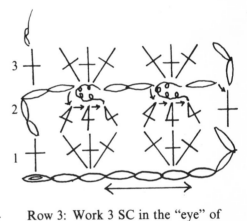

42 / Small Lozenge Stitch
(*multiple of 3 + 1 plus 2 chs*)

Row 1: Working on a chain foundation, work 3 SC in 4th ch from hook, * Skip 2 chs, 3 SC in next st. Repeat from * across, ending with Skip 1 st, SC in last ch, Ch 4, Turn.

Row 2: * Insert hook in next st, Pull Up thread, Insert hook in next st, Pull Up thread, Insert hook in next st, Pull Up thread, YO and through 4 loops, Ch 2. Repeat from * across, ending with Ch 1 (in place of Ch 2) and SC in last ch of turning ch, Ch 2, Turn.

Row 3: Work 3 SC in the "eye" of each sc group across, ending with SC in 3rd ch of turning ch, Ch 4, Turn.
Repeat Rows 2 and 3 for pattern.

43 / Medium Lozenge Stitch
(multiple of 3 + 1 plus 3 chs)

Row 1: Working on a chain foundation, work 3 DC in 5th ch from hook. * Skip 2 ch, 3 DC in next st. Repeat from * across, ending with Skip 1 st, DC in last st, Ch 4, Turn.

Row 2: * YO, Insert hook in next dc, Pull Up thread, YO and through 2 loops, YO, Insert hook in next dc, Pull Up thread, YO, through 2 loops, YO, Insert hook in next dc, Pull Up thread, YO and through 2 loops, YO and through 4 loops, Ch 2. Repeat from * across, ending with Ch 1 (instead of Ch 2), DC in 4th ch of turning ch, Ch 2, Turn.

Row 3: Work 3 DC in the "eye" of each dc group across, ending with DC in 3rd ch of turning ch, Ch 4, Turn.

Repeat Rows 2 and 3 for pattern.

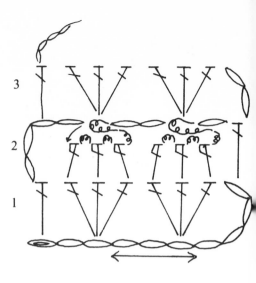

44 / Large Lozenge Stitch
(multiple of 3 + 1 plus 4 chs)

Row 1: Working on a chain foundation, work 3 TC in 6th ch from hook, * Skip 2 chs, work 3 TC in next st. Repeat from * across, ending with Skip 1 st, TC in last st, Ch 4, Turn.

Row 2: * YO twice, Insert hook in next tc, Pull Up thread, YO and through 2 loops, YO and through 2 loops, YO twice, Insert hook into next st, Pull Up thread, YO and through 2 loops, YO and through 2 loops. YO twice, Insert hook into next st, Pull Up thread, YO and through 2 loops, YO and through 2 loops, YO and through remaining loops, Ch 2. Repeat from * across ending with Ch 1 (instead of Ch 2) and TC in last ch of turning ch, Ch 3, Turn.

Row 3: Work 3 TC in the "eye" of each tc group across, ending with TC in 3rd ch of turning ch, Ch 4, Turn.

Repeat Rows 2 and 3 for pattern.

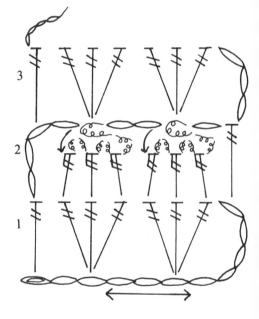

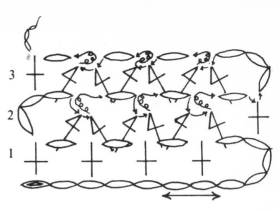

45 / Crossed Single Crochet
(*multiple of 2 + 1 plus 3 chs*)

Row 1: Working on a chain foundation, SC in 6th ch from hook. * Ch 1, Skip 1 ch, SC in next ch. Repeat from * across, Ch 3, Turn.

Row 2: Insert hook under next ch 1, Pull Up thread, Insert hook under next ch 1, Pull Up thread, YO and through 3 loops. * Ch 1, Insert hook under same ch as last "pull up," Pull Up thread, Insert hook under next ch 1, Pull Up thread, YO and through 3 loops. Repeat from * across, making last "pull up" under turning ch, and ending with Ch 1, SC in 4th ch of turning ch, Ch 3, Turn.

Row 3: Repeat Row 2, ending with SC at end of row in 2nd ch of turning ch, Ch 3, Turn.

Repeat Row 3 for pattern.

46 / Crossed Half Double Crochet
(*multiple of 2 + 1 plus 3 chs*)

Row 1: Working on a chain foundation, Skip 3 chs. * YO, Insert hook in next ch, Pull Up thread, YO, Insert hook in next st, Pull Up thread, YO, and through 5 loops on hook, Ch 1. Repeat from * across, ending with DC in last ch, Ch 2, Turn.

Row 2: YO, Insert hook under ch 1, Pull Up thread. YO, Insert hook under next ch 1, Pull Up thread, YO and through 5 loops on hook, Ch 1. * YO, Insert hook under same ch as last "pull up," Pull Up thread, YO, Insert hook under next ch 1, Pull Up thread, YO and through 5 loops, Ch 1. Repeat from * across, ending with last "pull up" under turning ch, DC in turning ch, Ch 2, Turn.

Repeat Row 2 for pattern.

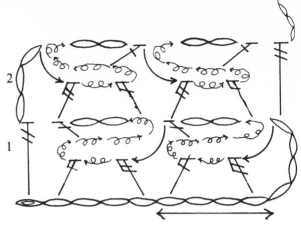

47 / Crossed Triple Crochet #1
(*multiple of 4 + 1 plus 4 chs*)

Row 1: Working on a chain foundation, Skip 4 chs. * YO 2 times, Insert hook in next st, Pull Up thread, YO and through 2 loops, Skip 2 sts, YO, Insert hook into next st, Pull Up thread, (YO and through 2 loops) 4 times. Ch 2, work DC under 2 loops pulled together by 2nd yo of ( ). Repeat from * across, ending with TC in last st, Ch 3, Turn.

Row 2: Work as for Row 1, working the stitches in the tops of the stitches of previous row and skipping the ch 2, Ch 3, Turn.
Repeat Row 2 for pattern.

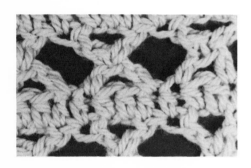

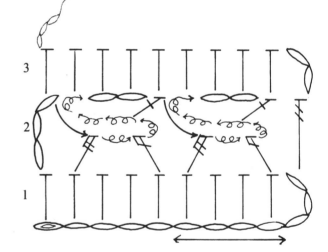

48 / Crossed Triple Crochet #2
(*multiple of 4 + 1 plus 3 chs*)

Row 1: Working on a chain foundation, HDC in 4th ch from hook and in each st across, Ch 3, Turn.
Row 2: Beginning with first st, work as for Row 1 in Crossed Triple Crochets #1 above, Ch 2, Turn.

Row 3: HDC in each st across, Ch 3, Turn.
Repeat Rows 2 and 3 for pattern.

49 / Crossed Bow Stitches
(*multiple of 2 + 1 plus 2 chs*)

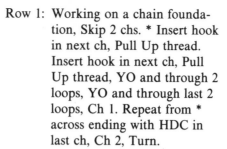
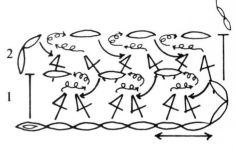

Row 1: Working on a chain foundation, Skip 2 chs. * Insert hook in next ch, Pull Up thread. Insert hook in next ch, Pull Up thread, YO and through 2 loops, YO and through last 2 loops, Ch 1. Repeat from * across ending with HDC in last ch, Ch 2, Turn.

Row 2: Insert hook under first ch 1, Pull Up thread, Insert hook under next ch, Pull Up thread, YO and through 2 loops, YO and through 2 loops, Ch 1, * Insert hook under same ch as last "pull up," Pull Up thread, Insert hook under next ch, Pull Up thread, YO and through 2 loops, YO and through 2 loops, Ch 1. Repeat from * across, ending with last "Pull Up" under turning ch, HDC in 3rd ch of turning ch, Ch 2, Turn.

Repeat Row 2 for pattern.

50 / Diamond Stitch
(*multiple of 2 + 1 plus 2 chs*)

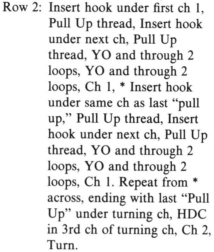
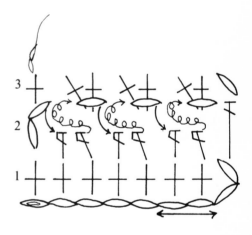

Row 1: Working on a chain foundation, work SC in 3rd ch from hook and in each ch across, Ch 2, Turn.

Row 2: * YO, Insert hook in next st, Pull Up thread, YO, Insert hook in next st, Pull Up thread, YO and through all 5 loops, Ch 1. Repeat from * across, ending with DC in turning ch, Ch 1, Turn.

Row 3: Work 2 SC under each ch 1 across, ending with SC under turning ch, Ch 2, Turn.

Repeat Rows 2 and 3 for pattern.

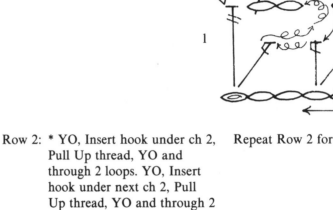

51 / Teepee Stitch
(multiple of 3 + 1 plus 4 chs)

Row 1: Working on a chain foundation, Skip 4 chs, * YO, Insert hook in next st, Pull Up thread, YO and through 2 loops, Skip 2 sts, YO, Insert hook in next st, Pull Up thread, YO and through 2 loops, YO and through 3 loops, Ch 2. Always working first "pull up" in same st as 2nd "pull up" of completed group, repeat from * across, ending with TC in same st as last "pull up," Ch 4, Turn.

Row 2: * YO, Insert hook under ch 2, Pull Up thread, YO and through 2 loops. YO, Insert hook under next ch 2, Pull Up thread, YO and through 2 loops, YO and through 3 loops, Ch 2. Working first "pull up" of next st in the same place as last "pull up" of last st, Repeat from * across, ending with last "pull up" under turning ch, Ch 2, TC in last ch of turning ch, Ch 4, Turn.

Repeat Row 2 for pattern.

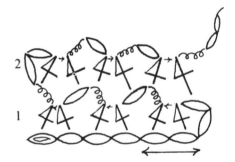

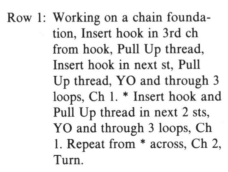

52 / Sophia Stitch
(multiple of 2 plus 2 chs)

Row 1: Working on a chain foundation, Insert hook in 3rd ch from hook, Pull Up thread, Insert hook in next st, Pull Up thread, YO and through 3 loops, Ch 1. * Insert hook and Pull Up thread in next 2 sts, YO and through 3 loops, Ch 1. Repeat from * across, Ch 2, Turn.

Row 2: * Insert hook in st at top of "group," Pull Up thread, Insert hook in ch, Pull Up thread, YO and through 3 loops, Ch 1. Repeat from * across, Ch 2, Turn.

Repeat Row 2 for pattern.

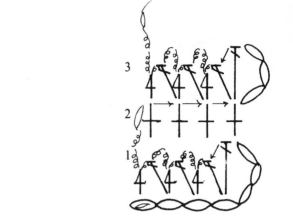

54 / Piqué Double Stitch
(multiple of 2 plus 3 chs)

Row 1: Working on a chain foundation, work DC in 4th ch from hook. * YO, Insert hook in same ch as last st was made, Pull Up thread, YO and through 1 loop, Insert hook into next ch, Pull Up thread, YO and through 3 loops, YO and through 2 loops. Repeat from * across, Ch 1, Turn.

Row 2: Work SC in each st across, ending with SC in 3rd ch of turning ch, Ch 3, Turn.

Row 3: Work as for Row 1, working first st of row in base of turning ch.

Repeat Rows 2 and 3 for pattern.

53 / Piqué Stitch
(multiple of 2 plus 3 chs)

Row 1: Working on a chain foundation, Skip 3 chs, * YO, Insert hook in next st, Pull Up thread, YO and through 2 loops, YO. Insert hook in next st, Pull Up thread, YO and through 2 loops, YO and through last 3 loops. Ch 1. Repeat from * across, Ch 2, Turn.

Row 2: SC in each st across, working last SC in turning ch, Ch 2, Turn.

Row 3: Work as for Row 1, working last "pull up" in 2nd ch of turning ch, Ch 2, Turn.

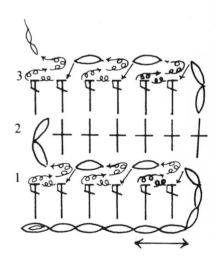

Repeat Rows 2 and 3 for pattern.

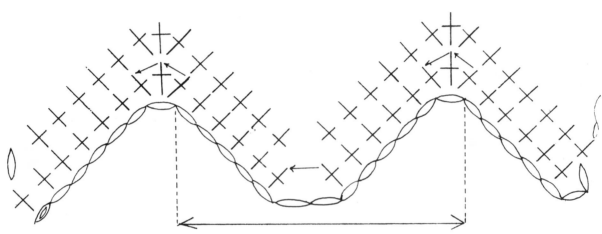

55 / Single Crochet Ripple Pattern
(multiple of 13 + 12 plus 2 chs)

Row 1: Working on a chain foundation, SC in 3rd ch from hook,
SC in each of next 4 chs.
* Work 3 SC in next ch, SC
in each of next 5 chs, Skip 2
chs, SC in each of next 5 chs.
Repeat from * across, ending
with 3 SC in next st, SC in
each of next 6 chs. Ch 1,
Turn.

Row 2: Skip next sc, * SC in each of
next 5 sc, work 3 SC in next
sc, SC in each of next 5 sc,
Skip 2 sc. Repeat from *
across, ending with SC in
each of next 5 sc, 3 SC in
next sc, SC in each of next 6
sc, Ch 1, Turn.

Repeat Row 2 for pattern.

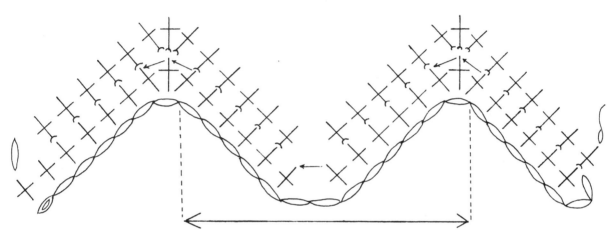

56 / Classic Ripple with Ridges
(*multiple of 13 + 12 plus 2 chs*)

Same as 55, except on 2nd and subsequent rows work all stitches in back loop of stitch.

Chapter 3 Advanced Pattern Stitches

This chapter includes a variety of pattern stitches, both simple and advanced. Some are richly textured; others are two-dimensional in effect. The Fisherman (or Aran) designs combine several elements to make attractive new patterns that are useful for sweaters, for afghans, and (in some cases) as borders. The stitches are grouped in categories as follows:

     1–24 Filet and Geometric Stitches
    25–41 Shell Stitches
    42–58 Popcorn, Cluster, and Puff Stitches
    59–65 Bullion and Rice Stitches
    66–73 Fancy Pattern Stitches
    74–95 Fisherman (Aran) Stitches

Note that in these patterns (as elsewhere in this book) capitalized words and abbreviations (SC, DC, ExSC, YO, etc.) represent a stitch that is to be made or an action to be taken. Abbreviations in small letters (sc, dc, tc, etc.) indicate a stitch that is to be *worked into*.

14″ × 14″ (35cm × 35cm) Basket Weave Pillow (*Plate 2*)

The woven design of this pillow looks complicated but is really very easy to do.
Material: 4 ounces (120 grams) of four-ply yarn (knitting worsted)
Hook size: H (UK 6, Int'l 5)
Gauge: 7 DC equals 2″ (5cm)
Make a foundation chain of 52 stitches. Work DC in 4th chain from hook and in each chain across (50 stitches including turning ch). Work rows 2 through 5 of Large Basket Weave (#76 in this chapter) 6 times. Tie off the yarn. Block the completed pillow top. For finishing instructions, see page 40.

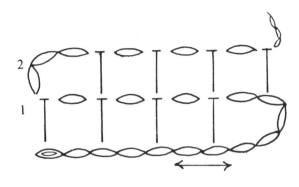

1 / Half Double Crochet Filet
(multiple of 2 plus 4 chs)

Row 1: Working on a chain foundation, HDC in 6th ch from hook, * Ch 1, Skip 1 st, HDC in next st. Repeat from * across, Ch 3, Turn.

Row 2: Skip ch 1, * HDC in next hdc, Ch 1. Repeat from * across, ending with HDC in 4th ch of turning ch, Ch 3, Turn.

Repeat Row 2 for pattern.

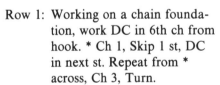

2 / Double Crochet Filet
(multiple of 2 plus 4 chs)

Row 1: Working on a chain foundation, work DC in 6th ch from hook. * Ch 1, Skip 1 st, DC in next st. Repeat from * across, Ch 3, Turn.

Row 2: Skip ch, * DC in next dc, Ch 1. Repeat from * across, ending with DC in 2nd ch past dc of turning ch, Ch 3, Turn.

Repeat Row 2 for pattern.

[Double Crochet Filet may be substituted for Triple Crochet Filet in working the projects suggested in Chapter 5.]

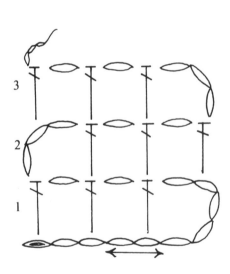

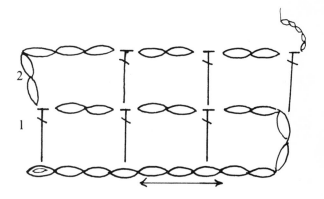

3 / Double Crochet Filet with Ch 2 Spaces
(*multiple of 3 plus 4 chs*)

Row 1: Working on a chain foundation, DC in 7th ch from hook. * Ch 2, Skip 2 chs, DC in next st. Repeat from * across, Ch 5, Turn.

Row 2: Skip 2 chs, * DC in next dc, Ch 2. Repeat from * across, ending with DC in 4th ch of turning ch, Ch 5, Turn.

Repeat Row 2 for pattern.

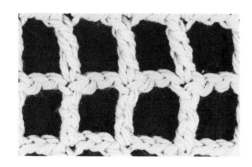

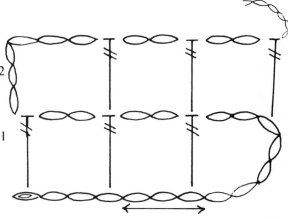

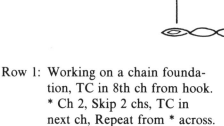

4 / Triple Crochet Filet with Ch 2 Spaces
(*multiple of 3 plus 5 chs*)

Row 1: Working on a chain foundation, TC in 8th ch from hook. * Ch 2, Skip 2 chs, TC in next ch, Repeat from * across. Ch 6, Turn.

Row 2: Skip 2 chs, * TC in next tc, Ch 2. Repeat from * across ending with TC in 5th ch of turning ch, Ch 6, Turn.

Repeat Row 2 for pattern.

[Triple Crochet Filet with Ch 2 Spaces is a favorite for making filet lace. See Chapter 5 for designs and project suggestions.]

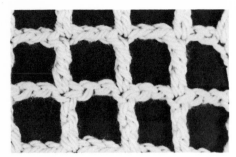

5 / Double Triple Crochet Filet
(multiple of 3 plus 5 chs)

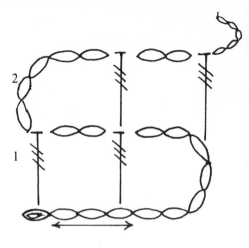

Row 1: Working on a chain foundation, TC in 8th ch from hook. * Ch 2, Skip 2 sts, TC in next st. Repeat from * across, Ch 5, Turn.
Row 2: * Skip 2 chs, TC in tc of previous row, Ch 2. Repeat from * across ending with TC in 5th ch of turning ch, Ch 5, Turn.
Repeat Row 2 for pattern.

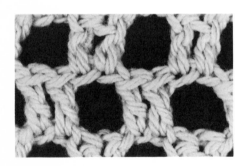

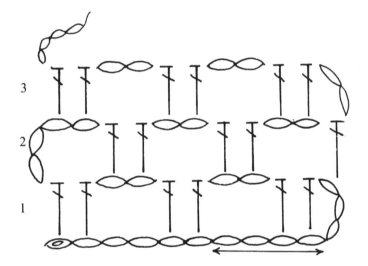

6 / Double Crochet Blocks
(multiple of 4 + 2 plus 3chs)

Row 1: Working on a chain foundation, DC in 4th ch from hook. DC in next ch. * Ch 2, Skip 2 sts, DC in each of next 2 sts. Repeat from * across, Ch 4, Turn.

Row 2: Skip dc, DC in each of next 2 chs, * Ch 2, Skip 2 dc, DC in each of next 2 chs. Repeat from * across until 2 dc remain. Ch 2, Skip dc, DC in top of turning ch, Ch 2, Turn.
Row 3: DC in each of next 2 chs. * Ch 2, Skip 2 dc, DC in each of next 2 chs. Repeat from * across until 2 dc remain, Ch 2, Skip 2 dc, DC in each of next 2 chs of turning ch, Ch 4, Turn.

Repeat Rows 2 and 3 for pattern.

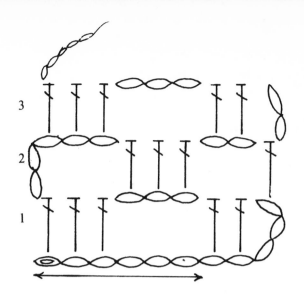

7 / Checks
(multiple of 6 + 2 plus 3 chs)

Row 1: Working on a chain foundation, DC in 4th ch from hook, DC in next st, * Ch 3, Skip 3 sts, DC in each of next 3 sts. Repeat from * across, Ch 5, Turn.

Row 2: Skip dcs, DC in each of next 3 chs. * Ch 3, DC in each of next 3 chs. Repeat from * across, ending with Ch 2, DC in last ch of turning ch, Ch 2, Turn.

Row 3: DC in each of next 2 chs. * Ch 3, Skip 3 dc, DC in each of next 3 chs. Repeat from * across, Ch 5, Turn.

Repeat Rows 2 and 3 for pattern.

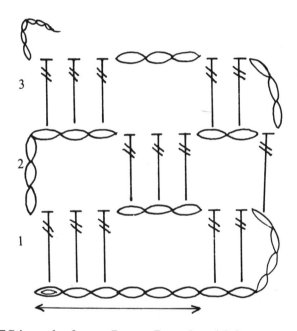

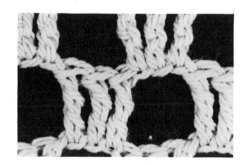

8 / Triple Crochet Blocks
(multiple of 6 + 2 plus 4 chs)

Row 1: Working on a chain foundation, TC in 5th ch from hook, TC in next st. * Ch 3, Skip 3 chs, TC in each of next 3 chs. Repeat from * across, Ch 6, Turn.

Row 2: * Skip 3 sts, TC in each of next 3 chs. Repeat from * across until 2 tc remain, Ch 2, Skip 2 sts, TC in 3rd ch of turning ch, Ch 3, Turn.

Row 3: TC in each of first 2 chs, * Ch 3, Skip 3 sts, TC in each of next 3 chs. Repeat from * across, ending with TC in each of nearest 3 chs, Ch 6, Turn.

Repeat Rows 2 and 3 for pattern.

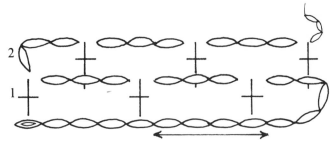

9 / Small Open Diamonds
(*multiple of 4 + 2 plus 4 chs*)

Row 1: Working on a chain foundation, SC in 6th ch from hook, * Ch 3, Skip 3 chs, SC in next ch. Repeat from * across, Ch 3, Turn.

Row 2: SC under first ch 3, * Ch 3, SC under next ch 3. Repeat from * across, ending with last SC under turning ch, Ch 3, Turn.

Repeat Row 2 for pattern.

[EDGING: Work Row 1. This edging makes a good base for fringe.]

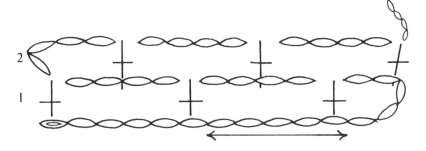

10 / Large Open Diamonds
(*multiple of 5 + 2 plus 4 chs*)

Row 1: Working on a chain foundation, SC in 6th ch from hook. * Ch 4, Skip 4 chs, SC in next ch. Repeat from * across, Ch 4, Turn.

Row 2: SC under first ch 4, * Ch 4, SC under next ch 4. Repeat from * across, ending with last SC under turning ch, Ch 4, Turn.

Repeat Row 2 for pattern.

[EDGING: Work Row 1 or Rows 1 and 2. This pattern is a good base for attaching fringe.]

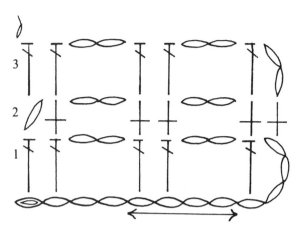

11 / Small Checkerboard
(*multiple of 4 + 1 plus 3 chs*)

Row 1: Working on a chain foundation, DC in 4th ch from hook.
* Ch 2, Skip 2 chs, DC in
each of next 2 chs. Repeat
from * across, Ch 1, Turn.

Row 2: SC in next dc, * Ch 2, SC in
each of next 2 dc. Repeat
from * across, ending with Ch
2, SC in next dc, SC in 3rd ch
of turning ch, Ch 2, Turn.

Row 3: DC in next sc, * Ch 2, DC in
each of next 2 sc. Repeat
from * across, ending with Ch
2, DC in last sc, DC in turning ch, Ch 1, Turn.

Repeat Rows 2 and 3 for pattern.

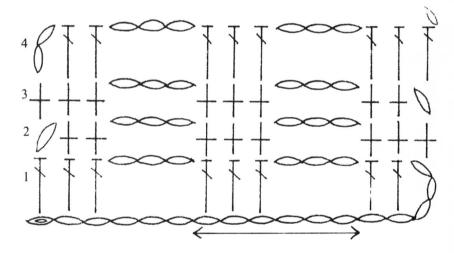

12 / Large Checkerboard
(*multiple of 6 + 2 plus 3 chs*)

Row 1: Working on a chain foundation, DC in 4th ch from hook,
DC in next ch. * Ch 3, Skip
3 chs, DC in each of next 3
chs. Repeat from * across, Ch
1, Turn.

Row 2: SC in each of next 2 dc, * Ch
3, SC in each of next 3 dc.
Repeat from * across, ending
with last SC in 3rd ch of turning ch, Ch 1, Turn.

Row 3: Same as Row 2, Ch 2, Turn.

Row 4: DC in each of next 2 sc, * Ch
3, DC in each of next 3 sc.
Repeat from * across, ending
with last DC in turning ch,
Ch 1, Turn.

Repeat Rows 2, 3, and 4 for pattern.

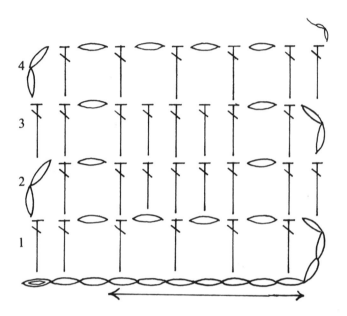

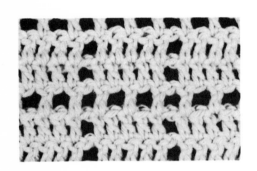

13 / Small Spaced Checks
(multiple of 7 + 3 plus 3 chs)

Row 1: Working on a chain foundation, DC in 4th ch from hook. * Ch 1, Skip ch, DC in next ch. Repeat from * across, ending with DC in last ch, Ch 2, Turn.

Row 2: DC in next dc, * Ch 1, (DC in next dc, DC in next ch) 2 times. DC in next dc, Repeat from * across, ending with Ch 1, DC in last dc, DC in 3rd ch of turning ch, Ch 2, Turn.

Row 3: DC in next dc, * Ch 1, DC in each of next 5 dc. Repeat from * across, ending with Ch 1, DC in last dc, DC in 2nd ch of turning ch, Ch 2, Turn.

Row 4: DC in next dc, * Ch 1, (DC, in next dc, Ch 1, Skip dc) 2 times, DC in next dc. Repeat from * across, ending with Ch 1, DC in last dc, DC in 2nd ch of turning ch, Ch 2, Turn.

Repeat Rows 2, 3, and 4 for pattern.

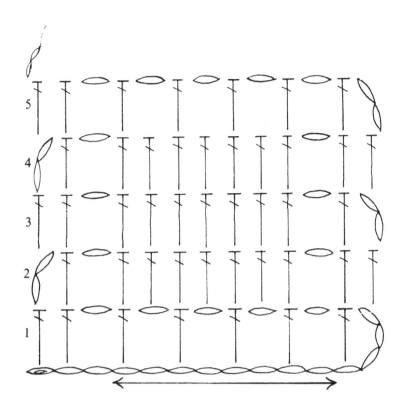

14 / Large Spaced Checks
(multiple of 8 + 4 plus 3 chs)

Row 1: Working on a chain foundation, DC in 4th ch from hook, * Ch 1, Skip 1 ch, DC in next ch. Repeat from * across, ending with DC in last ch, Ch 2, Turn.

Row 2: DC in next dc, * Ch 1, DC in next dc, (DC in next ch, DC in next dc) 3 times. Repeat from * across, ending with Ch 1, DC in last dc, DC in 3rd ch of turning ch, Ch 2, Turn.

Row 3: DC in next dc, Ch 1, * DC in each of next 7 dc, Ch 1. Repeat from * across, ending with DC in last dc, DC in 2nd ch of turning ch, Ch 2, Turn.

Row 4: Repeat Row 3.

Row 5: DC in next dc, * Ch 1, (DC in next dc, Ch 1, Skip dc) 3 times, DC in next dc. Repeat from * across, ending with Ch 1, DC in last dc and in 2nd ch of turning ch, Ch 2, Turn.

Repeat Rows 2 through 5 for pattern.

15 / Alternating Stitch #1
(multiple of 10 + 9 plus 2 chs)

Row 1: Working on a chain foundation, Skip 2 chs, SC in each of next 4 chs. * DC in each of next 5 chs, SC in each of next 5 chs. Repeat from * across, ending with DC in each of last 5 chs, Ch 2, Turn.

Row 2: SC in each of next 4 dc. * DC in each of next 5 sc, SC in each of next 5 dc. Repeat from * across, ending with DC in each of last 4 sc, DC in turning ch, Ch 2, Turn.

Repeat Row 2 for pattern.

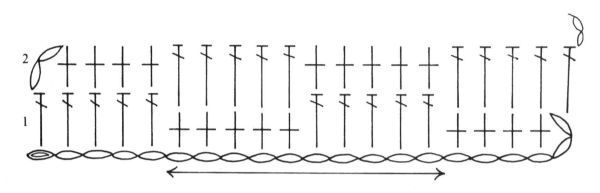

16 / Alternating Stitch #2
(multiple of 10 + 9 plus 2 chs)

Working on a chain foundation, work as for Alternating Stitch #1 above, except work all even numbered rows (2, 4, etc) in the *back loop* of stitch only.

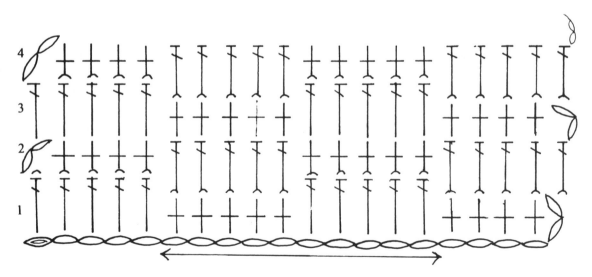

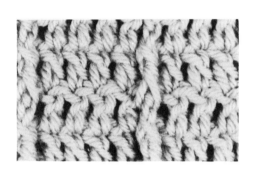

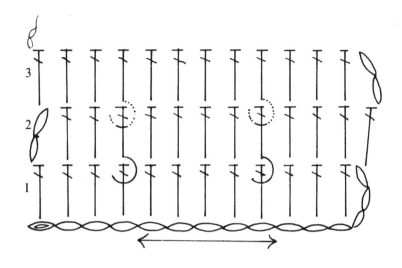

17 / Cord
(multiple of 5 + 7 plus 3 chs)

Row 1: Working on a chain foundation, DC in 4th ch from hook
and in each ch across, Ch 2,
Turn.

Row 2: DC in each of next 2 dc;
working from the *front,* work
a DC *around* next dc, * DC in
each of next 4 dc; working
from the *front,* work a DC
around next dc. Repeat from
* across, ending with DC in
last 3 dc and in turning ch,
Ch 2, Turn.

Row 3: DC in next 3 dc; working
from the *back,* work a DC
around the next dc. * DC in
each of next 4 dc; working
from *back,* work a DC *around*
the next dc. Repeat from *
across, ending with DC in
each of last 2 sts, DC in 2nd
ch of turning ch, Ch 2, Turn.

Repeat Rows 2 and 3 for pattern.

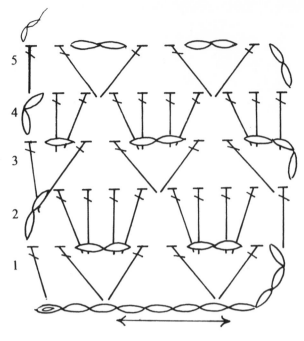

18 / May Baskets
(multiple of 4 + 1 plus 3 chs)

Row 1: Working on a chain foundation, work (DC, Ch 2, DC) in 6th ch from hook. * Skip 3 chs, (DC, Ch 2, DC) in next st. Repeat from * across, ending with Skip 1 st, DC in last ch, Ch 2, Turn.

Row 2: * Work 4 DC under ch 2. Repeat from * across, ending with DC in last ch of turning ch, Ch 3, Turn.

Row 3: DC *between* the first 2 dc. * (DC, Ch 2, DC) *between* each 4 dc group, Repeat from * across, ending with (DC, Ch 1, DC) under turning ch, Ch 2, Turn.

Row 4: Work 2 DC under ch 1. * Work 4 DC under ch 2. Repeat from * across, ending with 3 DC under turning ch, Ch 2, Turn.

Row 5: Work (DC, Ch 2, DC) *between* each group across, ending with DC in turning ch, Ch 2, Turn.

Repeat Rows 2 through 5 for pattern.

[**EDGING:** Work Rows 1 and 2.]

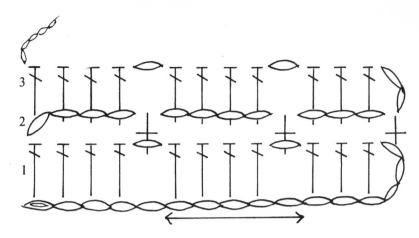

19 / Squares
(*multiple of 5 + 3 plus 3 chs*)

Row 1: Working on a chain foundation, DC in 4th ch from hook, DC in each of next 2 sts. * Ch 1, Skip 1 st, DC in each of next 4 sts. Repeat from * across, Ch 5, Turn.

Row 2: * SC under ch 1, Ch 4. Repeat from * across, ending with SC in last ch 1, Ch 3, SC in 3rd ch of turning ch, Ch 2, Turn.

Row 3: 3 DC under ch 4. * Ch 1, 4 DC under ch 4. Repeat from * across, Ch 5, Turn.

Repeat Rows 2 and 3 for pattern.

[EDGING: Work Row 1. If a fringe is to be added, attach it in the opening under the chain stitch.]

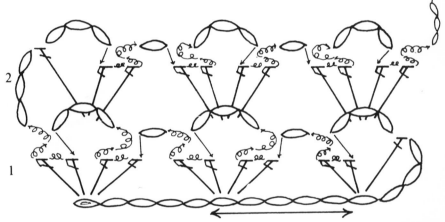

20 / Chain Links
(*multiple of 5 + 1 plus 3 chs*)

Row 1: Working on a chain foundation, DC in 4th ch from hook, Ch 3, work Half Cluster in same ch. [*To Make Half Cluster:* YO, Insert hook in st, Pull Up thread, YO and through 2 loops. YO, Insert hook in same st, Pull Up thread, YO and through 2 loops, YO and through 3 loops.] * Ch 1, Skip 4 chs, work (Half Cluster, Ch 3, Half Cluster) in next ch. Repeat from * across, Ch 3, Turn.

Row 2: DC under first ch 3, Ch 3, work Half Cluster under same ch 3, * Ch 1, work Half Cluster, Ch 3, Half Cluster under next ch 3. Repeat from * across, Ch 3, Turn.

Repeat Row 2 for pattern.

[EDGING: Work Row 1.]

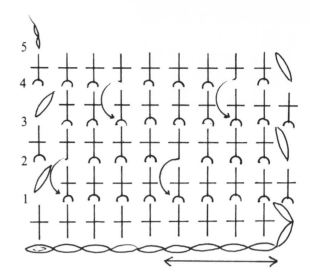

21 / Brick #1
(multiple of 4 + 1 plus 2 chs)

Row 1: Working on a chain foundation, SC in 3rd ch from hook and in each ch across, Ch 1, Turn.

Row 2: Working in *back loop only,* SC in each st (including turning chain) across, Ch 1, Turn.

Row 3: * Working in *back loop only,* SC in each of next 3 sts, SC into the next st on Row 1 (Skip st on Row 2). Repeat from * across, Ch 1, Turn.

Row 4: Work as for Row 2, Ch 1, Turn.

Row 5: SC in first st (*back loop only*), * Skip next st and work into *back loop only* of next st on Row 3, (skip st on Row 4). SC in next 3 sts. Repeat from * across, Ch 1, Turn.

Repeat Rows 2 through 5 for pattern.

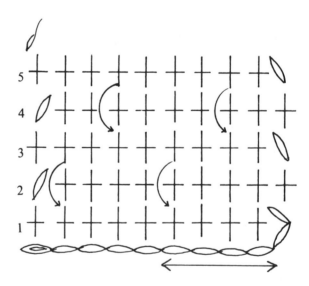

22 / Brick #2
(multiple of 4 + 1 plus 2 chs)

Row 1: SC in 3rd ch from hook and in each st across. Ch 1, Turn.

Row 2: SC in each st across, including turning ch, Ch 1, Turn.

Row 3: * SC in next 3 sts, SC in next st of Row 1 (Skip stitch on Row 2). Repeat from * across, ending with SC in turning ch, Ch 1, Turn.

Row 4: Work as for Row 1.

Row 5: SC in first st, * work SC in next st on Row 3, (Skip st on row 4). SC in next 3 sts. Repeat from * across, Ch 1, Turn.

Repeat Rows 2 through 5 for pattern.

23 / Ponytail #1
(multiple of 2 plus 3 chs)

Row 1: Working on a chain foundation, DC in 4th ch from hook and in each ch across, Ch 1, Turn.

Rows 2 and 3: SC in each st across, ending with SC in turning ch, Ch 1, Turn.

Row 4: DC (from front) *around* first dc of Row 1 (Skip st on Row 2 and 3). * SC in next st, DC (from front) *around* st on Row 1 (Skip sts on Row 2 and 3). Repeat from * across, ending with SC in turning ch, Ch 1, Turn.

Row 5: SC in each st across, working last SC in turning ch, Ch 1, Turn.

Repeat Rows 2 through 5 for pattern.

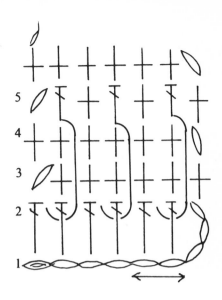

24 / Ponytail #2
(multiple of 2 plus 3 chs)

Row 1: Working on a chain foundation, work as for Row 1 through 4 of Ponytail Stitch #1.

Row 5: DC in each st across, Ch 1, Turn.

Rows 6 and 7: Work as for Rows 2 and 3.

Row 8: * SC in next st, DC (from front) *around* next st on Row 5, Skip next sc on Row 6 and 7. Repeat from * across, ending with SC in last sc and in turning ch, Ch 1, Turn.

Repeat Rows 2 through 8 for pattern.

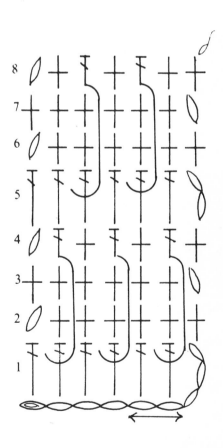

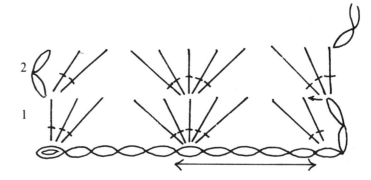

25 / Small Basic Shell #1
(*multiple of 5 + 1 plus 2 chs*)

Row 1: Working on a chain foundation, work 2 ExSC in 3rd ch
from hook. * Skip 4 sts, work
5 ExSC in next st. Repeat
from * across, ending with
only 3 ExSC in last st. Ch 2,
Turn.

Row 2: Work 2 ExSC in st at base of
ch. * Work 5 ExSC in middle
st of 5 sc shell of previous
row, Repeat from * across,
ending with 3 ExSC in 2nd ch
of turning ch, Ch 2, Turn.
Repeat Row 2 for pattern.

[**EDGING:** Work Row 1 or Rows 1
and 2.]

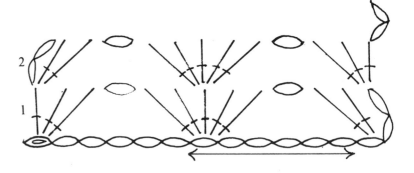

26 / Small Basic Shell #2
(*multiple of 6 + 1 plus 2 chs*)

Row 1: Working on a chain foundation, work 2 ExSC in 3rd ch
from hook, * Ch 1, Skip 5 sts,
work 5 ExSC in next st. Repeat from * across, ending
with only 3 ExSC in last st,
Ch 2, Turn.

Row 2: Work 2 ExSC in st at base of
turning ch, * Ch 1, work 5
ExSC in center st of shell of
previous row. Repeat from *
across, ending with Ch 1,
3 ExSC in 2nd ch of turning
ch, Ch 2, Turn.
Repeat Row 2 for pattern.

[**EDGING:** Work Row 1 or Rows 1
and 2. Fringe may be added under the
chain stitch.]

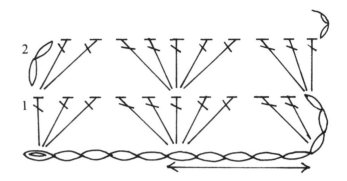

27 / Medium Basic Shell #1
(multiple of 5 + 1 plus 2 chs)

Row 1: Working on a chain foundation, work 2 DC in 3rd ch from hook. * Skip 4 sts, work 5 DC in next st. Repeat from * across, ending with only 3 DC in last ch. Ch 2, Turn.

Row 2: Work 2 DC in st at base of ch, * Work 5 DC in center st of dc shell of previous row. Repeat from * across, ending with 3 DC in 2nd ch of turning ch, Ch 2, Turn.

Repeat Row 2 for pattern.

[**EDGING:** Work Row 1 or Rows 1 and 2.]

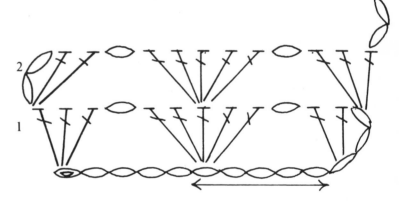

28 / Medium Basic Shell #2
(multiple of 5 + 1 plus 2 chs)

Row 1: Working on a chain foundation, work 2 DC in 3rd ch from hook. * Ch 1, Skip 4 chs, work 5 DC in next st. Repeat from * across, ending with only 3 DC in last ch, Ch 2, Turn.

Row 2: 2 DC in st at base of ch, * Ch 1, work 5 DC in center st of dc shell of previous row. Repeat from * across ending with Ch 1, 3 DC in 2nd ch of turning ch, Ch 2, Turn.

Repeat Row 2 for pattern.

[**EDGING:** Work Row 1 or Rows 1 and 2.]

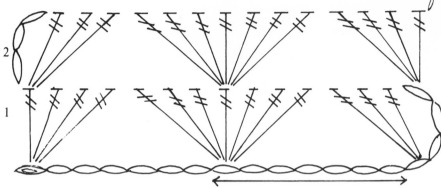

29 / Basic Shell #3 Triple Crochet
(*multiple of 7 + 1 plus 3 chs*)

Row 1: Working on a chain foundation, work 3 TC in 4th ch from hook. * Skip 6 sts, work 7 TC Shell in next st. Repeat from * across, ending with Skip 6 chs, 4 TC in last st, Ch 3, Turn.

Row 2: Work 3 TC in st at base of turning chain. * Work 7 TC Shell in middle st of 7 tc shell of previous row. Repeat from * across, ending with 4 TC in 3rd ch of turning ch, Ch 3, Turn.

Repeat Row 2 for pattern.

[EDGING: Work Row 1 or Rows 1 and 2.]

30 / Triple Shell with Filet Row
(*multiple of 8 + 1 plus 4 chs*)

Row 1: Working on a chain foundation, HDC in 5th ch from hook. * Ch 1, Skip 1 st, HDC in next st. Repeat from * across, Ch 4, Turn.

Row 2: Work 3 TC under first ch 1, Ch 1, * Skip 3 spaces, work 7 TC Shell under next ch 1, Ch 1, Repeat from * across, ending with Skip 3 spaces, 4 TC under turning ch, Ch 3, Turn.

Row 3: * HDC in next st, Ch 1, Skip 1 st. Repeat from * across, ending with HDC in 3rd ch of turning ch, Ch 4, Turn.

Repeat Rows 2 and 3 for pattern.

[EDGING: Work Rows 1 and 2.]

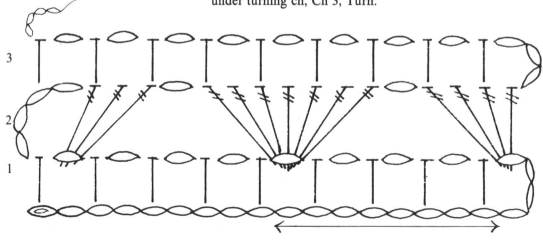

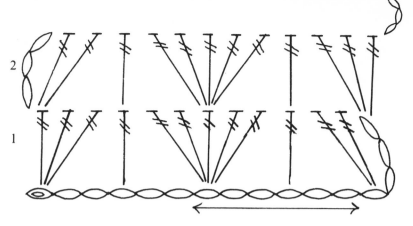

31 / Triple Shells and Bars
(*multiple of 6 + 1 plus 3 chs*)

Row 1: Working on a chain foundation, work 2 TC in 4th ch from hook. * Skip 2 chs, TC in next st. Skip 2 sts, work 5 TC Shell in next st. Repeat from * across until 6 sts remain, Skip 2 sts, TC in next st, Skip 2 sts, 3 TC in last st, Ch 3, Turn.

Row 2: 2 TC in base of turning ch, Skip 2 tc, * TC in next tc (the bar), work 5 TC Shell in center st of next shell. Repeat from * across, ending with TC in tc (the bar), 3 TC in 3rd ch of turning ch, Ch 3, Turn.

Repeat Row 2 for pattern.

[EDGING: Work Row 1 or Rows 1 and 2.]

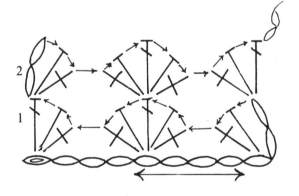

32 / Small Fancy Basic Shell
(*multiple of 4 + 1 plus 2 chs*)

Row 1: Working on a chain foundation, work (HDC, SC) in 3rd ch from hook. * Skip 3 sts, work (SC, HDC, DC, HDC, SC) Shell in next st. Repeat from * across ending with Skip 3 sts, (SC, HDC, DC) in last st, Ch 2, Turn.

Row 2: Work (HDC, SC) in st at base of ch. * Work (SC, HDC, DC, HDC, SC) Shell in center st of the shell of previous row. Repeat from * across ending with (SC, HDC, DC) in turning ch, Ch 2, Turn.

Repeat Row 2 for pattern.

[EDGING: Work Row 1.]

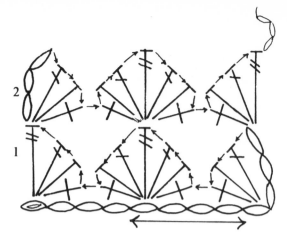

33 / Large Fancy Basic Shell
(multiple of 4 + 1 plus 3 chs)

Row 1: Working on a chain foundation, work (DC, HDC, SC) in 4th ch from hook. * Skip 3 sts, work (SC, HDC, DC, TC, DC, HDC, SC) Shell in next st. Repeat from * across ending with Skip 3 sts, (SC, HDC, DC, TC) in last st, Ch 3, Turn.

Row 2: Work (DC, HDC, SC) at base of turning ch, * Work (SC, HDC, DC, TC, DC, HDC, SC) Shell in center st of shell of previous row. Repeat from * across, ending with (SC, HDC, DC, TC) in 3rd ch of turning ch, Ch 3, Turn.
Repeat Row 2 for pattern.

[EDGING: Row 1 or Rows 1 and 2.]

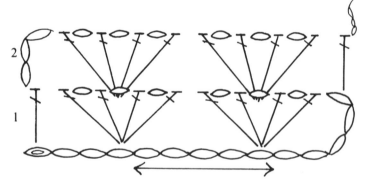

34 / Small Open Shell
(multiple of 5 + 1 plus 3 chs)

Row 1: Working on a chain foundation, Skip 5 chs. In next st work DC, (Ch 1, DC) 3 times to make Shell. * Skip 4 sts, work Shell in next st. Repeat from * across ending with Skip 2 chs, DC in last ch, Ch 3, Turn.

Row 2: Work a Shell under middle ch of shell of previous row, ending with DC in last ch of turning chain, Ch 3, Turn.
Repeat Row 2 for pattern.

[EDGING: Work Row 1 or Rows 1 and 2.]

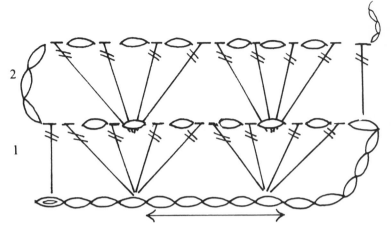

35 / Large Open Shell
(multiple of 5 + 1 plus 4 chs)

Row 1: Working on a chain foundation, Skip 6 chs. In next st, work TC, (Ch 1, TC) 3 times to make Shell. * Skip 4 sts, in next st work Shell. Repeat from * across ending with Skip 2 sts, TC in last st, Ch 3, Turn.

Row 2: Work a Shell under middle ch of each shell of previous row across, ending with TC in first ch past last shell, Ch 3, Turn.

Repeat Row 2 for pattern.

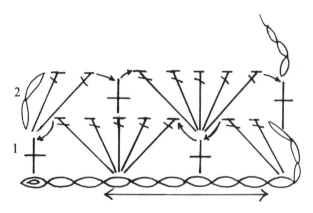

36 / Alternating Shell
(multiple of 6 + 4 plus 3 chs)

Row 1: Working on a chain foundation, work 2 DC in 4th ch from hook. * Skip 2 sts, SC in next st, Skip 2 sts, work 5 DC Shell in next st, Repeat from * across ending with Skip 2 sts, SC in last st, Ch 2, Turn.

Row 2: Work 2 DC in base of turning ch, * SC in 3rd dc of 5 dc shell, 5 DC in sc. Repeat from * across, ending with SC in last ch of turning ch, Ch 3, Turn.

Repeat Row 2 for pattern.

[EDGING: Work Row 1 or Rows 1 and 2.]

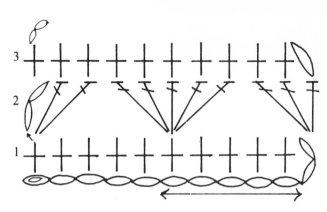

37 / Double Crochet Shells with Single Crochet Rows
(*multiple of 5 plus 2 chs*)

Row 1: Working on a chain foundation, SC in 3rd ch from hook and in each ch across, Ch 2, Turn.

Row 2: Work 2 DC in st at base of ch, Skip 4 sts, * Work 5 DC Shell in next st. Skip 4 sts. Repeat from * across, ending with 3 DC in last ch of turning ch, Ch 1, Turn.

Row 3: SC in each st across ending with SC in 2nd ch of turning ch, Ch 2, Turn.

Repeat Rows 2 and 3 for pattern.

[EDGING: Rows 1 and 2.]

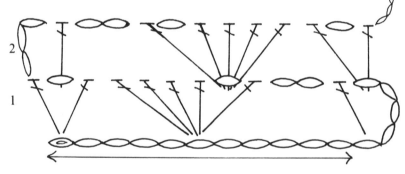

38 / Wings
(*multiple of 11 + 1 plus 4 chs*)

Row 1: Working on a chain foundation, DC in 5th ch from hook. * Ch 2, Skip 5 chs, work (DC, Ch 1, 4 DC) in next ch, Skip 4 chs, work (DC, Ch 1, DC) in next ch. Repeat from * across, Ch 3, Turn.

Row 2: DC under first ch 1 of previous row. * Ch 2, work (DC, Ch 1, 4 DC) under next ch 1. Work (DC, Ch 1, DC) under next ch 1. Repeat from * across, Ch 3, Turn.

Repeat Row 2 for pattern.

[EDGING: Work Rows 1 and 2.]

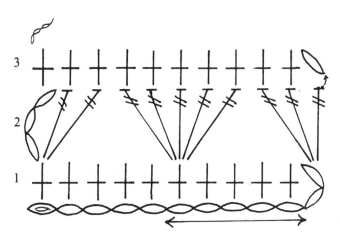

39 / Triple Shells with Single Crochet Rows
(*multiple of 5 plus 2 chs*)

Row 1: Working on a chain foundation, SC in 3rd ch from hook and in each st across, Ch 3, Turn.

Row 2: Work 2 TC in st at base of ch, Skip 4 sts, * 5 TC Shell in next st, Skip 4 sts. Repeat from * across, ending with 3 TC Shell in turning chain, Ch 1, Turn.

Row 3: SC in each st across ending with SC in turning ch, Ch 3, Turn.

Repeat Rows 2 and 3 for pattern.

[**EDGING:** Rows 1 and 2.]

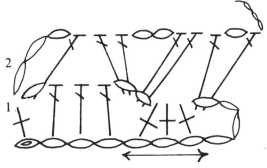

40 / Godet
(*multiple of 3 + 4 plus 4 chs*)

Row 1: Working on a chain foundation, SC in 5th ch from hook. SC into each of next 2 sts, * Ch 2, DC into each of next 3 sts, Ch 2, SC into each of next 3 sts. Repeat from * across, ending with DC in each of next 3 sts, Ch 1, SC in last ch, Ch 3, Turn.

Row 2: DC under first ch, * Work (2 DC, Ch 2, 2 DC) under each ch 2 across, ending with (DC, Ch 1, DC) under turning ch, Ch 3, Turn.

Repeat Row 2 for pattern.

[**EDGING:** Work Row 1 or Rows 1 and 2.]

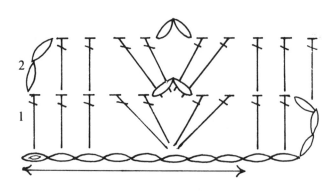

41 / Ribbon
(multiple of 8 + 2 plus 3 chs)

Row 1: Working on a chain foundation, DC in 4th ch from hook, DC in next ch. * Skip 2 sts, work (2 DC, Ch 2, 2 DC) Shell in next st, Skip 2 sts, DC in each of next 3 sts. Repeat from * across, Ch 2, Turn.

Row 2: DC in each of next 2 sts. * Work (2 DC, Ch 2, 2 DC) Shell under ch 2 of previous row, Skip 2 dc of shell, DC in each of next 3 sts. Repeat from * across, ending with DC in last 2 sts and DC in turning ch, Ch 2, Turn.

Repeat Row 2 for pattern.

[**EDGING:** Work Row 1 or Rows 1 and 2.]

42 / Small Popcorn #1
(multiple of 2 + 1 plus 3 chs)

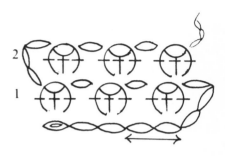

Row 1: Working on a chain foundation, work a Small Popcorn in
4th ch from hook. [*To Make
a Small Popcorn:* Work 3 SC
in same st, Pull Up a ½″ loop,
remove hook, Insert hook
under both loops of first sc of
group, and Pull dropped loop
through.] * Ch 1, Skip 1 st,
make Small Popcorn in next
st. Repeat from * across, Ch
3, Turn.

Row 2: * Work Small Popcorn in first
sc of group of previous row
(in same place the dropped
loop was pulled through), Ch
1. Repeat from * across, Ch
3, Turn.

Repeat Row 2 for pattern.

43 / Small Popcorn #2
(multiple of 2 + 1 plus 3 chs)

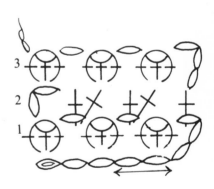

Row 1: Working on a chain foundation, work as for Row 1
above, Ch 2, Turn.

Row 2: Work 2 SC under each ch
across, ending with SC under
turning ch, Ch 3, Turn.

Row 3: * Work Small Popcorn in
next sc, Ch 1, Skip 1 sc. Repeat from * across, ending
with Small Popcorn in 2nd ch
of turning ch, Ch 2, Turn.

Repeat Rows 2 and 3 for pattern.

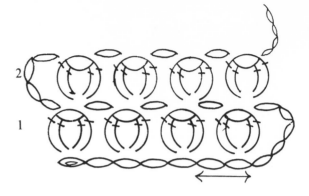

44 / Medium Popcorn #1
(*multiple of 2 + 1 plus 5 chs*)

Row 1: Working on a chain foundation, make a Medium Popcorn in 6th ch from hook. [*To Make a Medium Popcorn:* Make 4 DC in same st, Pull Up a loop about ½″, remove hook. Insert hook under both threads of first dc made and pull dropped loop through.] * Ch 1, Skip 1 st, make Medium Popcorn in next st, Repeat from * across, Ch 4, Turn.

Row 2: Work Medium Popcorn in first dc of 4 dc group of previous row (in same place the dropped loop was pulled through), Ch 1. Repeat across, Ch 4, Turn.
Repeat Row 2 for pattern.

45 / Medium Popcorn #2
(*multiple of 2 plus 4 chs*)

Row 1: Working on a chain foundation, work as for Row 1 of Medium Popcorn #1. Ch 2, Turn.

Row 2: Work 2 SC between each popcorn and SC under turning ch, Ch 4, Turn.

Row 3: * Work Medium Popcorn in next sc, Ch 1, Skip 1 st. Repeat from * across ending with last Popcorn in turning ch, Ch 2, Turn.
Repeat Rows 2 and 3 for pattern.

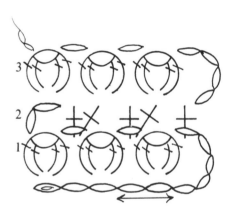

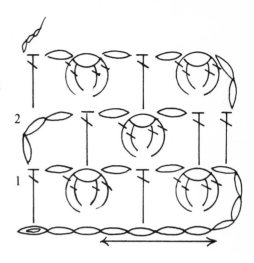

46 / Medium Popcorn #3
(*multiple of 4 + 3 plus 4 chs*)

Row 1: Working on a chain foundation, work a Medium Popcorn (see Pattern #44) in 5th ch from hook. * Ch 1, Skip ch, DC in next ch, Skip ch, Popcorn in next ch. Repeat from * across, ending with DC in last ch, Ch 3, Turn.
Row 2: * DC in next popcorn, Ch 1, work Popcorn in next dc, Ch 1. Repeat from * across, ending with DC in last popcorn and DC in turning ch, Ch 2, Turn.
Row 3: * Work Popcorn in next dc, Ch 1, DC in next popcorn, Ch 1. Repeat from * across, working last DC in 2nd ch of turning ch, Ch 3, Turn.
Repeat Rows 2 and 3 for pattern.

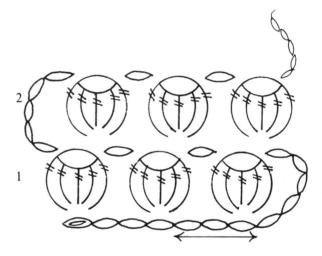

47 / Large Popcorn #1
(*multiple of 3 + 1 plus 5 chs*)

Row 1: Working on a chain foundation, make a Large Popcorn in 6th ch from hook. [*To Make a Large Popcorn:* Work 5 TC in same st, Pull Up a ½" loop, remove hook, Insert hook under both loops of first tc, and Pull dropped loop through.] * Ch 1, Skip 2 sts, make a Large Popcorn in next st. Repeat from * across, Ch 5, Turn.

Row 2: * Work Large Popcorn in next large popcorn, inserting hook in first st of 5 tc group (this will be the same st that the dropped loop was pulled through), Ch 1. Repeat from * across, Ch 5, Turn.
Repeat Row 2 for pattern.

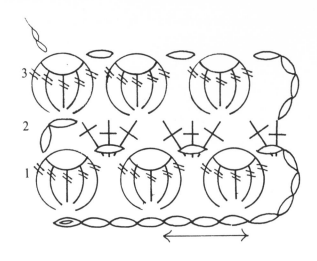

48 / Large Popcorn #2
(*multiple of 3 + 2 plus 4 chs*)

Row 1: Working on a chain foundation, work as for Row 1 of Large Popcorn #1, except Ch 2 to turn at end of row.

Row 2: Work 3 SC under ch 1 between each of the popcorns and 2 SC under the turning ch at end of row, Ch 4, Turn.

Row 3: Skip 1 st, work Large Popcorn in next st. * Ch 1, Skip 2 sts, work Large Popcorn in next st. Repeat from * across, ending with Popcorn in 2nd ch of turning ch, Ch 2, Turn.

Repeat Rows 2 and 3 for pattern.

49 / Small Cluster #1
(*multiple of 2 + 1 plus 3 chs*)

Row 1: Working on a chain foundation, make a Small Cluster in 4th ch from hook. [*To Make a Small Cluster:* (Insert hook in st, Pull Up thread, YO and through 1 loop) three times in same stitch. YO and through all loops on hook.] * Ch 1, Skip 1 st, make Small Cluster in next st. Repeat from * across, Ch 3, Turn.

Row 2: Skip first cluster. * Make Cluster (as in Row 1) in the "eye" formed by ch 1, then Ch 1. Repeat from * across, working the last Cluster in 3rd ch of turning ch, Ch 2, Turn.

Repeat Row 2 for pattern.

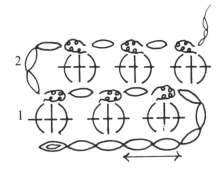

50 / Small Cluster #2
(multiple of 2 + 1 plus 3 chs)

Row 1: Work as for Row 1 in Small Cluster #1. Ch 2, Turn.
Row 2: Work 2 SC between the clusters of previous row, ending with SC under turning ch, Ch 3, Turn.
Row 3: * Work Cluster in next st, Skip 1 st, Ch 1. Repeat from * across, ending with last Cluster in 2nd ch of turning ch, Ch 2, Turn.
Repeat Rows 2 and 3 for pattern.

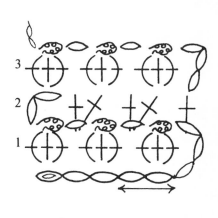

51 / Medium Cluster #1
(multiple of 2 + 1 plus 4 chs)

Row 1: Working on a chain foundation, make a Medium Cluster in 5th ch from hook. [*To Make a Medium Cluster:* (YO, Insert hook in stitch, Pull Up thread, YO and through 2 loops) 4 times in same st. YO and through all loops on hook.] * Ch 1, Skip 1 st, make Cluster in next st. Repeat from * across, Ch 4, Turn.
Row 2: * Make a Cluster in the "eye" of previous row, Ch 1. Repeat from * across, ending with last Cluster in 4th ch of turning ch, Ch 4, Turn.
Repeat Row 2 for pattern.

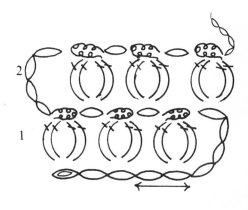

52 / Medium Cluster #2
(multiple of 2 + 1 plus 4 chs)

Row 1: Work as for Row 1 above, Ch 2, Turn.
Row 2: SC between first 2 clusters, work 2 SC between each cluster across ending with 2 SC under turning ch, Ch 3, Turn.
Row 3: Work Medium Cluster in next sc, * Skip 1 sc, Ch 1, work Medium Cluster in next sc. Repeat from * across working last Cluster in 2nd ch of turning ch. Ch 2, Turn.
Repeat Rows 2 and 3 for pattern.

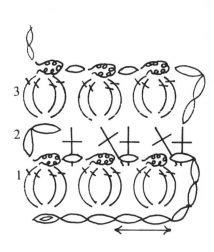

53 / Medium Cluster #3
(multiple of 4 + 2 plus 4 chs)

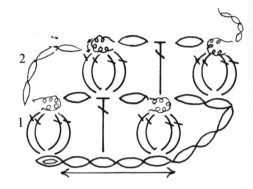

Row 1: Working on a chain foundation, make a Medium Cluster in the 6th ch from hook. * Ch 1, Skip 1 st, DC in next st, Ch 1, Skip 1 st, make Cluster in next st. Repeat from * across, Ch 4, Turn.

Row 2: * Make a Cluster in dc, Ch 1, DC in last yo of cluster (*not* in the "eye" of the cluster), Ch 1. Repeat from * across, ending with Cluster in next to last ch of turning ch, Ch 4, Turn.

Repeat Row 2 for pattern.

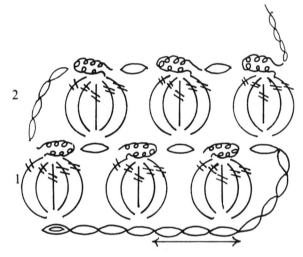

54 / Large Cluster #1
(multiple of 3 + 2 plus 4 chs)

Row 1: Working on a chain foundation, make a Large Cluster in 6th ch from hook. [*To Make a Large Cluster:* (YO 2 times, Insert hook into st, Pull Up thread. YO and through 2 loops 2 times) 5 times in same stitch, YO and through all loops on hook.] * Ch 1, Skip 2 sts, make Large Cluster in next st. Repeat from * across, Ch 4, Turn.

Row 2: * Make Large Cluster in the "eye" (formed by ch 1) of cluster of previous row, Ch 1. Repeat from * across, ending with last Cluster in first ch past last cluster of previous row, Ch 4, Turn.

Repeat Row 2 for pattern.

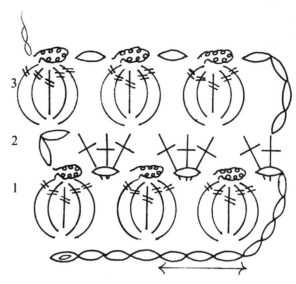

55 / Large Cluster #2
(multiple of 3 + 1 plus 5 chs)

Row 1: Working on a chain foundation, work as for Row 1 above, Ch 2, Turn.

Row 2: Make 3 SC between the clusters of previous row, ending with 2 SC under turning ch, Ch 4, Turn.

Row 3: Skip 1 st, * work Large Cluster in next st, Ch 1, Skip 2 sts. Repeat from * across, working last Cluster in 2nd ch of turning ch, Ch 2, Turn.

Repeat Rows 2 and 3 for pattern.

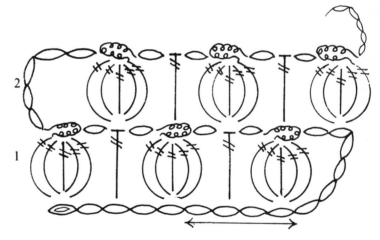

56 / Large Cluster #3
(multiple of 4 + 2 plus 4 chs)

Row 1: Working on a chain foundation, make a Large Cluster in 7th ch from hook. (See Large Cluster #1) * Ch 1, Skip 1 st, TC in next st, Ch 1. Skip 1 st, make a Large Cluster in next st. Repeat from * across, Ch 5, Turn.

Row 2: * Make a Large Cluster in the next tc, Ch 1, TC in last yo of cluster of previous row (*not* the ch 1 "eye"), Ch 1. Repeat from * across, ending with Large Cluster in 2nd ch past last cluster of previous row, Ch 5, Turn.

Repeat Row 2 for pattern.

57 / Puff (or Bobble)
(multiple of 2 + 1 plus 4 chs)

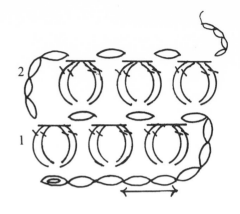

Row 1: Working on a chain foundation work Puff in 5th ch from hook. [*To Make a Puff Stitch:* (YO, Insert hook into st, Pull Up thread about ½″) 4 times in same st, YO and through all loops on hook.] * Ch1, Skip 1 st, make Puff in next st, Ch 1 (you will have 2 chs between puffs). Repeat from * across, Ch 4, Turn.

Row 2: * Work Puff in space between puffs of previous row, Ch 1. Repeat from * across ending with Puff under turning ch, Ch 4, Turn.

Repeat Row 2 for pattern.

[Note: Pull Up thread ½″ for baby yarn (one-ply), ¾″ for sport yarn (two-ply), and 1″ for worsted weight (four-ply).]

58 / Horizontal Puff
(multiple of 4 + 1 plus 4 chs)

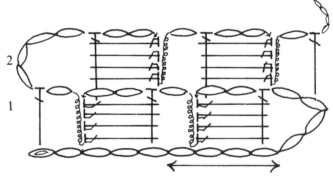

Row 1: Working on a chain foundation, DC in 5th ch from hook, Ch 2. * Make Horizontal Puff. [*To Make Horizontal Puff:* (YO, Insert hook *around* dc just completed, Pull Up thread ¾″) 4 times in same st. YO and through all loops on hook, Ch 1 to "tie" the st.] Skip 3 sts, DC in next st, Ch 2. Repeat from * across, ending with DC in last st, Ch 4, Turn.

Row 2: * DC under ch 2 loop on top of puff, Ch 2, make Horizontal Puff around dc. Repeat from * across, ending with DC in 2nd ch past last puff of previous row, Ch 4, Turn.

Repeat Row 2 for pattern.

[Horizontal Puff makes a tall, lacy stitch.]

Note: Bullion and rice stitches at first may seem difficult to work, but using a "fat" hook with a thick shank makes them much easier to do. When making the yarn-overs, wrap the thread around the fattest part of the hook and keep the tension loose as you draw the yarn through. It takes a little practice to perfect this maneuver.

59 / Small Rice Stitch
(an odd number of sts plus 3 chs)

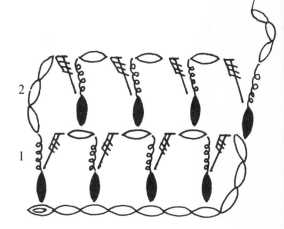

Row 1: Working on a chain foundation, wrapping yarn around fattest part of hook, YO 3 times, Insert hook in 4th ch from hook, Pull Up thread and bring it on through all the loops on the hook (Rice stitch). Ch 1, Skip 1 st. Repeat across. Ch 3, Turn.

Row 2: Working in each ch across, make stitch as in Row 1. Ch 1 between sts. Make last st in turning ch, Ch 3, Turn.

Repeat Row 2 for pattern.

[EDGING: This pattern makes an excellent edging for attaching fringe, *but Rice Stitch is not recommended for beginners.*]

60 / Medium Rice Stitch
(multiples of 2 + 1 plus 4 chs)

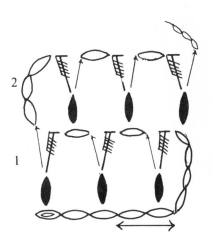

Row 1: Working on a chain foundation, YO 5 times, Insert hook in 5th ch from hook, Pull Up thread and carry it through all loops on hook (Rice stitch). * Ch 1, Skip 1 st, YO 5 times, Insert hook in next st, Pull Up thread and carry it through all loops on the hook (Rice st). Repeat from * across, Ch 3, Turn.

Row 2: * Work Rice st as in Row 1, working the sts *between* the rice sts of previous row, Ch 1. Repeat from * across, ending with last Rice st under turning ch, Ch 3, Turn.

Repeat Row 2 for pattern.

61 / Small Bullion Stitch
(any number of sts plus 3 chs)

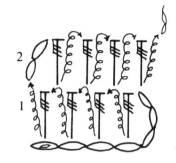

See Note above #59 before beginning.

Row 1: Working on a chain foundation, YO 3 times, Insert hook in 4th ch from hook, Pull Up thread, YO and through 5 loops. * YO 3 times, Insert hook in next st, Pull Up thread, YO and through 5 loops. Repeat from * across, Ch 2, Turn.

Row 2: Work as for Row 1, making each Bullion *between* each bullion of previous row and the last Bullion under the turning ch, Ch 2, Turn.

Repeat Row 2 for pattern.

62 / Medium Bullion Stitch #1
(any number of sts plus 3 chs)

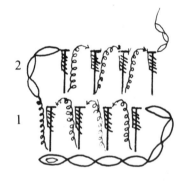

See Note above #59 before beginning.

Row 1: On a chain foundation, YO 5 times. Insert hook in 4th ch from hook, Pull Up thread, YO and through 7 loops. *YO 5 times, Insert hook in next st, Pull Up thread. YO and through 7 loops. Repeat from * across, Ch 3, Turn.

Repeat Row 1 for pattern, working each Bullion between bullions of previous row. Make last Bullion under turning chain, Ch 3, Turn.

63 / Medium Bullion Stitch #2
(any number of sts plus 3 chs)

See Note above #59 before beginning.

Row 1: On a chain foundation, YO 5 times. Insert hook in 4th ch from hook, Pull Up thread, YO and through 7 loops. * YO 5 times, Insert hook in next st, Pull Up thread, YO and through 7 loops. Repeat from * across, Ch 1, Turn.

Row 2: SC in each st across, Ch 3, Turn.

Row 3: Repeat Row 1, working Bullion in each sc of previous row. Make last Bullion under turning ch, Ch 1, Turn.

Repeat Rows 2 and 3 for pattern.

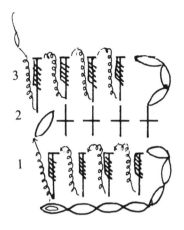

64 / Picket Fence
(any number of sts plus 2 chs)

Row 1: Work Bullion Stitch in any desired size (Small Bullion was used in the photograph and diagram shown here). Ch 1, Turn.

Row 2: SC across (Ch same number of chs used in Bullion stitch in Row 1) Ch 2, Turn.

Repeat Rows 1 and 2 for pattern, always making last Bullion in last ch of turning ch.

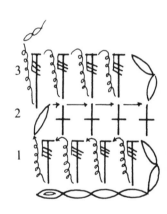

65 / Wheat Sheaf (Tied Bullion)
(any number of sts plus 4 chs)

See Note above #59 before beginning.

Row 1: Working on a chain foundation, Skip 4 chs, * YO 5
times, Insert hook in next ch,
Pull Up thread, YO and
through 3 loops, YO and
through remaining loops. Repeat from * across, Ch 2,
Turn.

Row 2: SC in each st across, Ch 3,
Turn.

Row 3: Work Wheat Sheaf (as in
Row 1) in each st across and
in 2nd ch of turning ch, Ch 2,
Turn.

Repeat Rows 2 and 3 for pattern.

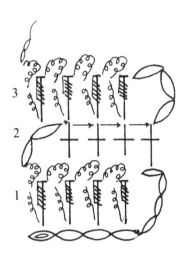

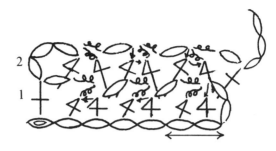

66 / Kathrine Stitch
(*multiple of 2 + 1 plus 2 chs*)

Row 1: Working on a chain foundation, Insert hook in 3rd ch from hook, Pull Up thread. Insert hook in next st, Pull Up thread, YO and through 2 loops, YO and through remaining loops. * Ch 1, Insert hook into next st, Pull Up thread, Insert hook in next st, Pull Up thread, YO and through 2 loops, YO and through remaining loops. Repeat from * across ending with Ch 1, SC in last st, Ch 3, Turn.

Row 2: * Insert hook under first ch 1, Pull Up thread, Insert hook under next ch 1, Pull Up thread, YO and through 2 loops, YO and through remaining loops, Ch 1. Always making first "pull up" under same ch as last "pull up," repeat from * across, ending with SC in turning ch, Ch 3, Turn.

Repeat Row 2 for pattern.

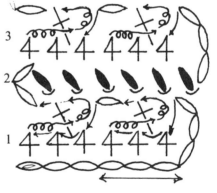

67 / Cane Stitch
(*multiple of 3 plus 3 chs*)

Row 1: Working on a chain foundation, Skip 3 chs, * Insert hook and Pull Up thread in each of next 3 chs, YO and through 3 loops, YO and through 2 loops. Work SC between first and 2nd "pull ups," Ch 1. Repeat from * across, Ch 2, Turn.

Row 2: Working *loosely* and Inserting hook under *front* loop only, Sl St in each st across, ending with last Sl St in turning ch, Ch 3, Turn.

Row 3: * Insert hook and Pull Up thread in next 3 sts, YO and through 3 loops, YO and through 2 loops. SC between first and 2nd "pull ups," Ch 1. Repeat from * across, Ch 1 more (2 chs) at end of row, Turn.

Repeat Rows 2 and 3 for pattern.

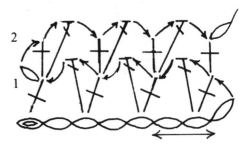

68 / Suzette Stitch
(multiple of 2 + 1 plus 1 ch)

Row 1: Working on a chain foundation, in 2nd chain from hook work (SC, DC), * Skip 1 st, work (SC, DC) in next st. Repeat from * across ending with Skip 1 st, SC in last st, Ch 1, Turn.

Row 2: Work (SC, DC) in st at base of ch and in each sc across. SC in last st, Ch 1, Turn.
Repeat Row 2 for pattern.

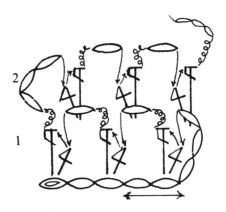

69 / Elizabeth Stitch
(multiple of 2 + 1 plus 3 chs)

Row 1: Working on a chain foundation, Insert hook in 4th ch from hook, Pull Up thread, YO. Insert hook into same stitch, Pull Up thread, YO and through all the loops on the hook. * Ch 1, Skip 1 st, Insert hook in next st, Pull Up thread, YO, Insert hook in same st, Pull Up thread, YO and through all loops on hook. Repeat from * across, Ch 3, Turn.

Row 2: * Insert hook under ch 1, Pull Up thread, YO, Insert hook into same space, Pull Up thread, YO and through all the loops on hook. Ch 1. Repeat from * across ending with last st under turning ch, Ch 3, Turn.
Repeat Row 2 for pattern.

70 / Fancy "A" Stitch
(*multiple of 2 + 1 plus 4 chs*)

Row 1: Working on a chain foundation, start an "A" Stitch in
5th ch from hook. [*To Make
an "A" Stitch:* YO. Insert
hook in stitch, Pull Up
thread, YO and through 2
loops, Skip 1 st, YO, Insert
hook in next st, Pull Up
thread, YO and through 2
loops, YO and through 3
loops. *This completes the "A"
Stitch.*] Ch 1, * Making first
"pull up" in same st as last
"pull up" of previous stitch,
work an "A" St, Ch 1, Repeat
from * across, ending with
DC in last st, Ch 3, Turn.

Row 2: * YO, Insert hook under ch 1,
Pull Up thread, YO and
through 2 loops, YO. Insert
hook under next ch 1, Pull
Up thread, YO and through 2
loops, YO and through 3
loops, Ch 1. Working first
"pull up" under same ch as
last one of previous st, repeat
from * across, ending with
last "pull up" in 4th ch of
turning ch and working DC
in same ch, Ch 3, Turn.

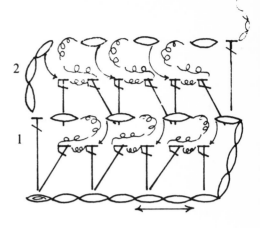

Repeat Row 2 for pattern.

71 / Half Daisy Stitch
(*multiple of 3 + 1 plus 1 ch*)

Row 1: Working on a chain foundation, and starting with 2nd ch
from hook, Pull Up thread in
each of next 4 chs. YO and
through 5 loops on hook,
* Ch 1. Inserting hook

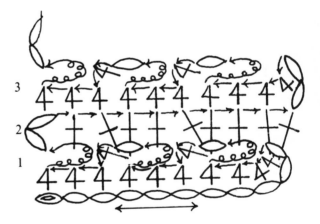

through the "eye" made by
the last ch 1, Pull Up thread.
Pull Up thread in next 3 chs,
YO and through 5 loops. Re-
peat from * across, Ch 2,
Turn.

Row 2: * SC in "eye" of first daisy, 2
SC under ch 1. Repeat from *
across, ending with 2 SC
under turning ch, Ch 2, Turn.

Row 3: Starting with 2nd ch from
hook, Pull Up thread in *each*
of next 4 sts, YO and through

5 loops on hook. * Ch 1, Inserting hook through the
"eye" made by the last ch 1,
Pull Up thread, Pull Up
thread in next 3 sts, YO and
through 5 loops. Repeat from
* across, ending with last
"pull up" in 2nd ch of turning
ch, Ch 2, Turn.

Repeat Rows 2 and 3 for pattern.

72 / Victorian Shells (Shell in Line)
(multiple of 2 + 1 plus 3 chs)

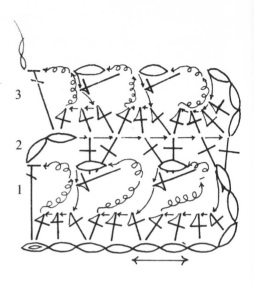

Row 1: Working on a chain foundation, Skip 2 chs, (Insert hook
and Pull Up thread) in each
of next 4 sts, YO and through
4 loops, YO and through 2
loops, * Ch 1. In-sert hook in "eye" of previous
group, Pull Up thread, Insert
hook and Pull Up thread in
same st as last "pull up" of
previous group, Insert hook
and Pull Up thread in each of
next 2 sts, YO and through 4
loops, YO and through 2
loops. Repeat from * across
ending with DC in same st as
last "pull up," Ch 2, Turn.

Row 2: 2 SC under each ch across,
ending with 2 SC under turning ch, Ch 3, Turn.

Row 3: Work as for Row 1, ending
with last "pull up" and DC in
2nd ch of turning ch, Ch 2,
Turn.

Repeat Rows 2 and 3 for pattern.

[**EDGING:** Work Rows 1 and 2.]

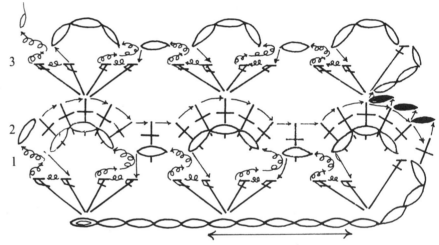

73 / Francie
(multiple of 5 + 1 plus 3 chs)

Row 1: Working on a chain foundation, DC in 4th ch from hook,
Ch 3, and make a Half Cluster. [*To Make Half Cluster:*
YO, Insert hook in same st,
Pull Up thread, YO and
through 2 loops, YO, Insert
hook in same st, Pull Up
thread, YO and through 2
loops, YO and through 3
loops. This completes the
Half Cluster.] * Ch 1, Skip 4
sts, work (Half Cluster, Ch 3,
Half Cluster) in next st. Repeat from * across, Ch 1,
Turn.

Row 2: * 5 SC under ch 3, SC under
ch 1. Repeat from * across,
ending with 5 SC under ch 3,
SC in 3rd ch of turning ch, no
chs, Turn.

Row 3: Sl St into each of next 3 sts,
Ch 3, (DC, Ch 3, Half Clus-
ter) in next st, * Ch 1. (Half
Cluster, Ch 3, Half Cluster) in
center sc of 5 sc group. Repeat from * across, Ch 1,
Turn.

Repeat Rows 2 and 3 for pattern.

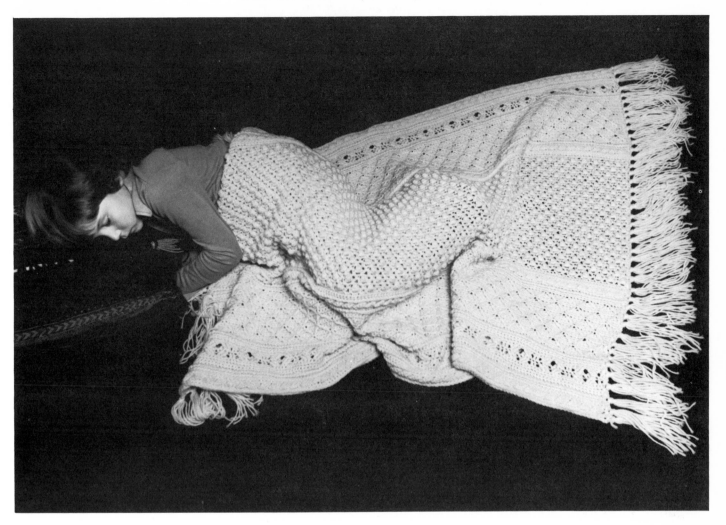

Fisherman Afghan (*Plate 5*)

45″ × 66″ (114 cm × 168 cm)
Material: 40 ounces (1200 grams) of Fisherman unscoured four-
    ply yarn (knitting worsted)
Hook Sizes: H (UK 6, Int'l 5) and I (UK 5, Int'l 5.5)
Gauge: 4 SC equal 1″ (2.5cm)
This afghan incorporates many of the Fisherman crochet stitch
patterns which follow in this chapter. Some of them are new;
others have been specially adapted for doing Fisherman crochet
designs. The advantage of Fisherman crochet is that only one pattern is worked at a time. You do not have to keep changing patterns within the row as you do when knitting Aran patterns.
When changing stitch patterns as many times as must be done in
this afghan, however, you may find you are "losing" stitches.
Count stitches at the start of each pattern section to make sure
you still have the right number.

With the exception of Single Crochet, which is explained in the Basic Stitches in Chapter 1, instructions for all the pattern stitches used in the afghan are to be found in this chapter. Included are:

Low Ridge (#90)	Shadow Box (#84)
Cable (#89)	Diamond Pattern (#87)
Knurl Stitch (#92)	Fisherman Popcorn (#93)

With the H hook, make a foundation chain of 163 stitches. Work SC in 3rd ch from hook and in each chain across for a total of 162 stitches, including the turning chain. Work Rows 2 and 3 of Low Ridge; work Rows 3 and 4 of Cable; work Rows 2 and 3 of Low Ridge; work 1 row of SC (do not turn at end of row); work Rows 2 and 3 of Knurl; work Rows 2 through 5 of Shadow Box; work 2 rows of SC (do not turn at end of second row); work Rows 2 and 3 of Knurl; work Rows 2 through 9 of Diamond 3 times; work 2 rows of SC (do not turn at end of second row); work Rows 2 and 3 of Knurl; work 1 row of SC; work Rows 3 and 4 of Cable; work Rows 2 and 3 of Low Ridge.

Change to I hook. Work Rows 2 through 5 of Fisherman Popcorn 5 times; work "finishing row" of Fisherman Popcorn.

Change back to H hook. Work 1 row SC; work Rows 2 and 3 of Low Ridge; work Rows 3 and 4 of Cable; work 1 row SC (do not turn at end of row); work Rows 2 and 3 of Knurl; work Rows 2 through 9 of Diamond 3 times; work 2 rows of SC (do not turn at end of second row); work Rows 2 and 3 of Knurl; work Rows 2 through 5 of Shadow Box (do not turn at end of Row 5); work Rows 2 and 3 of Knurl; work 1 row SC, work Rows 2 and 3 of Low Ridge; work Rows 3 and 4 of Cable; work Rows 2 and 3 of Low Ridge.

Ch 3, turn corner, and work along end as follows: * Skip 1 row, SC in next row. Ch 1. Repeat from * across ends, working last SC in end ch of foundation ch. Attach yarn at corner of other end of afghan and work in same manner. Block.

Fringe: Cut yarn in 14″ (35cm) lengths. Using 5 strands. fold the strands in half and attach them under each ch 1 across the ends of the afghan, using a reverse double half-hitch as described on page 32.

74 / Small Basket Weave
(multiple of 4 + 3 plus 3 chs)

Row 1: Working on a chain foundation, DC in 4th ch from hook
and in each st across, Ch 2,
Turn.

Row 2: * Working from the *Front,*
DC *around* each of next 2 dc.
Working from the *Back,* DC
around each of next 2 dc. Repeat from * across, ending
with 2 DC (front) in last 2 dc
and HDC in normal manner
in 2nd ch of turning ch, Ch 2,
Turn.

Repeat Row 2 for pattern.

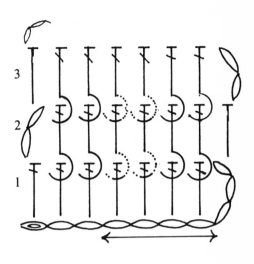

75 / Medium Basket Weave
(multiple of 4 + 1 plus 3 chs)

Row 1: Working on a chain foundation, DC in 4th ch from hook
and in each ch across, Ch 2,
Turn.

Row 2: * Working from *Front,* work
DC *around* each of next 2 dc,
working from *Back,* DC
around each of next 2 dc.
Repeat from * across, ending
with HDC in 3rd ch of turning ch, Ch 2, Turn.

Row 3: Repeat Row 2, HDC in 2nd
ch of turning ch, Ch 2, Turn.

Row 4: * Working from *Back,* DC
around each of next 2 dc,
working from *Front,* DC
around each of next 2 dc. Repeat from * across, ending
with HDC in 2nd ch of turning ch, Ch 2, Turn.

Row 5: Repeat Row 4.

Repeat Rows 2 through 5 for pattern.

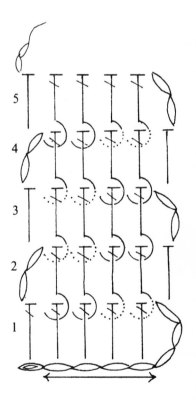

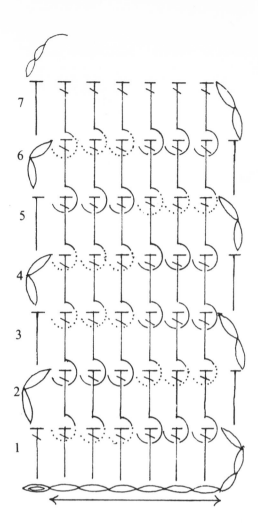

76 / Large Basket Weave
(multiple of 6 + 1 plus 3 chs)

Row 1: Working on a chain foundation, DC in 4th ch from hook
and in each ch across, Ch 2,
Turn.

Rows 2, 3, and 4: * Working from
Back, DC *around* each of
next 3 dc, working from
Front, DC *around* each of
next 3 dc. Repeat from *
across, ending with HDC in
turning ch, Ch 2, Turn.

Rows 5, 6, and 7: * Working from
Front, DC *around* each of
next 3 dc, working from *Back,*
DC *around* each of next 3 dc.
Repeat from * across, ending
with HDC in 2nd ch of turning ch, Ch 2, Turn.

Repeat Rows 2 through 7 for pattern.

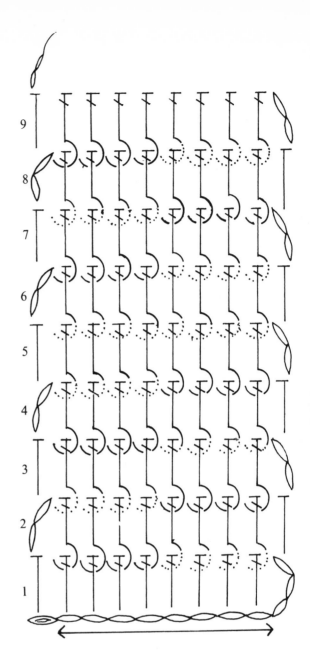

77 / Extra Large Basket Weave
(*multiple of 8 + 1 plus 3 chs*)

Row 1: Working on a chain foundation, DC in 4th ch from hook
and in each ch across, Ch 2,
Turn.

Row 2: * Working from *Front*, DC
around each of next 4 dc,
working from *Back*, DC
around each of next 4 dc. Repeat from * across, ending
with HDC in 2nd ch of turning ch, Ch 2, Turn.
Rows 3, 4, and 5: Same as Row 2.
Rows 6, 7, 8, and 9: * Working from
Back, DC *around* each of next
4 dc, working from *Front*, DC
around each of next 4 dc. Repeat from * across, ending
with HDC in 2nd ch of turning ch, Ch 2, Turn.

Repeat Rows 2 through 9 for pattern.

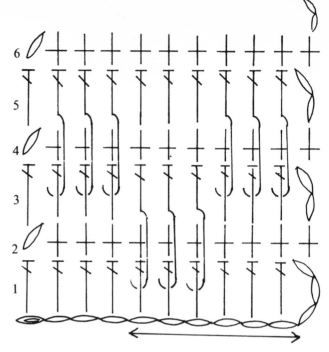

78 / Check Relief
(*multiple of 6 + 4 plus 3 chs*)

Row 1: Working on a chain foundation, DC in 4th ch from hook and in each ch across, Ch 1, Turn.

Row 2: SC in each dc across and in 3rd ch of turning ch, Ch 2, Turn.

Row 3: * DC in each of next 3 sc. Working from *Front,* work DC *around* each of next 3 dc of 2nd row below (Row 1 of pattern). Skip 3 sc on Row 2. Repeat from * across, ending with DC in each of last 3 sc, DC in turning ch, Ch 1, Turn.

Row 4: SC in each dc across, ending with last sc in 2nd ch of turning ch, Ch 2, Turn.

Row 5: * Working from *Front,* work DC *around* each of next 3 dc on 2nd row below (Row 3 of pattern). Skip 3 sc on Row 4, DC in each of next 3 sc. Repeat from * across, ending with DC around each of next 3 dc of 2nd row below and DC in turning ch, Ch 1, Turn.

Row 6: SC in each dc across ending with SC in 2nd ch of turning ch, Ch 2, Turn.

Repeat Rows 3 through 6 for pattern.

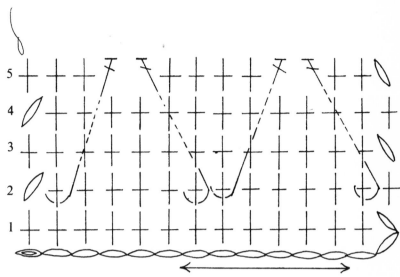

79 / Chevron

(multiple of 6 + 1 plus 2 chs)

Row 1: Working on a chain foundation, SC in 3rd ch from hook and SC in each ch across, Ch 1, Turn.

Rows 2, 3, and 4: SC in each st across, ending with SC in turning ch, Ch 1, Turn.

Row 5: SC in each of next 2 sc, DC in 2nd sc of 3rd row below (Row 2 of the pattern). * Skip 4 sc in 3rd row below and DC in next sc of Row 2. Skip 2 sc on top row, SC in each of next 4 sc, DC in sc next to the sc in which last dc was worked on 3rd row below (Row 2 of pattern). Repeat from * across, ending with SC in last 2 sc and SC in turning ch, Ch 1, Turn.

Repeat Rows 2 through 5 for pattern.

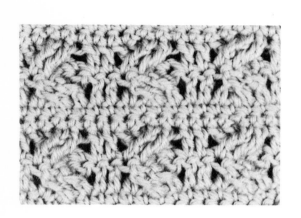

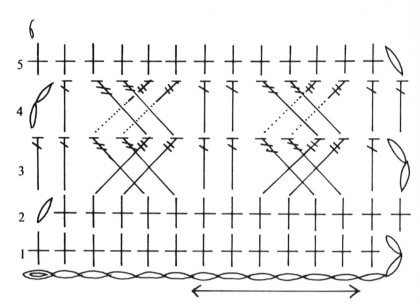

80 / Fish Hook

(multiple of 6 + 1 plus 2 chs)

Row 1: Working on a chain foundation, SC in 3rd ch from hook
and in each ch across, Ch 1,
Turn.

Row 2: SC in each st across, including turning ch, Ch 2, Turn.

Row 3: DC in next st, * Skip 2 sc, TC
in each of next 2 sc. Work
Front TC in each of 2 skipped
sts, DC in next 2 sc. Repeat
from * across, ending with
last DC in turning ch, Ch 2,
Turn.

Row 4: DC in next st, * Skip 2 sts,
TC in each of next 2 sts, work
Back TC in each of 2 skipped
sts, DC in each of next 2 sts.
Repeat from * across, ending
with last DC in turning ch,
Ch 1, Turn.

Row 5: SC in each st across, including turning ch, Ch 1, Turn.

Repeat Rows 2 through 5 for pattern.

81 / Arrow
(multiple of 4 + 3 plus 2 chs)

Row 1: Working on a chain foundation, SC in 3rd ch from hook and in each ch across, Ch 2, Turn.

Row 2: DC in each st across, ending with DC in turning ch, Ch 2, Turn.

Row 3: DC in next dc, * Skip 3 dc, TC in next dc. Working from *Back,* DC in each of 3 skipped dc. Repeat from * across, ending with DC in last dc and DC in turning ch, Ch 2, Turn.

Row 4: DC in next dc, * Skip next 3 dc, TC in next tc. Working from *Front,* DC in each of 3 skipped dc. Repeat from * across, ending with DC in last dc, DC in turning ch, Ch 1, Turn.

Row 5: SC in each st across, Ch 2, Turn.

Repeat Rows 2 through 5 for pattern.

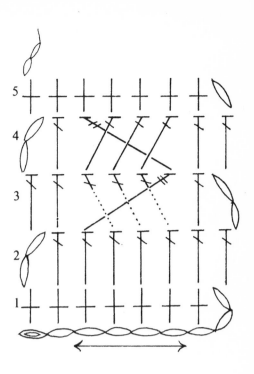

82 / Zig-Zag
(multiple of 6 + 1 plus 2 chs)

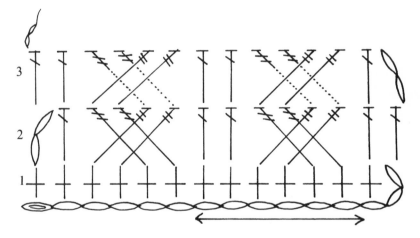

Row 1: Working on a chain foundation, SC in 3rd ch from hook and in each ch across, Ch 2, Turn.

Row 2: DC in next sc, * Skip next 2 sts, TC in each of next 2 sts. Working from *Front,* TC in each of 2 skipped sts, DC in each of next 2 sts, Repeat from * across, ending with last DC in 2nd ch of turning ch, Ch 2, Turn.

Row 3: DC in next dc. * Skip 2 sts, TC in each of next 2 sts. Working from *Back,* TC in each of 2 skipped sts, DC in each of next 2 sts. Repeat from * across, ending with last DC in 2nd ch of turning ch, Ch 2, Turn.

Repeat Rows 2 and 3 for pattern.

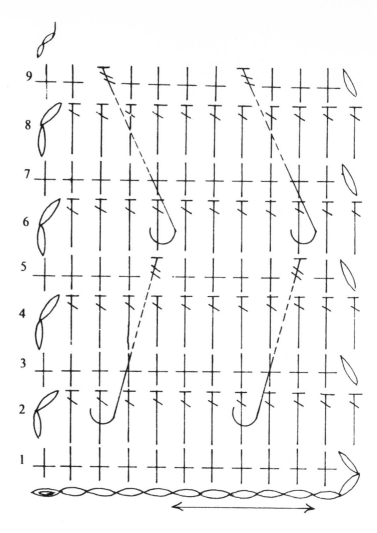

83 / Sea Breeze
(*multiple of 5 + 1 plus 2 chs*)

Row 1: Working on a chain foundation, SC in 3rd ch from hook and in each ch across, Ch 2, Turn.

Row 2: DC in each st across, ending with last DC in 2nd ch of turning ch, Ch 1, Turn.

Row 3: SC in each st across, ending with last SC in 2nd ch of turning ch, Ch 2, Turn.

Row 4: DC in each st across, ending with last DC in turning ch, Ch 1, Turn.

Row 5: SC in next dc, work Long (4½ chs long) TC *around* 5th dc on 3rd row below (Row 2 of pattern). * Skip dc, SC in each of next 4 dc, Skip 4 dc on 3rd row below. Work Long TC in next dc on 3rd row below. Repeat from * across, ending with SC in last 3 dc and in turning ch, Ch 2, Turn.

Row 6: Repeat Row 2.

Row 7: Repeat Row 3.

Row 8: Repeat Row 4.

Row 9: SC in each of next 3 dc, work Long TC in 3rd dc on 3rd row below. * Skip dc, SC in each of next 4 dc. Skip 4 dc on 3rd row below. Work Long TC in next st on 3rd row below. Repeat from * across, ending with SC in last dc, SC in turning ch, Ch 2, Turn.

Repeat Rows 2 through 9 for pattern.

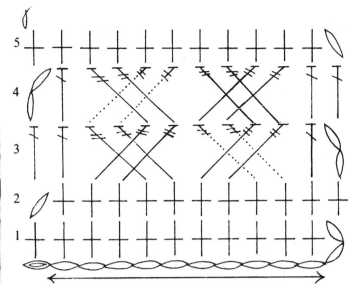

84 / Shadow Box
(multiple of 10 + 1 plus 2 chs)

Row 1: Working on a chain foundation, SC in 3rd ch from hook and in each ch across, Ch 1, Turn.

Row 2: SC in each st across, ending with SC in turning ch, Ch 2, Turn.

Row 3: DC in next st, * Skip 2 sts, work TC in each of next 2 sts. Working from *Back,* TC in each of skipped sts, Skip 2 sts, work TC in each of next 2 sts, work *Front* TC in each of skipped sts. DC in each of next 2 sts. Repeat from * across, working last DC in turning ch, Ch 2, Turn.

Row 4: Same as Row 3, Ch 1, Turn.

Row 5: SC in each st across, Ch 1, Turn.

Repeat Rows 2 through 5 for pattern.

85 / Bow Tie

This pattern is the reverse side of #84 Shadow Box (above).

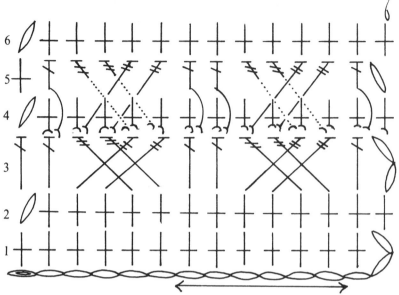

86 / Fishbone
(multiple of 6 + 1 plus 2 chs)

Row 1: Working on a chain foundation, SC in 3rd ch from hook and in each ch across, Ch 1, Turn.

Row 2: SC in each st across, ending with SC in turning ch, Ch 2, Turn.

Row 3: DC in next sc. * Skip 2 sc, TC in each of next 2 sc. Working from *Front,* TC in each of 2 skipped sc, DC in each of next 2 sc. Repeat from * across, working last DC in turning ch, Ch 1, Turn.

Row 4: Working in *back loop* only, SC in each st across, working last SC in turning ch, Ch 1, Turn.

Row 5: Working *all stitches* of this row in loops *not worked* in Row 3, Skip first loop, DC behind next sc. * Skip next 2 loops, TC in next 2 loops. Working from *Back,* TC in each of 2 skipped loops, DC in each of next 2 loops. Repeat from * across ending with SC in turning ch, Ch 1, Turn.

Row 6: SC in each st across, ending with SC in turning ch, Ch 1, Turn.

Repeat Rows 2 through 6 for pattern.

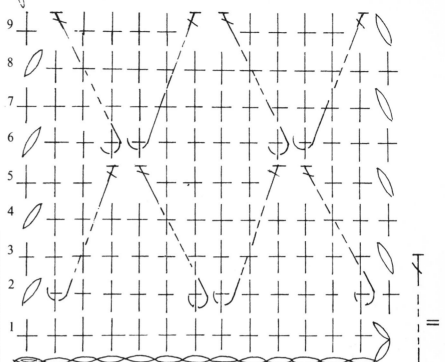

87 / Diamond Pattern
(*multiple of 6 + 1 plus 2 chs*)

Row 1: Working on a chain foundation, SC in 3rd ch from hook and in each ch across, Ch 1, Turn.

Rows 2, 3, and 4: SC in each st across, including turning ch, Ch 1, Turn.

Row 5: SC in each of next 2 sts, work Long DC (length of 4 chs) *around* 2nd sc of 3rd row below (Row 2 of pattern). Skip 4 sc on 3rd row below, work Long DC in next sc on 3rd row below. * Skip 2 sc on top row, SC in each of next 4 sc on top row. Work Long DC *around* sc next to last dc on 3rd row below, Skip 4 sc on 3rd row below. Work Long DC in next sc on 3rd row below. Repeat from * across, ending with SC in each of last 2 sc and SC in turning ch, Ch 1, Turn.

Rows 6, 7, and 8: SC in each st across, working last SC in turning ch, Ch 1, Turn.

Row 9: Work Long DC in 4th sc of 3rd row below (Row 6 of pattern). Skip sc, * work SC in each of next 4 sc on top row, make Long DC in sc next to last long dc on 3rd row below. Skip 4 sc on 3rd row below, work Long DC in next sc. Skip 2 sc on top row. Repeat from * across, ending with: Work SC in each of next 4 sc, make Long DC in sc next to last long dc, Skip sc on top row, work SC in turning ch, Ch 1, Turn.

Repeat Rows 2 through 9 for pattern.

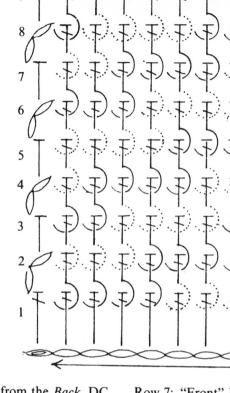

88 / Stair
(multiple of 8 + 1 plus 3 chs)

Row 1: Working on a chain foundation, DC in 4th ch from hook and each ch across, Ch 2, Turn.

Row 2: * Working from the *Front,* DC *around* each of next 4 dc. Working from the *Back,* DC *around* each of next 4 dc. Repeat from * across, ending with HDC in 3rd ch of turning ch, Ch 2. Turn.

Row 3: Working from the *Back,* DC *around* next dc. * Working from the *Front,* DC *around* next 4 dc; working from the *Back,* DC *around* next 4 dc. Repeat from * across, ending with only 3 "Back" DC, HDC in turning ch, Ch 2, Turn.

Row 4: Working from the *Front,* DC around next 2 dc; * working from the *Back,* DC around the next 4 dc; working from the *Front,* DC around the next 4 dc. Repeat from * across, ending with "Front" DC in each of last 2 dc, HDC in turning ch, Ch 2, Turn.

Row 5: Work "Back" DC in each of next 3 dc, * Work "Front" DCs in each of next 4 dc, work "Back" DCs in each of next 4 dc. Repeat from * across ending with "Back." DC in last dc, HDC in turning ch, Ch 2, Turn.

Row 6: * Work "Back" DC in each of next 4 dc, "Front" DC in each of next 4 dc. Repeat from * across, HDC in turning ch, Ch 2, Turn.

Row 7: "Front" DC in next dc, * work "Back" DC in each of next 4 dc, "Front" DC in each of next 4 dc. Repeat from * across, ending with "Front" DC in each of last 3 dc, HDC in turning ch, Ch 2, Turn.

Row 8: Work "Back" DC in each of next 2 dc, * "Front" DC in each of next 4 dc, "Back" DC in each of next 4 dc. Repeat from * across, ending with "Back" DC in last 2 dc, HDC in turning ch, Ch 2, Turn.

Row 9: Work "Front" DC in each of next 3 dc, * "Back" DC in each of next 4 dc, "Front" DC in each of next 4 dc. Repeat from * across, ending with "Front" DC in last dc, HDC in turning ch, Ch 2, Turn.

Repeat Rows 2 through 9 for pattern.

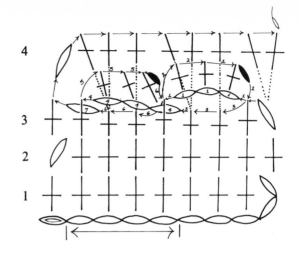

89 / Cable
(multiple of 4 plus 2 chs)

Row 1: Working on a chain foundation, SC in 3rd ch from hook and in each ch across, Ch 1, Turn.

Row 2: SC in each sc across, ending with last SC in turning ch, Ch 1, Turn.

Row 3: SC in next st, Ch 3, Skip 2 scs, SC in next st, Turn. SC in each of just completed 3 chs, Sl St in next sc (sc before ch was begun), Turn. Working from the *Back,* SC in each of 2 skipped sts. * Ch 3, Skip the st where the previous ch was attached and the next 2 sts, SC in next st, Turn. SC in each of just completed 3 chs, Sl St in sc where the previous ch was attached, Turn. SC in each of 2 skipped sts. Repeat from * across, ending with Ch 1, SC in turning ch, Ch 1, Turn.

Row 4: Skip next sc, * Work 2 SC in next sc (*behind* cable), SC in next sc (*behind same* cable). (Skip sc where ch was attached on previous row.) Repeat from * across, ending with 2 SC in turning ch, Ch 1, Turn.

Repeat Rows 3 and 4 for pattern.

90 / Low Ridge
(any number plus 2 chs)

Row 1: Working on a chain foundation, SC in 3rd ch from hook and in each ch across, Ch 1, Turn.

Row 2: Working in front loop only, Sl St *loosely* in each st across, working last Sl St in turning ch, Ch 1, Turn.

Row 3: Working in the loop *not worked* in Row 2, SC behind each sl st across, SC in turning ch, Ch 1, Turn.

Rows 4 and 5: SC in each st across, Ch 1, Turn.

Repeat Rows 2 and 3 or 2 through 5 for pattern.

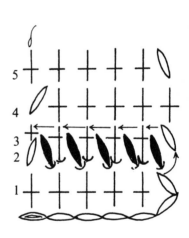

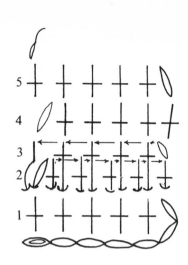

91 / High Ridge
(any number plus 2 chs)

Row 1: Working on a chain foundation, SC in 3rd ch from hook and in each ch across, Ch 1, Turn.

Row 2: Working in front loop only, SC in each st across, Ch 1, Turn.

Row 3: Working in loop *not worked* in Row 2, work SC behind each sc of Row 2, Ch 1, Turn.

Row 4: SC in each st across, Ch 1, Turn.

Row 5: Same as Row 4. Repeat Rows 2 and 3 or 2 through 5 for pattern.

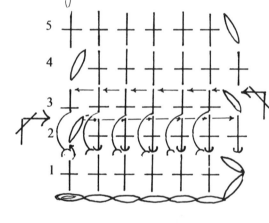

92 / Knurl Stitch
(any number plus 2 chs)

Row 1: Working on a chain foundation, SC in 3rd ch from hook and in each ch across, Ch 1, *do not turn.*

Row 2: Working in front loop only, SC in reverse direction, i.e., Insert hook in stitch to the right of the turning ch, Pull Up thread and complete as SC. Work last SC in turning ch, Ch 1, *do not turn.*

Row 3: SC in loop *not worked* in Row 2 across, SC in turning ch, Ch 1, Turn.

Rows 4 and 5: SC in each st across, Ch 1, Turn.

Repeat Rows 2 and 3 or 2 through 5 for pattern.

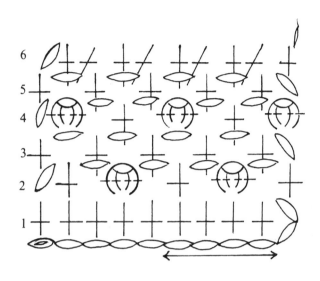

93 / Fisherman Popcorn
(multiple of 4 + 1 plus 2 chs)

Row 1: Working on a chain foundation, SC in 3rd ch from hook
and in each ch across, Ch 1,
Turn.

Row 2: * SC in next sc, Ch 1, Skip sc,
work (4 SC) Popcorn in next
sc, Ch 1, Skip sc. Repeat from
* across, ending with SC in
turning ch, Ch 1, Turn.

Row 3: * SC under ch, Ch 1. Repeat
from * across, ending with SC
in turning ch, Ch 1, Turn.

Row 4: * Work Popcorn under next
ch, Ch 1, SC under next ch,
Ch 1. Repeat from * across,
ending with Popcorn in turning ch, Ch 1, Turn.

Row 5: Same as Row 3, Ch 1, Turn.
Repeat Rows 2 through 5 for pattern.

Finishing Row: Work 2 SC under each
ch across, ending with SC in turning
ch.

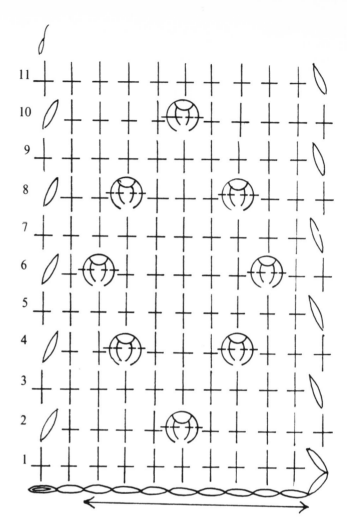

94 / Popcorn Diamond
   (*multiple of 8 + 2 plus 2 chs*)

Row 1: Working on a chain foundation, SC in 3rd ch from hook
   and in each ch across, Ch 1,
   Turn.
Row 2: SC in each of next 4 sc,
   * work a 4 SC Popcorn in
   next sc, SC in each of next 7
   sc. Repeat from * across, ending with SC in each of last 4
   sc and SC in turning ch, Ch
   1, Turn.

Row 3: SC in each sc and popcorn
   across, ending with SC in
   turning ch, Ch 1, turn.
Row 4: SC in each of next 2 sc,
   * work Popcorn in next sc,
   SC in each of next 3 sc, work
   Popcorn in next sc, SC in
   each of next 3 sc. Repeat
   from * across, ending with SC
   in each of last 2 sc and SC in
   turning ch, Ch 1, Turn.
Row 5: Repeat Row 3.
Row 6: SC in next sc, * work Popcorn in next sc, SC in each of
   next 5 sc, work Popcorn in
   next sc, SC in next sc. Repeat
   from * across, ending with SC
   in last sc and SC in turning
   ch, Ch 1, Turn.
Row 7: Repeat Row 3.
Row 8: Repeat Row 4.
Row 9: Repeat Row 3.

Row 10: Repeat Row 2.
Row 11: Repeat Row 3.
Repeat Rows 2 through 11 for pat-
tern.

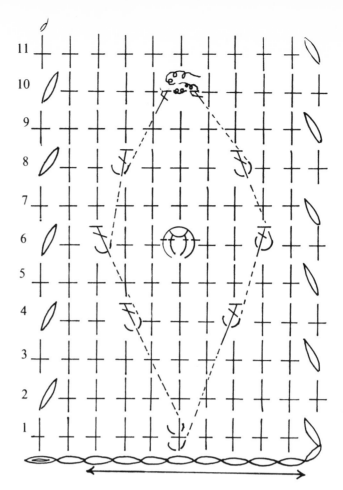

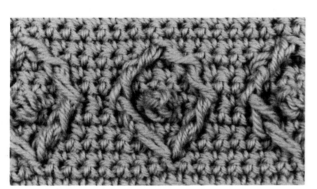

95 / Fish Eye
(*multiple of 8 + 2 plus 2 chs*)

Row 1: Working on a chain foundation, SC in 3rd ch from hook
and in each ch across, Ch 1,
Turn.

Rows 2 and 3: SC in each sc across
ending with SC in turning ch,
Ch 1, Turn.

Row 4: SC in each of next 2 sc, Skip
5 sc on Row 1, * Work Long
DC *around* next sc on Row 1.
Skip next sc on Row 4. SC in
each of next 3 sc, work Long
DC *around* same st on Row 1
in which the last dc was
made. Skip next sc on Row 4.
SC in each of next 3 sc, Skip
7 sc on Row 1. Repeat from *
across, ending with SC in last
2 sc and SC in turning ch, Ch
1, Turn.

Row 5: SC in each sc and dc across,
ending with SC in turning ch,
Ch 1, Turn.

Row 6: * SC in next sc. Work Long
DC *around* first long dc of
Row 4. Skip next sc on Row
6, SC in each of next 2 sc,
work Popcorn (with 4 SC) in
next sc, SC in each of next 2
sc. Work Long DC *around*
next long dc of Row 4, Skip
next sc on Row 6. Repeat
from * across, ending with SC
in last sc, SC in turning ch,
Ch 1, Turn.

Row 7: Repeat Row 5.

Row 8: SC in each of next 2 sc,
* work Long DC *around* next
long dc of Row 6, Skip next
sc on Row 8. SC in each of
next 3 sc, work Long DC
around next long dc of Row 6,
Skip next sc on Row 8, SC in
each of next 2 sc. Repeat
from * across, ending with SC
in each of last 2 sc and SC in
turning ch, Ch 1, Turn.

Row 9: Repeat Row 5.

Row 10: SC in each of next 4 sc.
* YO, Insert hook *around*
next long dc, Pull Up thread,
YO and through 2 loops.
YO, Insert hook *around* next
long dc, Pull Up thread, YO
and through 2 loops, YO
and through 3 loops. Skip
next sc on Row 10, work SC
in each of next 7 sc. Repeat
from * across, ending with
SC in each of last 4 sc and
SC in turning ch, Ch 1,
Turn.

Row 11: Repeat Row 5.

Repeat Rows 2 through 11 for pattern.

A variation of the Popcorn Stitch, tufted crochet uses a tuft or popcorn consisting of four Extended Single Crochet stitches to achieve the effect of the candlewick counterpanes of the 19th century. Any graphed cross-stitch or filet pattern may be adapted for tufted with the following changes: The design must be expanded either by regraphing and adding one stitch between each cross-stitch shown in the pattern and one row between each graphed row, or else each line as well as each square of the graphed design must be counted as a stitch and as a row. For the tufts to show there must be an Extended Single Crochet stitch between each graphed needlepoint or cross-stitch, and all the tufts must be worked on the same side of piece. In the tufted crochet graphs shown here, this separation has already been taken into account. Each X represents a tuft, and each blank square is an ExSC.

To Make a Tuft Stitch: Work 4 ExSC in the same stitch, remove the hook from the loop, insert the hook under the top 2 loops of the first stitch of the group, and pull the dropped loop through the first stitch. This completes the Tuft.

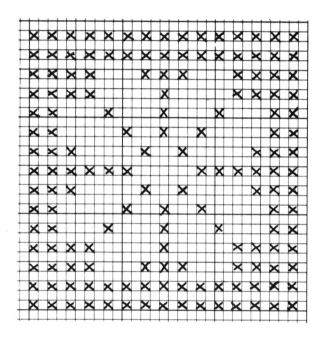

Small Tufted Pillow

10″ × 10″ (25cm × 25cm)
This pillow is a "negative" design, because the design motif is developed as a flat area and the tufts form the background.
Material: 4 ounces (120 grams) of four-ply yarn (knitting worsted)
Hook size: H (UK 6, Int'l 5)
Gauge: 3 ExSC equal 1″ (2.5cm)
Make a foundation chain of 32 chs, work ExSC in 3rd chain from hook and in each chain across. (This row is the first row of the graph and should contain 31 sts, including the turning chain.) Ch 2, Turn. The turning chain always represents the first square of each row on the graph. Work a Tuft Stitch for each X in the graph and ExSC where squares are blank. Ch 2 at the end of all rows. Continue to follow the graph until the pattern is completed. Tie off the yarn, and block the piece.

131

16″ × 16″ (40cm × 40cm)

This pillow has what is known as a "positive" design because the tufts form the design motifs.

Material: 8 ounces (240 grams) of four-ply yarn (knitting worsted)
Hook size: H (UK 6, Int'l 5)
Gauge: 3 ExSC equal 1″ (2.5cm)

Make a foundation chain of 48 chs. Work ExSc in 3rd chain from hook and in each ch across. This completes the first row of the graph and it should total 47 stitches, including the turning chain. Ch 2, Turn. (The turning chain always represents the first square of each row on the graph.) Work Tuft Stitch where indicated by the Xs, and ExSC where the squares are blank. Ch 2 at the end of all rows. Continue to follow the graph until all the squares are completed, tie off the yarn, and block the pillow top.

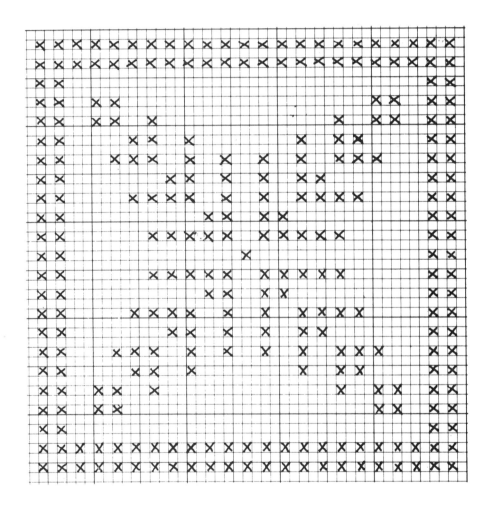

Tufted Crochet Afghan

42″ × 60″ (100cm × 150cm)

This afghan design features a border of butterflies. For an elegant, personalized gift you might want to insert a monogram, following graphs in Chapter 5. The graphed pattern shows only one quarter of the design, but the entire afghan can be made from it by following the directions given below.

Material: 40 ounces (1200 grams) of four-ply yarn (knitting worsted)

Hook size: H (UK 6, Int'l 5)

Gauge: 3 ExSC equals 1″ (2.5cm)

Make a foundation chain of 128 stitches, work ExSC in 3rd ch from hook and in each ch across. This is the first row on the graph and should contain 127 stitches, including the turning chain. (The turning chain is always the first square on the graph.) On the second row, follow the graph from right to left until the stitch marked Center is completed. Continue the row by following the graph back from left to right, beginning with the stitch to the right of the Center stitch and work back to the beginning stitch. Continue to work the rows in this manner, following the graph upward until the row marked Center Row is completed, then work the next row below Center Row again. Follow the graph back down from top to bottom to complete the design and tie off the yarn and block the afghan.

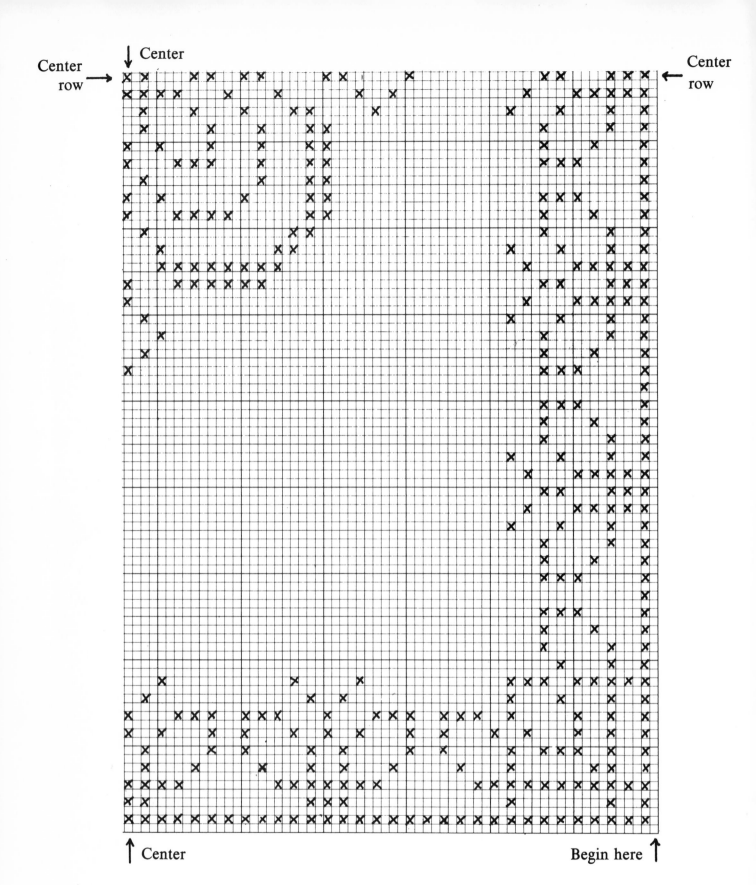

Center row →   ↓ Center   Center row ←

↑ Center   Begin here ↑

Pattern for afghan of tufted crochet. The graph shows one quarter of the symmetrical design.

Chapter 4   Lace Stitches

Lace stitches are an important element in the crocheter's repertoire. They provide unlimited possibilities for making shawls, stoles, edgings, afghans, curtain panels, blouses, vests, table runners, or whatever your creativity suggests. Be careful, however, to make the individual stitches snugly, for if they are loose and "stringy" the pattern will not hold its shape. Shawls and stoles are probably the most popular uses for these stitches. General instructions and dimensions for making them may be found in Chapter 2.

Japanese Fans Shawl (*Plate 4*)

42″ × 28″ (105cm × 70cm)
Material: 4 ounces (120 grams) rayon thread
Hook size: E (UK 9, Int'l 3.5)
Gauge: 1 pattern (14 stitches) equals 2″ (5 cm)
Make a foundation chain of 395 stitches. Work in Japanese Fan pattern (Stitch Pattern #29 in this chapter) for 5 rows. Decrease one "fan" at end of every 6th and 7th row by *not working* the last "fan" (Ch 5, SC, Ch 5, etc.) at the end of Row 6 and *not working* last "fan" on Row 7 as shown in the diagrams. Work Rows 2 and 3 a total of 30 times (60 rows), continuing to decrease every 6th and 7th row.

Dropping one "fan" at the end of Row 6.

Dropping one "fan" at the end of Row 7.

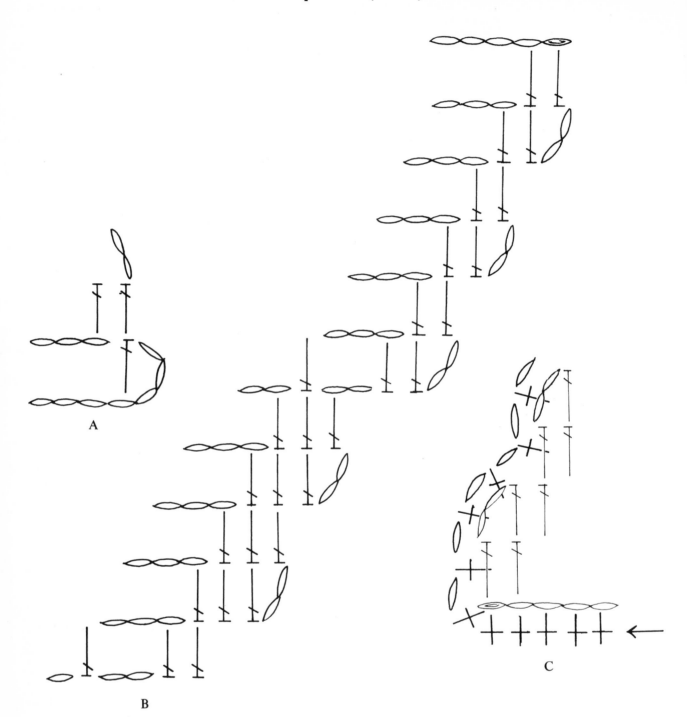

A

B

C

60″ × 32″ (150cm × 80cm)

The design for this rounded triangular shawl is adapted from a pattern discovered in a handicraft shop in the old city of Jaffa, Israel.

Material: 12 ounces (370 grams) of two-ply yarn (sport weight or one of many new novelty yarns)

Hook size: F (UK 8, Int'l 4)

Gauge: 16 stitches (one pattern) equals 4″ (10cm)

Make a foundation chain of 196 stitches and work in Carmel Grape Pattern (Stitch Pattern #49 in this chapter), shaping at the end of the 2nd row by decreasing as shown in Figure A. At the end of the 3rd and subsequent rows, decrease as shown in Figure B.

Repeat Rows 2 through 11 five times, shaping as you work. Two full patterns and 2 half patterns will remain, making a flat area at the bottom corner. When the fringe is attached, the corner will appear rounded.

Work around the entire piece, working 1 SC in every chain of the foundation chain, 2 SC in the end chains, and work (Ch 1, SC) under tc, (Ch 1, SC, Ch 1, SC) under the turning chain (Figure C) .

Cut strands of yarn in 15″ (38cm) lengths. Fold the strands in half in groups of five, and attach them under every chain 1 to form fringe.

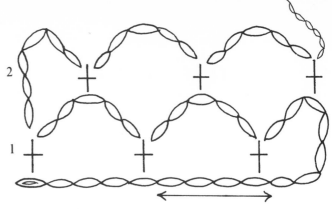

1 / Arch
(*multiple of 4 + 3 plus 5 chs*)

Row 1: Working on a *loose* chain foundation, work SC in 8th ch from hook, * Ch 5, Skip 3 chs, SC in next ch. Repeat from * across, Ch 6, Turn.

Row 2: * SC in 3rd ch of ch 5 loop, Ch 5. Repeat from * across ending with SC in 3rd ch past last sc, Ch 6, Turn.

Repeat Row 2 for pattern.

[**EDGING:** Work Row 1.]

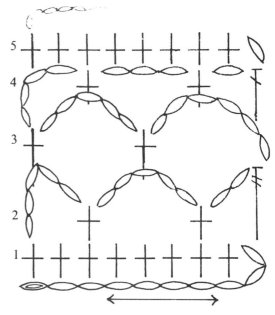

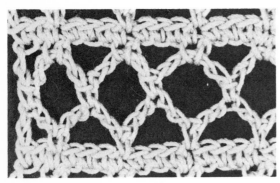

2 / Lace
(*multiple of 4 + 4 plus 2 chs*)

Row 1: Working on a chain foundation, SC in 3rd ch from hook and in each ch across, Ch 5, Turn.

Row 2: Skip first sc, * SC in next sc, Ch 5, Skip 3 sc. Repeat from * across, ending with SC in next to last st, Ch 2, TC in 2nd ch of turning ch, Ch 6, Turn.

Row 3: * SC under ch 5, Ch 5. Repeat from * across, ending with SC under turning ch, Ch 4, Turn.

Row 4: * SC under ch 5, Ch 3. Repeat from * across, ending with SC under turning ch, Ch 1, DC in 2nd ch of turning ch, Ch 1, Turn.

Row 5: SC in each ch and sc across, including 3rd and 4th chs of turning ch, Ch 5, Turn.

Repeat Rows 2 through 5 for pattern.

[**EDGING:** Work Rows 1 through 5 to make an insertion band or Rows 1 and 2 to make a lace edging.]

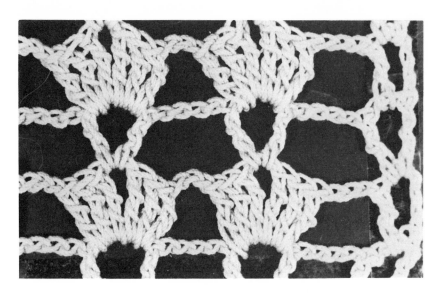

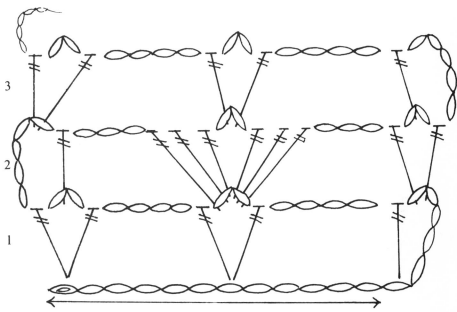

3 / Shells and Trellis
(*multiple of 12 + 1 plus 5 chs*)

Row 1: Working on a chain foundation, work TC in 6th ch from hook. * Ch 4, Skip 5 chs, work (TC, Ch 2, TC) in next st. Repeat from * across, Ch 5, Turn.

Row 2: Work TC under first ch 2. * Ch 3, work (3 TC, Ch 2, 3 TC) under next ch 2, Ch 3, (TC, Ch 2, TC) under next ch 2. Repeat from * across, ending with last (TC, Ch 2, TC) under turning ch, Ch 5, Turn.

Row 3: Work TC under first ch 2. * Ch 4, (TC, Ch 2, TC) under next ch 2, Repeat from * across, ending with last (TC, Ch 2, TC) under turning ch, Ch 5, Turn.

Repeat Rows 2 and 3 for pattern.

[EDGING: Work Rows 1 and 2.]

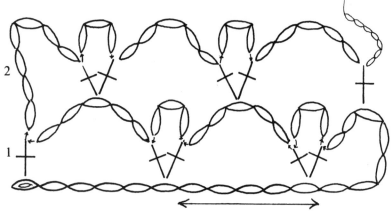

4 / Picot Mesh
(*multiple of 5 + 3 plus 5 chs*)

Row 1: Working on a *loose* chain foundation, Skip 7 chs. * Work (SC, Ch 3, SC) in next st, Ch 5, Skip 4 chs. Repeat from * across, ending with SC in last ch, Ch 7, Turn.

Row 2: * Work (SC, Ch 3, SC) in 3rd ch of ch 5, Ch 5. Repeat from * across ending with SC in 3rd ch past last sc, Ch 7, Turn.

Repeat Row 2 for pattern.

[**EDGING:** Work Row 1. Fringe may be attached under the picot.]

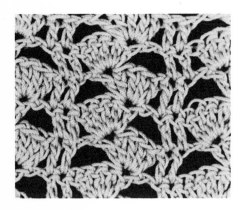

5 / Crazy Lace
(*multiple of 8 + 1 plus 3 chs*)

Row 1: Working on a chain foundation, DC in 4th ch from hook, * Skip 2 chs, 5 DC in next ch, Ch 1, Skip 3 chs, DC in each of next 2 chs. Repeat from * across, Ch 2, Turn.

Row 2: DC in first dc, * work 5 DC in first dc of 5 dc group, Ch 1, DC in each of next 2 dc. Repeat from * across, working last DC in turning ch, Ch 2, Turn.

Repeat Row 2 for pattern.

[**EDGING:** Work Row 1.]

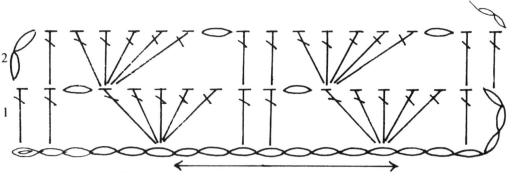

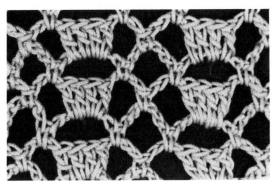

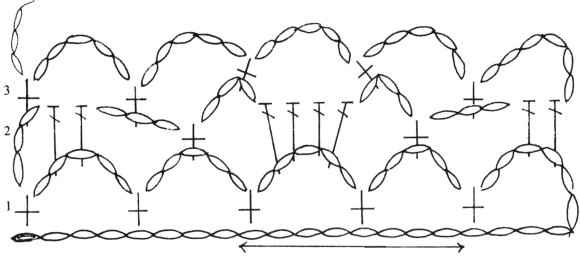

6 / Camelot
(*multiple of 8 + 4 plus 6 chs*)

Row 1: Working on a chain foundation, SC in 10th ch from hook, * Ch 5, Skip 3 chs, SC in next ch. Repeat from * across, Ch 3, Turn.

Row 2: 2 DC under first ch 5, * Ch 3, SC under next ch 5, Ch 3, 4 DC under next ch 5. Repeat from * across ending with only 2 DC under turning ch, Ch 6, Turn.

Row 3: * SC under ch 3, Ch 5. Repeat from * across, ending with SC under turning ch, Ch 3, Turn.

Repeat Rows 2 and 3 for pattern.

[EDGING: Work Rows 1 and 2.]

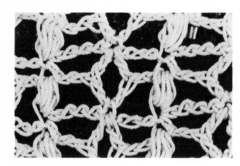

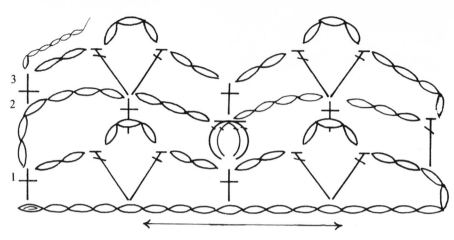

7 / Puff Rib

(*multiple of 8 + 1 plus 4 chs*)

Row 1: Working on a chain foundation, Skip 8 chs, * work (DC, Ch 3, DC) in next st. Ch 2, Skip 3 chs, SC in next st, Ch 2, Skip 3 chs. Repeat from * across, ending with SC in last ch, Ch 6, Turn.

Row 2: SC under ch 3, * Ch 3, work Puff stitch in next SC [*To Make a Puff Stitch:* ** YO, Insert hook in st, Pull Up thread about ½″, repeat from ** 3 times more in same st, YO and through 9 loops.] Ch 4. SC under ch 3. Repeat from * across, ending with Ch 3, DC in 3rd ch past last dc, Ch 4, Turn.

Row 3: * (DC, Ch 3, DC) in sc, Ch 2, SC in top of puff, Ch 2. Repeat from * across, ending with SC in 3rd ch of turning ch, Ch 6, Turn.

Repeat Rows 2 and 3 for pattern.

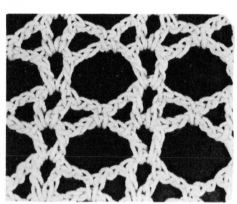

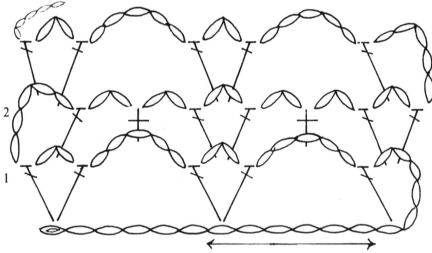

8 / Old Lace

(*multiple of 6 + 1 plus 5 chs*)

Row 1: Working on a chain foundation, DC in 6th ch from hook. * Ch 5, Skip 5 chs, work (DC, Ch 2, DC) in next ch. Repeat from * across, Ch 5, Turn.

Row 2: DC under first ch 2, * Ch 2, SC under ch 5, Ch 2, work (DC, Ch 2, DC) under ch 2. Repeat from * across, working last (DC, Ch 2, DC) under turning ch, Ch 5, Turn.

Row 3: DC under first ch 2, * Ch 5, work (DC, Ch 2, DC) under ch 2 between the next 2 dc. Repeat from * across, working last (DC, Ch 2, DC) under turning ch, Ch 5, Turn.

Repeat Rows 2 and 3 for pattern.

[**EDGING:** Work Rows 1 and 2.]

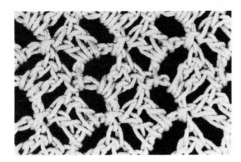

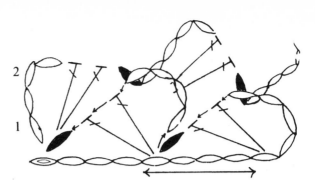

9 / Braid Lace
(*multiple of 4 + 1 plus 4 chs*)

Row 1: Working on a ch foundation, work 2 DC in 5th ch from hook. * Skip 3 chs, Sl St in next ch, Ch 4. Work 2 DC in same ch as sl st. Repeat from * across, ending with Sl St in last ch, Ch 4, Turn.

Row 2: Work 2 DC in sl st, * Sl St under next ch 4, Ch 4, work 2 DC under same ch 4 as sl st was made. Repeat from * across, ending with Sl St under turning ch, Ch 4, Turn.

Repeat Row 2 for pattern.

[**EDGING:** Work Rows 1 and 2.]

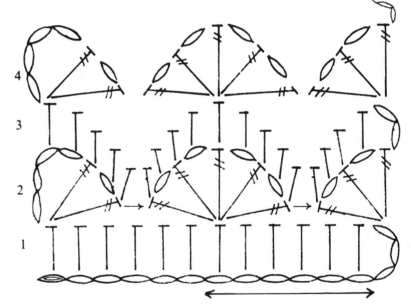

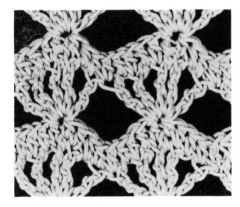

10 / Open Scallops
(*multiple of 6 plus 3 chs*)

Row 1: Working on a chain foundation, HDC in 4th ch from hook and in each ch across, Ch 4, Turn.

Row 2: Work (TC, Ch 1, TC) in hdc at base of ch. * Skip 5 hdc, work (TC, Ch 1, TC, Ch 1, TC, Ch 1, TC, Ch 1, TC) in next hdc. Repeat from * across, ending with (TC, Ch 1, TC, Ch 1, TC) in 3rd ch of turning ch, Ch 2, Turn.

Row 3: HDC in each ch and tc across. Work HDC in each of 3rd and 4th ch of turning ch, Ch 4, Turn.

Row 4: Work (TC, Ch 1, TC) in hdc at base of ch. * Skip 8 hdc, work (TC, Ch 1, TC, Ch 1, TC, Ch 1, TC, Ch 1, TC) in next hdc. Repeat from * across, ending with (TC, Ch 1, TC, Ch 1, TC) in turning ch, Ch 2, Turn.

Repeat Rows 3 and 4 for pattern.

[**EDGING:** Work Rows 2 and 3.]

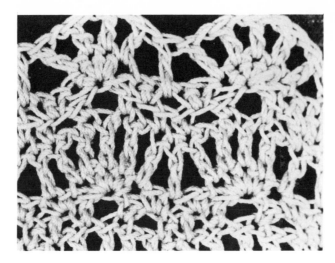

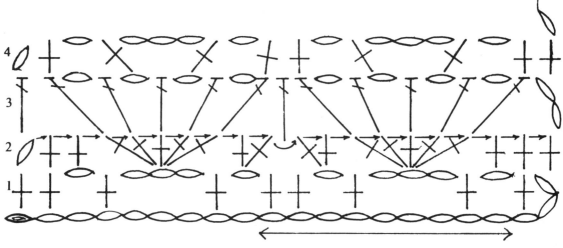

11 / Pompadour
(*multiple of 9 + 1 plus 2 chs*)

Row 1: Working on a chain foundation, SC in 3rd ch from hook, * Ch 1, Skip 1 ch, SC in next ch, Ch 3, Skip 3 chs, SC in next ch, Ch 1, Skip 1 ch, SC in each of next 2 chs. Repeat from * across, Ch 1, Turn.

Row 2: SC in first sc, SC in next ch, * Work 5 SC in 2nd ch of ch 3, Skip next sc, work 2 SC in next ch, Skip 2 sc, 2 SC in next ch. Repeat from * across, ending with 5 SC in middle ch, and SC in next ch 1, SC in last sc and SC in 2nd ch of turning ch, Ch 2, Turn.

Row 3: * (DC, Ch 1) in each sc of 5 sc group (do not ch 1 after the 5th dc), DC between the 2 sc groups. Repeat from * across, ending with DC in turning ch, Ch 1, Turn.

Row 4: SC in first dc, Ch 1, Skip 1 (ch & dc) * SC in next ch, Ch 3, Skip dc, SC in next ch, Ch 1, Skip 1 (dc & ch) SC in next dc, Skip 1 dc, SC in next dc, Ch 1, Skip (ch & dc). Repeat from * across, ending with last SC in 2nd ch of turning ch, Ch 1, Turn.

Repeat Rows 2 through 4 for pattern.

[**EDGING:** Work Rows 1, 2, and 3.]

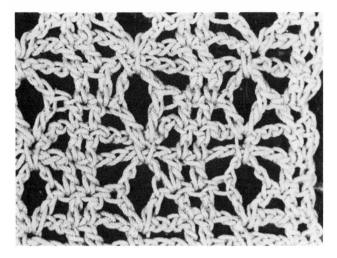

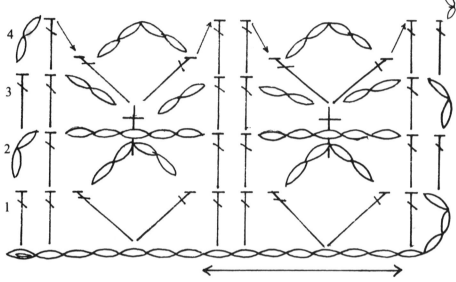

12 / Jigsaw Lace
(multiple of 7 + 1 plus 3 chs)

Row 1: Working on a chain foundation, DC in 4th ch from hook. * Skip 2 chs, work (DC, Ch 4, DC) in next ch, Skip 2 chs, work DC in each of next 2 chs. Repeat from * across, Ch 2, Turn.

Row 2: DC in next dc, * Ch 5, Skip (dc, ch 4, dc), DC in each of next 2 dc. Repeat from * across, working last DC in 3rd ch of turning ch, Ch 2, Turn.

Row 3: DC in next dc, * Ch 2, SC under both ch 5 and ch 4 of Rows 2 and 3, Ch 2, DC in each of next 2 dc. Repeat from * across, ending with last DC in 2nd ch of turning ch, Ch 2, Turn.

Row 4: DC in next dc, * (DC, Ch 4, DC) in next sc, DC in each of next 2 dc. Repeat from * across, Ch 2, Turn.

Repeat Rows 2 through 4 for pattern.

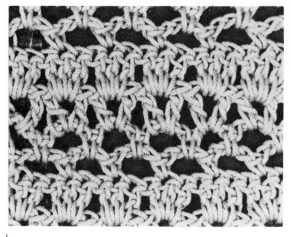

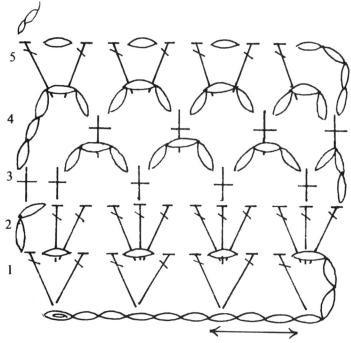

13 / Lacy V's
   (*multiple of 3 + 1 plus 3 chs*)

Row 1: Working on a chain foundation, DC in 4th ch from hook. * Skip 2 chs, work (DC, Ch 1, DC) in next ch. Repeat from * across, Ch 2, Turn.

Row 2: Work 2 DC under ch 1, * work 3 DC under next ch 1. Repeat from * across, working last 3 DC under turning ch, Ch 3, Turn.

Row 3: SC in next dc, * Ch 3, Skip 2 dc, SC in next dc. Repeat from * across, ending with SC in 2nd ch of turning ch, Ch 5, Turn.

Row 4: * SC under ch 3, Ch 3. Repeat from * across, ending with SC under turning ch, Ch 4, Turn.

Row 5: DC under ch 3 * work (DC, Ch 1, DC) under next ch 3. Repeat from * across, ending with last (DC, Ch 1, DC) under turning ch, Ch 2, Turn.

Repeat Rows 2 through 5 for pattern.

[**EDGING:** Work Rows 1, 2, and 3.]

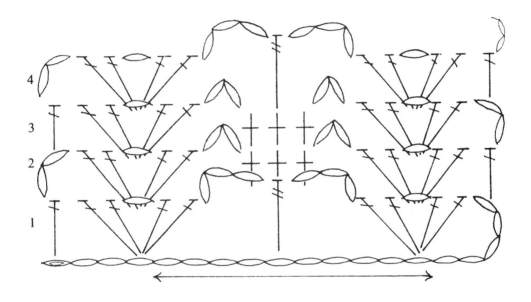

14 / Web Lace
(*multiple of 10 + 6 plus 3 chs*)

Row 1: Working on a chain foundation, Skip 5 chs. * Work (2 DC, Ch 1, 2 DC) in next ch, Ch 3, Skip 4 chs, TC in next ch, Ch 3, Skip 4 chs. Repeat from * across, ending with (2 DC, Ch 1, 2 DC) in next ch, Skip 2 chs, DC in last ch, Ch 2, Turn.

Row 2: * (2 DC, Ch 1, 2 DC) under ch 1, Ch 2, SC under ch 3, SC in tc, SC under ch 3, Ch 2. Repeat from * across, ending with (2 DC, Ch 1, 2 DC) under last ch 1, DC in last ch of turning ch, Ch 2, Turn.

Row 3: * (2 DC, Ch 1, 2 DC) under ch 1, Ch 2, SC in each of next 3 sc, Ch 2. Repeat from * across, ending with (2 DC, Ch 1, 2 DC) under last ch 1, DC in 2nd ch of turning ch, Ch 2, Turn.

Row 4: * Work (2 DC, Ch 1, 2 DC) under ch 1, Ch 3, Skip sc, TC in next sc (middle sc), Ch 3. Repeat from * across, ending with (2 DC, Ch 1, 2 DC) under last ch 1, DC in 2nd ch of turning ch, Ch 2, Turn.

Repeat Rows 2 through 4 for pattern.

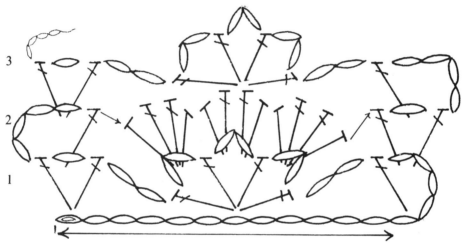

15 / Shell Clusters
(multiple of 12 + 1 plus 4 chs)

Row 1: Working on a chain foundation, DC in 5th ch from hook. * Ch 2, Skip 5 chs, work (DC, Ch 2, DC, Ch 2, DC, Ch 2, DC) in next ch, Ch 2, Skip 5 chs, work (DC, Ch 1, DC) in next ch. Repeat from * across, Ch 4, Turn.

Row 2: DC under ch 1, * Skip ch 2, work (HDC, 2 DC, HDC) under each of next 3 ch 2s, Skip ch 2, work (DC, Ch 1, DC) under next ch 1. Repeat from * across, ending with last (DC, Ch 1, DC) under turning chain, Ch 4, Turn.

Row 3: DC under first ch 1, * Ch 2, Skip (dc, hdc, 2 dc, 2 hdc) and work (DC, Ch 2, DC, Ch 2, DC, Ch 2, DC) in next dc, Ch 2, work (DC, Ch 1, DC) under next ch 1. Repeat from * across, working last (DC, Ch 1, DC) under turning chain, Ch 4, Turn.

Repeat Rows 2 and 3 for pattern.

[EDGING: Work Rows 2 and 3.]

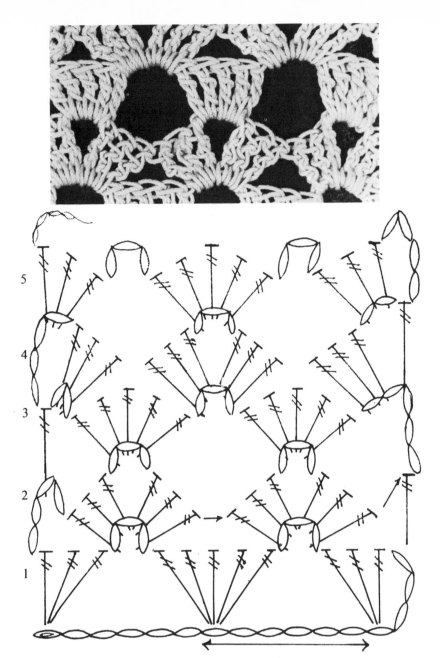

16 / Lace Shell
(*multiple of 6 + 1 plus 3 chs*)

Row 1: Working on a chain foundation, work 3 TC in 4th ch
from hook, * Ch 3, Skip 5
chs, work 5 TC in next ch.
Repeat from * across, ending
with 3 TC in last ch (instead
of 5 TC), Ch 4, Turn.

Row 2: * Work (3 TC, Ch 3, 3 TC)
under ch 3. Repeat from *
across, ending with TC in 3rd
ch of turning ch, Ch 5, Turn.

Row 3: * Work 5 TC under ch 3, Ch
3. Repeat from * across, ending with Ch 2 (instead of Ch
3), TC under turning ch, Ch
4, Turn.

Row 4: Work 3 TC under ch 2,
* work (3 TC, Ch 3, 3 TC)
under ch 3. Repeat from *
across, ending with (3 TC, Ch
2, TC) under turning ch, Ch
4, Turn.

Row 5: Work 3 TC under ch
2, * Ch 3, 5 TC under
ch 3. Repeat from *
across, ending with
Ch 3, 3 TC under
turning ch, Ch 4,
Turn.

Repeat Rows 2 through 5 for pattern.

[EDGING: Work Row 2.]

151

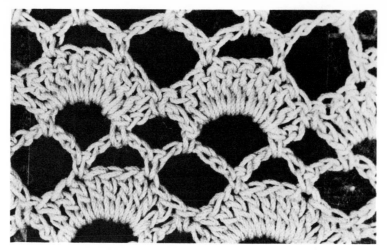

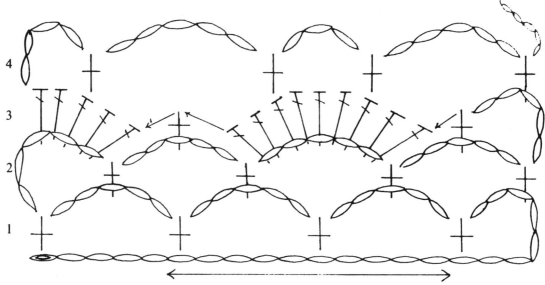

17 / Happiness
(multiple of 10 + 8 plus 5 chs)

Row 1: Working on a chain foundation, SC in 8th ch from hook. * Ch 5, Skip 4 chs, SC in next ch. Repeat from * across, Ch 5, Turn.

Row 2: * SC under ch 5, Ch 5. Repeat from * across, ending with SC under turning ch, Ch 5, Turn.

Row 3: * SC under ch 5, work 9 DC under next ch 5. Repeat from * across, ending with SC under ch 5, work 5 DC under turning ch, Ch 4, Turn.

Row 4: SC in 2nd dc, * Ch 5, Skip (2 dc, sc, 2 dc) SC in next dc, Ch 3, Skip 3 dc, SC in next dc. Repeat from * across ending with Ch 5, SC under turning ch, Ch 5, Turn.

Repeat Rows 2 through 4 for pattern.

[**EDGING:** Work Rows 1, 2, and 3.]

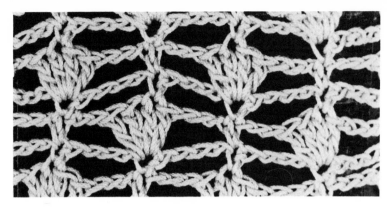

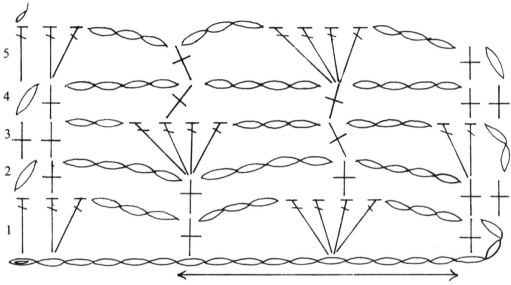

18 / Rachel
(multiple of 10 + 7 plus 2 chs)

Row 1: Working on a chain foundation, SC in 3rd ch from hook. * Ch 3, Skip 4 chs, work 4 DC in next ch, Ch 3, Skip 4 chs, SC in next ch. Repeat from * across, ending with Ch 3, Skip 4 chs, work 2 DC in next ch, DC in last ch, Ch 1, Turn.

Row 2: SC in next dc. * Ch 4, SC in next sc, Ch 4, Skip 2 dc, SC in next dc. Repeat from * across, ending with Ch 4, SC in last sc, SC in turning ch, Ch 2, Turn.

Row 3: Work 2 DC in next sc, * Ch 3, SC in next sc, Ch 3, work 4 DC in next sc. Repeat from * across, ending with Ch 2, SC in last sc, SC in turning ch, Ch 1, Turn.

Row 4: SC in next sc, * Ch 4, SC in 2nd dc (of 4 dc), Ch 4, SC in next sc. Repeat from * across, ending with Ch 4, SC in 2nd dc, SC in turning ch, Ch 1, Turn.

Row 5: SC in next sc, * Ch 3, work 4 DC in next sc, Ch 3, SC in next sc. Repeat from * across, ending with Ch 3, 2 DC in next sc, DC in turning ch, Ch 1, Turn.

Repeat Rows 2 through 5 for pattern.

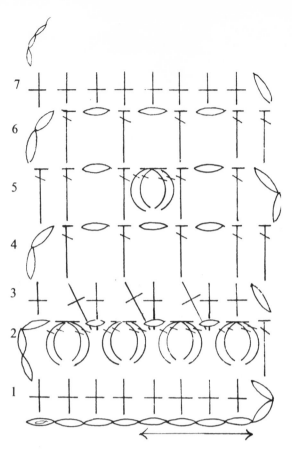

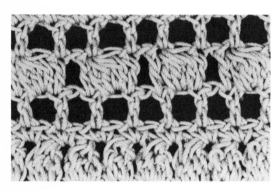

19 / Wrought Iron Grill
(multiple of 4 plus 2 chs)

Row 1: Working on a chain foundation, SC in 3rd ch from hook and in each ch across, Ch 3, Turn.

Row 2: * Work Cluster in next sc. [*To Make Cluster:* (YO, Insert hook, Pull Up thread, YO and through 2 loops) 4 times. YO and through 5 loops.] Ch 1. Skip sc, Repeat from * across, ending with Cluster in last sc, DC in turning ch, Ch 1, Turn.

Row 3: SC in next cluster, * work 2 SC under next ch. Repeat from * across, ending with SC in 3rd ch of turning ch, Ch 2, Turn.

Row 4: * DC in next sc, Ch 1, Skip sc. Repeat from * across, ending with DC in last sc and DC in turning ch, Ch 2, Turn.

Row 5: * DC in next dc, Ch 1, DC in next dc, work Cluster in next ch. Repeat from * across, ending with DC in next dc, Ch 1, DC in last dc, DC in turning ch, Ch 2, Turn.

Row 6: * DC in next dc, Ch 1. Repeat from * across, ending with DC in last dc, DC in turning ch, Ch 1, Turn.

Row 7: SC in each dc and ch across ending with last SC in turning ch, Ch 3, Turn.

Repeat Rows 2 through 7 for pattern.

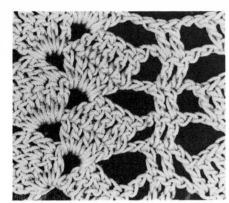

20 / Shell Ladders
(multiple of 17 + 2 plus 3 chs)

Row 1: Working on a chain foundation, DC in 4th ch from hook, DC in next ch. * Ch 2, Skip 6 chs, work 5 DC in next ch, Ch 2, DC in each of next 5 chs, Ch 2, Skip 3 chs, DC in each of next 2 chs. Repeat from * across, Ch 2, Turn.

Row 2: DC in next 2 dc, * Ch 2, Skip (2 chs, 5 dc) work 5 DC under next ch 2, Ch 2, DC in each of next 5 dc, Ch 2, DC in each of next 2 dc. Repeat from * across, ending with DC in 3rd ch of turning ch, Ch 2, Turn.

Repeat Row 2 for pattern.

[EDGING: Work Rows 1 and 2.]

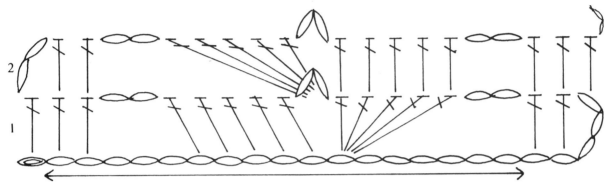

21 / Triple Fish Scale
(multiple of 8 + 1 plus 3 chs)

Row 1: Working on a chain foundation, DC in 4th ch from hook. * Skip 3 chs, work (DC, Ch 3, DC) in next ch, Skip 3 chs, work (DC, Ch 1, DC) in next ch. Repeat from * across, Ch 3, Turn.

Row 2: DC under ch 1, * work 6 TC under ch 3, work (DC, Ch 1, DC) under next ch 1. Repeat from * across, working last (DC, Ch 1, DC) under turning ch, Ch 3, Turn.

Row 3: DC under ch 1, * work (DC, Ch 3, DC) between 3rd and 4th tc, work (DC, Ch 1, DC) under next ch 1. Repeat from * across, working last (DC, Ch 1, DC) under turning ch, Ch 3, Turn.

Repeat Rows 2 and 3 for pattern.

[EDGING: Work Rows 1 and 2.]

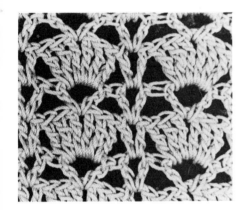

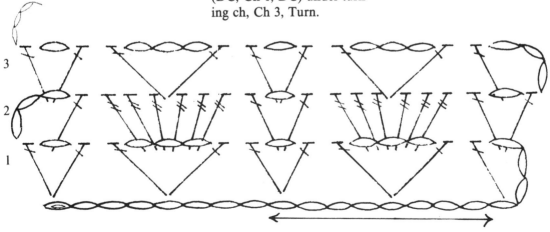

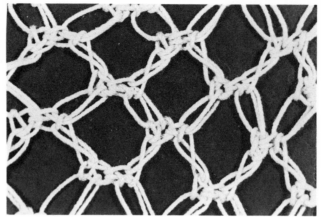

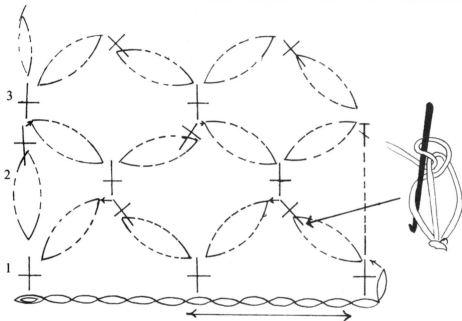

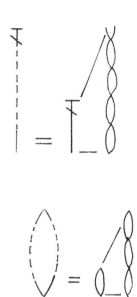

22 / Solomon's Knot
(multiple of 6 + 1 plus 1 ch)

Row 1: Working on a chain foundation, SC in 2nd ch from hook.
* Make a Long Ch. [*To Make
a Long Chain:* Pull the loop
already on the hook out to
the length of 3 chs and Pull
the thread through as you
normally would to make a
chain stitch.] Work SC under
back thread of just completed
ch. Make Long Ch as above,
Skip 5 chs, SC in next ch. Repeat from * across, make
Long Ch to turn. Turn.

Row 2: SC under back thread of just
completed ch, make Long Ch,
* SC in sc between 2 long chs
of last row. Make Long Ch,
SC under back thread of just
completed ch, make Long Ch,
Skip next sc on last row. Repeat from * across, ending
with SC in next sc, make
Long Ch, work Long DC
(length of 4½ chs) in sc on
last row, make Long Ch,
Turn.

Row 3: Same as Row 2, except ending with SC in last sc, Long
Ch, Turn. Repeat Rows 2 and
3 for pattern.

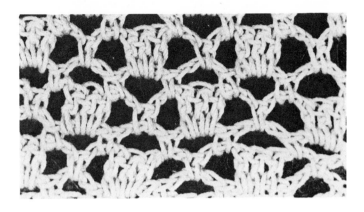

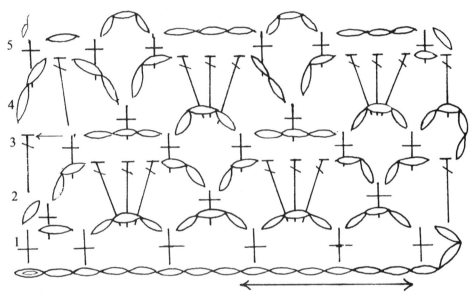

23 / Lace Triangles
(multiple of 6 + 3 plus 2 chs)

Row 1: Working on a chain foundation, SC in 3rd ch from hook.
* Ch 3, Skip 2 chs, SC in next
ch. Repeat from * across,
ending with Ch 1, Skip 1 ch,
SC in last ch, Ch 1, Turn.

Row 2: SC under first ch 1. * Ch 2,
work 3 DC under next ch 3,
Ch 2, SC under next ch 3.
Repeat from * across, ending
with Ch 2, DC in 2nd ch of
turning ch, Ch 4, Turn.

Row 3: * SC under ch 2, Ch 3. Repeat from * across, ending
with SC under last ch 2, DC
in turning ch, Ch 2, Turn.

Row 4: DC in first sc, * Ch 2, SC
under ch 3, Ch 2, work 3 DC
under next ch 3, Repeat from
* across, ending with Ch 1,
DC under turning ch, Ch 1,
Turn.

Row 5: SC under ch 1, * Ch 3, SC
under ch 2. Ch 3, SC under
next ch 2. Repeat from *
across, ending with Ch 1, SC
under turning ch, Ch 1, Turn.

Repeat Rows 2 through 5 for pattern.

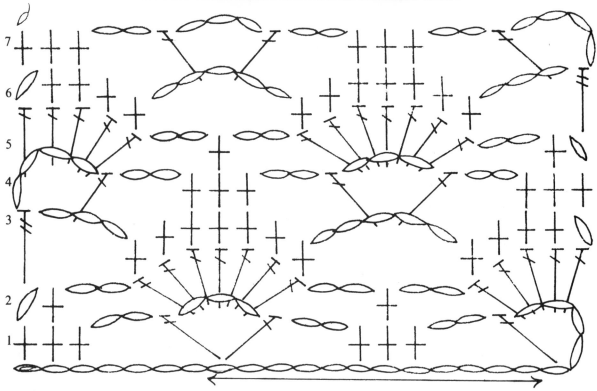

24 / Lace with Alternating Shells
(*multiple of 12 + 8 plus 4 chs*)

Row 1: Working on a chain foundation, DC in 5th ch from hook. * Ch 2, Skip 4 chs, SC in each of next 3 chs, Ch 2, Skip 4 chs, work (DC, Ch 3, DC) in next ch. Repeat from * across, ending with Ch 2, Skip 4 chs, SC in each of last 3 chs, Ch 1, Turn

Row 2: SC in next sc, * Ch 2, work 7 DC under ch 3, Ch 2, Skip 1 sc, SC in next sc. Repeat from * across, ending with Ch 2, work 5 DC under turning ch, Ch 1, Turn.

Row 3: SC in each of next 4 dc, * Ch 5, SC in each of next 7 dc. Repeat from * across, ending with Ch 3, TC in turning ch, Ch 4, Turn.

Row 4: DC under ch 3, Ch 2, * Skip 2 sc, SC in each of next 3 sc, Ch 2, work (DC, Ch 3, DC) under ch 5, Ch 2. Repeat from * across, ending with Skip 2 sc, SC in each of last 2 sc and in turning ch, Ch 1, Turn.

Row 5: Repeat Row 2.
Row 6: Repeat Row 3.
Row 7: Repeat Row 4.
Repeat Rows 2 through 7 for pattern.

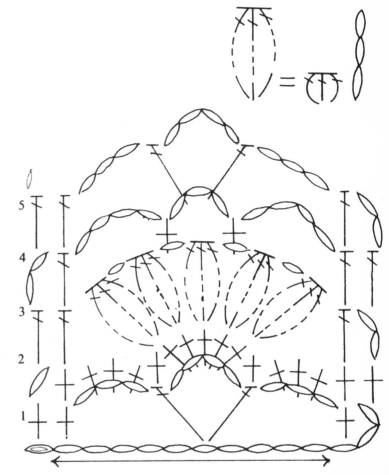

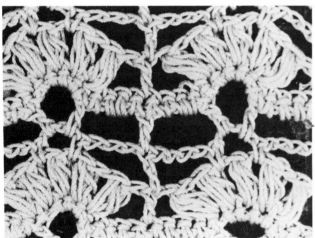

25 / Cluster Fans
(multiple of 10 + 2 plus 2 chs)

Row 1: Working on a chain founda-
tion, SC in 3rd ch from hook.
* Ch 3, Skip 4 chs, work (DC,
Ch 4, DC) in next ch, Ch 3,
Skip 4 chs, SC in next ch. Re-
peat from * across, ending
with SC in last ch, Ch 1,
Turn.

Row 2: SC in next st, * Work 3 SC
under ch 3, SC in dc, work 5
SC under ch 4, SC in dc,
work 3 SC under ch 3, SC in
next st. Repeat from * across,
ending with SC in turning ch,
Ch 2, Turn.

Row 3: DC in next sc. * Skip 4 sc,
work Long Small Puff, Ch 1,
in each of next 5 sc. [*To
Make Long Small Puff*: (YO,
Insert hook, Pull Up thread
about the length of 3 chs) 3
times. YO and through 7
loops.] Do not Ch 1 after last
puff. Skip 4 sc, DC in next sc.
Repeat from * across ending
with DC in turning ch, Ch 2,
Turn.

Row 4: DC in next dc, * Ch 4, Skip
(puff, ch 1, puff) SC under
next ch 1, Ch 3, Skip puff, SC
under next ch 1, Ch 4, DC in
next dc. Repeat from * across,
ending with DC in turning ch,
Ch 2, Turn.

Row 5: DC in next dc, * Ch 3, work
(DC, Ch 4, DC) under ch 3,
Ch 3, DC in next dc. Repeat
from * across, ending with
DC in turning ch, Ch 1, Turn.

Repeat Rows 2 through 5 for pattern.

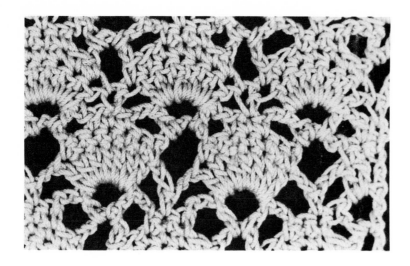

26 / Rainbow Fans
(multiple of 8 plus 2 chs)

Row 1: Working on a chain foundation, SC in 3rd ch from hook * Skip 2 chs, work (2 DC, Ch 3, 2 DC) in next ch, Skip 2 chs, SC in each of next 3 chs. Repeat from * across, ending with only 2 SC in last 2 chs, Ch 3, Turn.

Row 2: * Work 7 DC under ch 3, Skip (2 dc, sc) SC in next sc. Repeat from * across, working last SC in turning ch, Ch 6, Turn.

Row 3: * SC in each of next 7 dc, Ch 5. Repeat from * across ending with Ch 2, SC in 3rd ch of turning ch, Ch 5, Turn.

Row 4: DC under ch 2, * Ch 2, Skip 2 sc, SC in each of next 3 sc, Ch 2, work (DC, Ch 3, DC) under ch 5, Repeat from * across, ending with only (DC, Ch 2, DC) under turning ch, Ch 3, Turn.

Row 5: Work 2 DC under ch 2, * Ch 2, SC in 2nd sc of 3 sc group, Ch 2, work 7 DC under ch 3. Repeat from * across, ending with only 3 DC under turning ch, Ch 1, Turn.

Row 6: SC in each of next 2 dc, * Ch 5, SC in each of next 7 dc. Repeat from * across ending with SC only in next 2 dc and SC in 3rd ch of turning ch, Ch 1, Turn.

Row 7: SC in next sc, * Ch 2, work (DC, Ch 3, DC) under ch 5, Ch 2, Skip 2 sc, SC in each of next 3 sc. Repeat from * across ending with only Skip 1 sc, SC in next sc, SC in turning ch, Ch 3, Turn.

Repeat Rows 2 through 7 for pattern.

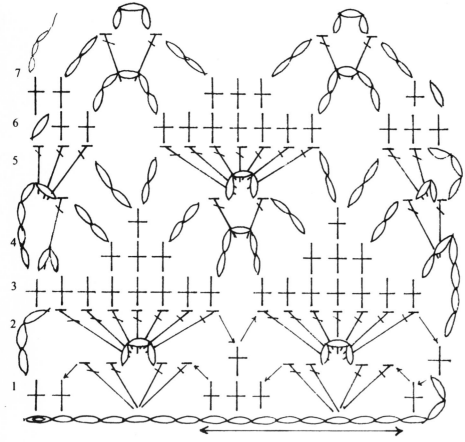

27 / Fancy Shells with Picots
(multiple of 8 + 1 plus 5 chs)

Row 1: Working on a chain foundation, SC in 8th ch from hook. * Ch 4, Skip 3 chs, SC in next ch. Repeat from * across, ending with Ch 2, Skip ch, TC in last ch, Ch 2, Turn.

Row 2: Work 4 DC under ch 2. * SC under ch 4, work (4 DC, Ch 3, SC in last dc made, 4 DC) under next ch 4. Repeat from * across, ending with SC under next ch 4, work (4 DC, Ch 3, SC in last dc made, DC) under turning ch, Ch 5, Turn.

Row 3: SC in 3rd dc, * Ch 4, Skip (2 dc, sc, 2 dc) SC in next dc, Ch 4, Skip 2 dc (includes picot), SC in next dc. Repeat from * across, ending with Ch 4, Skip (2 dc, sc, 2 dc) SC in next dc, Ch 1, TC in turning ch, Ch 1, Turn.

Row 4: * Work (4 DC, Ch 3, SC in last dc made, 4 DC) under ch 4, SC under next ch 4. Repeat from * across, ending with last SC under turning ch, Ch 5, Turn.

Row 5: Skip 2 dc, * SC in next dc, Ch 4, Skip 2 dc (including picot), SC in next dc, Ch 4, Skip (2 dc, sc, 2 dc). Repeat from * across, ending with Skip 2 dc (including picot), SC in next dc, Ch 2, TC in turning ch, Ch 2, Turn.

Repeat Rows 2 through 5 for pattern.

[**EDGING:** Work Rows 1 and 2.]

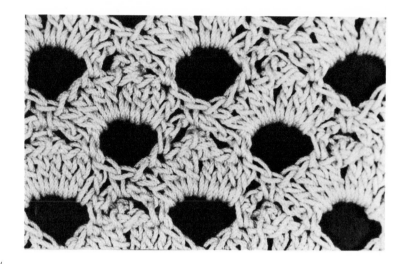

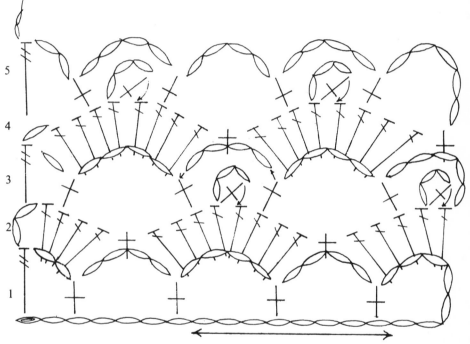

28 / Fancy Fans
(multiple of 6 + 2 plus 2 chs)

Row 1: Working on a chain foundation, SC in 3rd ch from hook and in each ch across, Ch 1, Turn.

Row 2: * SC in next sc, Skip 2 sc, work 7 Long DC (pulling up stitches to length of 3 chs) in next sc. Skip 2 sc. Repeat from * across, ending with SC in last sc and SC in 2nd ch of turning ch, Ch 4, Turn.

Row 3: SC in 2nd dc (of 7 dc group), SC in next 4 dc, * Ch 1, Skip (dc, sc, dc), SC in each of next 5 dc. Repeat from * across ending with Ch 1, Skip (dc, sc) TC in turning ch, Ch 3, Turn.

Row 4: Work 4 Long DC under ch 1, * SC in 3rd sc (of 5 sc group), work 7 Long DC under next ch 1. Repeat from * across, ending with only 5 Long DC under turning ch, Ch 1, Turn.

Row 5: SC in each of next 3 dc, * Ch 1, Skip (dc, sc, dc), SC in each of next 5 dc. Repeat from * across, ending with Ch 1, Skip (dc, sc, dc), SC in each of last 3 dc and in 3rd ch of turning ch, Ch 1, Turn.

Row 6: SC in next sc, * Work 7 Long DC under ch 1, Skip 2 sc, SC in next sc. Repeat from * across, ending with SC in turning ch, Ch 4, Turn.

Repeat Rows 3 through 6 for pattern.

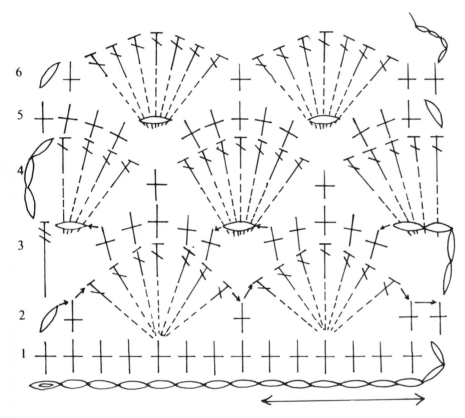

29 / Japanese Fans
(multiple of 14 + 1 plus 1 ch)

Row 1: Working on a chain founda-
tion, SC in 2nd ch from hook,
* Skip 6 chs, work 13 Long
DC (each dc should be the
length of 6 chs) in next ch,
Skip 6 chs, SC in next ch. Re-
peat from * across, Ch 7,
Turn.

Row 2: Work Long DC in sc at base
of turning ch, * Ch 5, Skip 6
long dc, SC in next long dc,
Ch 5, work (Long DC, Ch 1,
Long DC) in sc. Repeat from
* across (do not work in turning ch), Ch 1, Turn.

Row 3: SC under first ch 1, * Work
13 Long DC in next sc, SC
under next ch 1. Repeat from
* across, ending with SC
under turning ch, Ch 7, Turn.

Repeat Rows 2 and 3 for pattern.

[EDGING: Work Row 1.]

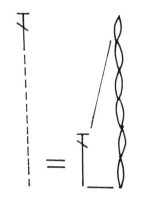

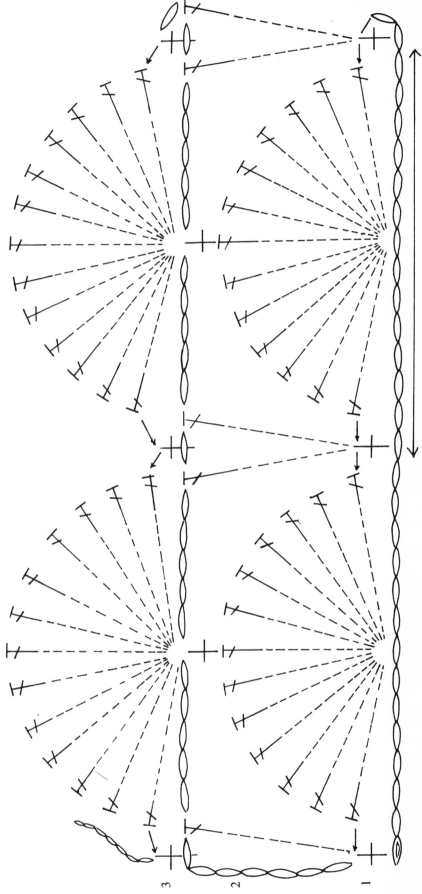

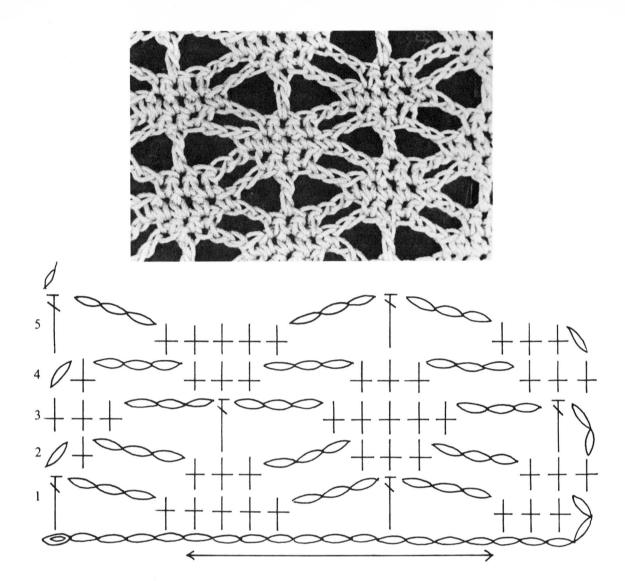

30 / Sunburst

(multiple of 11 + 8 plus 2 chs)

Row 1: Working on a chain foundation, SC in 3rd ch from hook,
SC in each of next 2 sc, * Ch
3, Skip 3 chs, DC in next ch,
Ch 3, Skip 3 chs, SC in each
of next 5 chs. Repeat from *
across, ending with Ch 3,
Skip 3 chs, DC in last ch, Ch
1, Turn.

Row 2: SC in first ch (of ch 3), * Ch
3, Skip 1 sc, SC in each of
next 3 sc, Ch 3, SC in ch before dc, SC in dc, SC in first
ch past dc. Repeat from *
across, ending with Ch 3,
Skip 1 sc, SC in next 2 sc and
in 2nd ch of turning ch, Ch 2,
Turn.

Row 3: DC in next sc, * Ch 3, Skip
next sc, SC in ch before next
sc, SC in each of next 3 sc
and SC in first ch past sc, Ch
3, DC in center sc of 3 sc. Repeat from * across ending
with Ch 3, SC in 3rd ch (of 3
chs), SC in sc and in turning
ch, Ch 1, Turn.

Row 4: SC in next sc, * Ch 3, SC in
3rd ch of ch 3, SC in dc, SC
in ch past dc, Ch 3, Skip 1 sc,
SC in next 3 sc. Repeat from
* across, ending with Ch 3,
SC in last ch of ch 3, SC in
dc and SC in 2nd ch of turning ch, Ch 1, Turn.

Row 5: SC in each of next 2 sc and in
first ch * Ch 3, DC in middle
sc of 3 sc, Ch 3, SC in last ch
of ch 3, SC in each of next 3
sc and SC in first ch. Repeat
from * across, ending with Ch
3, DC in turning ch, Ch 1,
Turn.

Repeat Rows 2 through 5 for pattern.

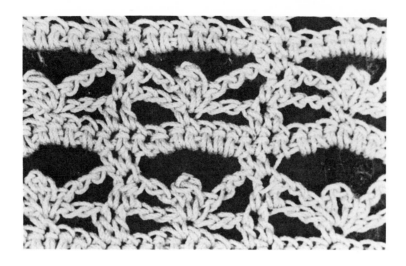

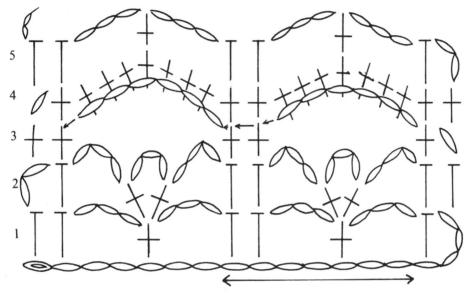

31 / Garden Gates with Picots
(multiple of 7 + 1 plus 3 chs)

Row 1: Working on a chain foundation, work HDC in 4th ch from hook. * Ch 3, Skip 2 chs, SC in next st, Ch 3, Skip 2 chs, HDC in each of next 2 chs. Repeat from * across, Ch 2, Turn.

Row 2: HDC in hdc, * Ch 3, work (SC, Ch 3, SC) in next sc, Ch 3, HDC in each of next 2 hdc. Repeat from * across, working last HDC in turning ch, Ch 1, Turn.

Row 3: SC in hdc, * Ch 6, SC in each of next 2 hdc. Repeat from * across, working last SC in turning ch, Ch 1, Turn.

Row 4: SC in next sc, * work 7 SC under ch 6, SC in each of next 2 sc. Repeat from * across, working last SC in turning ch, Ch 2, Turn.

Row 5: HDC in sc, * Ch 3, SC in 4th sc of 7 sc group, Ch 3. Skip 3 sc, HDC in each of next 2 sc. Repeat from * across, working last HDC in turning ch, Ch 2, Turn.

Repeat Rows 2 through 5 for pattern.

[EDGING: Work Rows 1 through 4.]

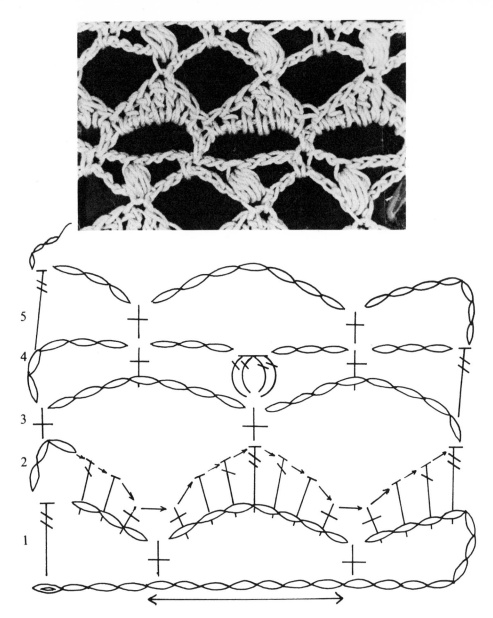

32 / Arches and Puffs
(multiple of 7 + 1 plus 7 chs)

Row 1: Working on a chain foundation, SC in 11th ch from hook. * Ch 7, Skip 6 chs, SC in next ch. Repeat from * across, ending with Ch 3, Skip 3 chs, TC in last ch, Ch 3, Turn.

Row 2: Work (DC, HDC, SC) under ch 3. * Work (SC, HDC, DC, TC, DC, HDC, SC) under ch 7. Repeat from * across, ending (SC, HDC, DC, TC) under turning ch, Ch 8, Turn.

Row 3: * SC in center tc of first full shell, Ch 7. Repeat from * across, ending with SC in 2nd ch of turning ch, Ch 5, Turn.

Row 4: * SC under ch 7, Ch 3, work Puff in sc. [*To Make Puff:* (YO, Insert hook, Pull Up thread) in same st 4 times. YO and through all loops on hook.] Ch 3, Repeat from * across, ending with SC under ch 7, Ch 3, TC in first ch of turning ch, Ch 7, Turn.

Row 5: * SC in sc, Ch 7. Repeat from * across, ending with only Ch 3, TC in 2nd ch of turning ch, Ch 3, Turn.

Repeat Rows 2 through 5 for pattern.

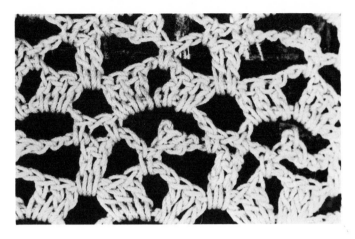

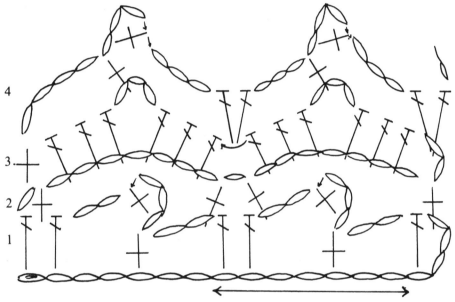

33 / Picot Lace
(multiple of 7 + 1 plus 3 chs)

Row 1: Working on a chain foundation, DC in 4th ch from hook,
* Ch 2, Skip 2 chs, SC in next
ch, Ch 3, SC in first ch of just
completed ch 3, Ch 2, Skip 2
chs, DC in next 2 chs. Repeat
from * across, Ch 1, Turn.

Row 2: SC between first 2 dc, * Ch 7,
SC under ch just before next
dc, Ch 1, SC under ch 2 past
dc. Repeat from * across,
ending with Ch 7, SC under
turning ch, Ch 2, Turn.

Row 3: * Work (3 DC, Ch 3, 3 DC)
under ch 7. Repeat from *
across, ending with SC in
turning ch, Ch 4, Turn.

Row 4: * SC under ch 3, Ch 3, SC in
first ch of just completed ch 3,
Ch 3, 2 DC between 3rd and
4th dc. Ch 3, Repeat from *
across, ending with last 2 DC
under turning ch, Ch 1, Turn.

Repeat Rows 2 through 4 for pattern.

[**EDGING:** Work Rows 1, 2, and 3.]

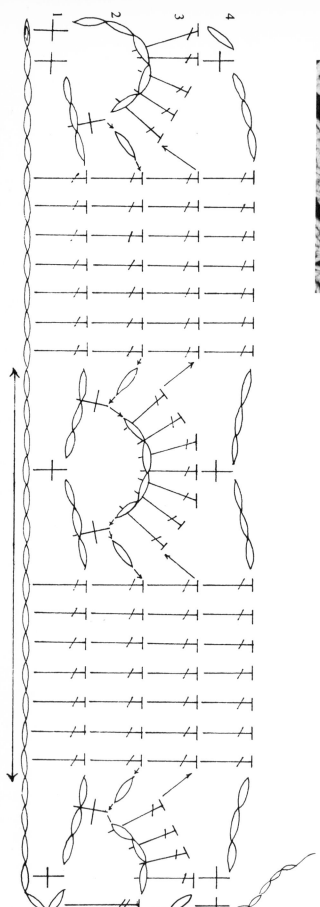

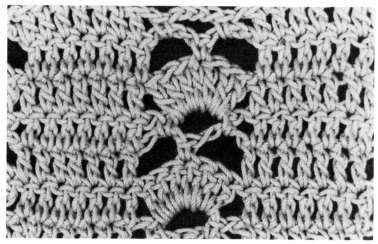

34 / Sunrise
(multiple of 14 + 2 plus 2 chs)

Row 1: Working on a chain foundation, SC in 3rd ch from hook, * Ch 3, Skip 3 chs, DC in each of next 7 chs, Ch 3, Skip 3 chs, SC in next ch. Repeat from * across, ending with SC in last ch, Ch 5, Turn.

Row 2: SC under ch 3, * Ch 1, DC in each of next 7 dc, Ch 1, SC under next ch 3, Ch 4, SC under next ch 3. Repeat from * across, ending with only Ch 3, TC in 2nd ch of turning ch, Ch 2, Turn.

Row 3: Work 4 DC under ch 3, * DC in each of next 7 dc, work 7 DC under ch 4. Repeat from * across, ending with only 5 DC under turning ch, Ch 1, Turn.

Row 4: SC in next dc, Ch 3, * Skip 3 dc, DC in each of next 7 dc, Ch 3, Skip 3 dc, SC in next dc, Ch 3. Repeat from * across, ending with DC in each of next 7 dc, Ch 3, Skip 3 dc, SC in next dc, SC in 2nd ch of turning ch, Ch 5, Turn.

Repeat Rows 2 through 4 for pattern.

[EDGING: Work Rows 1, 2, and 3 to make a solid edging.]

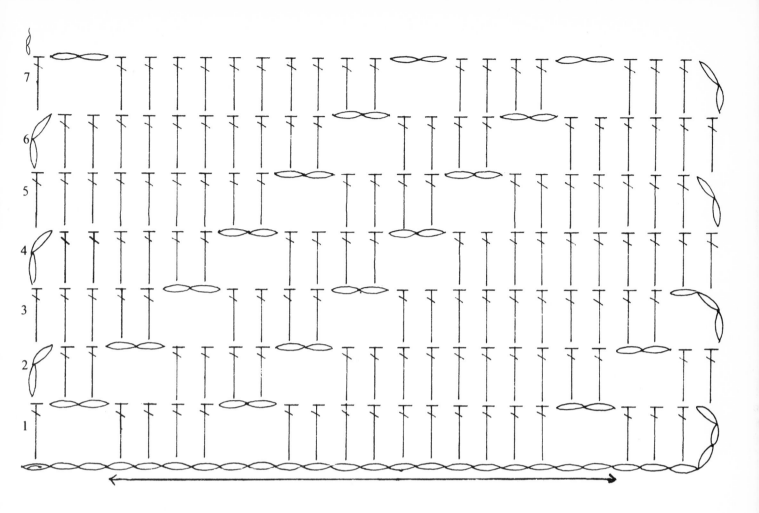

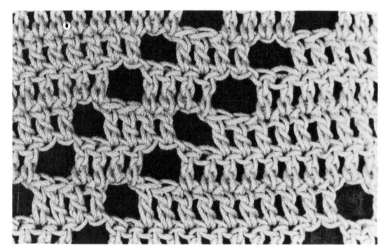

35 / Double Stair Step
(multiple of 18 + 6 plus 3 chs)

Row 1: Working on a chain foundation, DC in 4th ch from hook
and in each of next 2 chs,
* Ch 2, Skip 2 chs, DC in
each of next 10 chs, Ch 2,
Skip 2 chs, DC in each of
next 4 chs. Repeat from *
across, ending with Ch 2,
Skip 2 chs, DC in last ch, Ch
2, Turn.

Row 2: DC in each of next 2 chs,
* Ch 2, Skip 2 dc, DC in each
of next 2 dc and next 2 chs,
Ch 2, Skip 2 dc, DC in each
of next 8 dc and next 2 chs.
Repeat from * across, ending
with Ch 2, Skip 2 dc, DC in
last dc and in 3rd ch of turning ch, Ch 3. Turn.

Row 3: * DC in each of next 2 chs and next 8 dc, Ch 2, Skip 2 dc, DC in each of next 2 chs and next 2 dc, Ch 2, Skip 2 dc. Repeat from * across, ending with DC in each of next 2 chs, next 2 dc and 2nd ch of turning ch, Ch 2, Turn.

Row 4: DC in each of next 4 dc and next 2 chs, * Ch 2, Skip 2 dc, DC in each of next 2 dc and next 2 chs, Ch 2, Skip 2 dc, DC in each of next 8 dc and next 2 chs. Repeat from * across, working last 2 DC in 3rd and 2nd chs of turning ch, Ch 2, Turn.

Row 5: DC in each of next 7 dc, * Ch 2, Skip 2 dc, DC in each of next 2 chs and next 2 dc, Ch 2, Skip 2 dc, DC in each of next 2 chs and next 8 dc. Repeat from * across, ending with only 6 DC in last 6 dc and DC in 2nd ch of turning ch, Ch 2, Turn.

Row 6: * DC in each of next 8 dc and next 2 chs, Ch 2, Skip 2 dc, DC in each of next 2 dc and next 2 chs, Ch 2, Skip 2 dc.

Repeat from * across, ending with DC in each of last 5 dc and 2nd ch of turning ch, Ch 2, Turn.

Row 7: DC in each of next 3 dc, * Ch 2, Skip 2 dc, DC in each of next 2 chs and next 2 dc, Ch 2, Skip 2 dc, DC in each of next 2 chs and next 8 dc. Repeat from * across, ending with Ch 2, Skip 2 dc, DC in 2nd ch of turning ch, Ch 2, Turn.

Repeat Rows 2 through 7 for pattern.

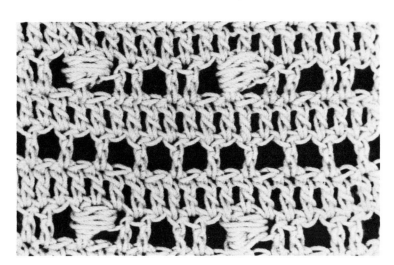

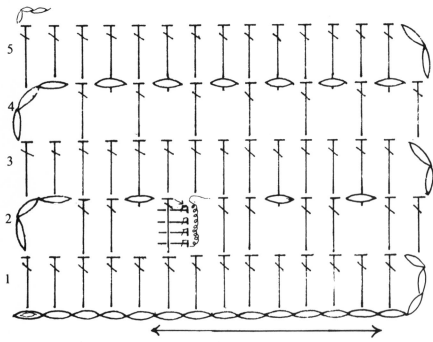

36 / Bean
(multiple of 8 + 6 plus 3 chs)

Row 1: Working on a chain foundation, DC in 4th ch from hook and each ch across, Ch 3, Turn.

Row 2: Skip 1 dc, * DC in each of next 2 dc, Ch 1, Skip dc, DC in next dc. Work a Bean around dc just completed. [*To Make a Bean* in the same way as horizontal puff: (YO, Insert hook around dc, Pull Up thread about the length of 2 chs) 4 times. YO and through all 9 loops on hook to complete Bean.] Skip dc, work DC in each of next 2 dc, Ch 1. Repeat from * across, ending with Skip 1 st, DC in each of next 2 dc, Skip dc, Ch 1, DC in next dc, DC in 3rd ch of turning ch, Ch 2, Turn.

Row 3: DC in each dc, ch, and bean across, working last 2 DC in 3rd and 2nd turning chs, Ch 3, Turn.

Row 4: * Skip dc, DC in next dc, Ch 1. Repeat from * across, working last DC in 2nd ch of turning ch, Ch 2, Turn.

Row 5: DC in each ch and dc across, working last 2 DC in 3rd and 2nd chs of turning ch, Ch 3, Turn.

Repeat Rows 2 through 5 for pattern.

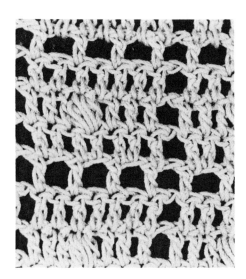

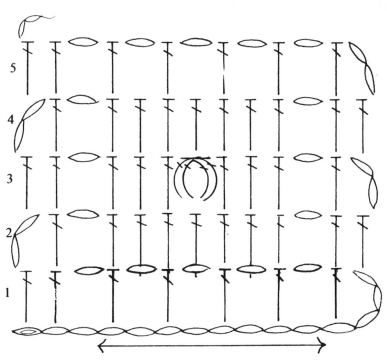

37 / Puffs in Squares
(multiple of 8 + 4 plus 3 chs)

Row 1: Working on a chain foundation, DC in 4th ch from hook. * Ch 1, Skip ch, DC in next ch. Repeat from * across, DC in last ch, Ch 2, Turn.

Row 2: DC in next dc, Ch 1. * (DC in next dc, DC under ch 1) 3 times, DC in dc, Ch 1. Repeat from * across, ending with DC in last dc and DC in turning ch, Ch 2, Turn.

Row 3: DC in next dc, Ch 1. * DC in each of next 3 dc, work Medium Puff in next dc. [*To Make Medium Puff:* (YO, Insert hook, Pull Up thread) 4 times. YO and through all 9 loops to complete Puff.] DC in each of next 3 dc, Ch 1. Repeat from * across ending with DC in last dc and DC in turning ch, Ch 2, Turn.

Row 4: DC in next dc, Ch 1. * DC in each of next (3 dc, puff, 3 dc), Ch 1. Repeat from * across, ending with DC in last dc and DC in turning ch, Ch 2, Turn.

Row 5: DC in next dc, Ch 1 * (DC in next dc, Ch 1, Skip dc) 4 times. Repeat from * across ending with DC in last dc and DC in turning ch, Ch 2, Turn.

Repeat Rows 2 through 5 for pattern.

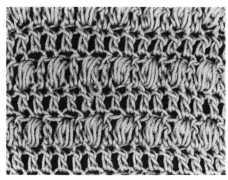

38 / Puffs 'n' Ridges
(multiple of 2 plus 3 chs)

Row 1: Working on a chain foundation, work Medium Puff in 4th ch from hook.[*To Make Puff:* (YO, Insert hook, Pull Up thread,) 4 times. YO, and through 9 loops on hook.] * DC in next ch, work Medium Puff in next ch. Repeat from * across, ending with DC in last ch, Ch 2, Turn.

Row 2: Working in *front* loop only, DC in each st across, Ch 2, Turn.

Row 3: Working all stitches in *back* loop only, * Work Medium Puff in next dc, DC in next dc. Repeat from * across, ending with last DC in turning ch, Ch 2, Turn.

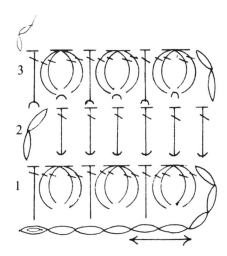

Repeat Rows 2 and 3 for pattern.

39 / Lozenge Lace
(multiple of 4 plus 2 chs)

Row 1: Working on a chain foundation, SC in 3rd ch from hook and in each ch across, Ch 3, Turn.

Row 2: * Skip 1 sc, DC in next sc, Ch 1. Repeat from * across, ending with DC in 2nd ch of turning ch, Ch 3, Turn.

Row 3: * SC in dc, Ch 3, Skip (ch 1, dc, ch 1). Repeat from * across, ending with Ch 1, SC in 2nd ch of turning ch, Ch 3, Turn.

Row 4: DC under first ch, * 4 DC under ch 3. Repeat from * across, ending with 3 DC under turning ch, Ch 3, Turn.

Row 5: YO, Insert hook in first dc, Pull Up thread, YO and through 2 loops. YO, Insert hook in next dc, Pull Up thread, YO and through 2 loops, YO and through 3 loops, Ch 2, * (YO, Insert hook in next dc, Pull Up thread, YO and through 2 loops) 4 times, YO and through 5 loops, Ch 3. Repeat from * across, ending with (YO, Insert hook in next dc, Pull Up thread, YO and through 2 loops) 2 times (final "pull up" will be in turning ch), YO and through 3 loops, Ch 1, Turn.

Row 6: SC in each st across, including 3rd Ch of turning ch, Ch 3, Turn.

Repeat Rows 2 through 6 for pattern.

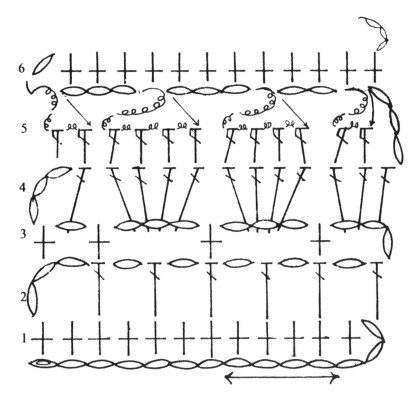

40 / Epergne

(multiple of 8 + 1 plus 1 ch)

Row 1: Working on a chain foundation, SC in 2nd ch from hook. * Ch 8, Skip 7 ch, SC in next ch. Repeat from * across, Ch 7, Turn.

Row 2: *Work 3 TC under ch 7, Ch 6. Repeat from * across, ending with 3 TC under ch 7, Ch 2, DTC in last sc, Ch 4, Turn.

Row 3: Work 2 TC under ch 2, * Ch 4, work (2 TC, Ch 2, 2 TC) under ch 6. Repeat from * across, ending with Ch 4, 2 TC, under turning ch, Ch 1, TC in 4th ch of turning ch, Ch 4, Turn.

Row 4: 2 TC under ch 1, * Ch 3, work (2 TC, Ch 2, 2 TC) under ch 2 (between tc). Repeat from * across, ending with Ch 3, (2 TC, Ch 1, TC) under turning ch, Ch 4, Turn.

Row 5: Work 2 TC under ch 1, * Ch 2, SC under both ch 3 and ch 4 (of Rows 3 and 4), Ch 2, work (2 TC, Ch 2, 2 TC) under ch 2. Repeat from * across, ending with only (2 TC, Ch 1, TC) under turning ch, Ch 9, Turn.

Row 6: * SC under 3rd ch 2, Ch 8. Repeat from * across, ending with SC under turning ch, Ch 7, Turn.

Repeat Rows 2 through 6 for pattern, working DTC of Row 2 in first ch of turning ch at end of Row 6 .

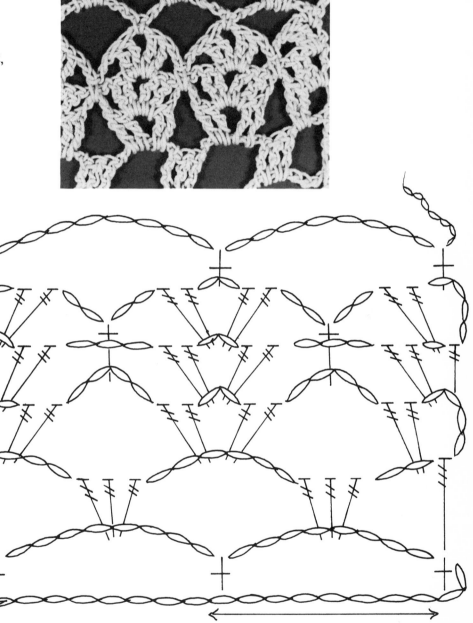

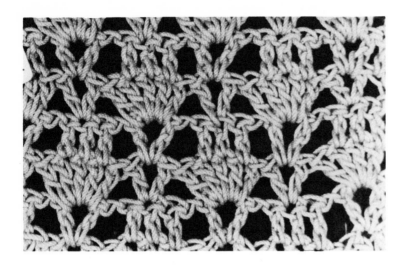

41 / Spaced Iris
(multiple of 7 + 2 plus 3 chs)

Row 1: Working on a chain founda-
tion, DC in 4th ch from hook.
DC in each of next 2 chs,
* Skip 2 chs, work 5 DC in
next ch, Skip 3 ch, work (DC,
Ch 1, DC) in next ch. Repeat
from * across, ending with
Skip 3 ch, work 3 DC in next
ch, DC in each of last 2 chs,
Ch 2, Turn.

Row 2: DC in next 3 dc, * Ch 1,
work (DC, Ch 1, DC) under
next ch 1, Ch 1, Skip 2 dc,
DC in each of next 3 dc, Repeat from * across, ending
with Ch 1, Skip 2 dc, work
(DC, Ch 1, DC) in next dc,
DC in 3rd ch of turning ch,
Ch 2, Turn.

Row 3: Work 4 DC under first ch 1,
* Skip (dc, ch 1, dc) work
(DC, Ch 1, DC) in next dc,
Skip (dc, ch 1, dc), work 5
DC under next ch 1. Repeat
from * across, ending with
Skip (dc, ch 1, dc), work (DC,
Ch 1, DC) in next dc, DC in
2nd ch of turning ch, Ch 2,
Turn.

Row 4: * Work (DC, Ch 1, DC)
under ch 1, Ch 1, Skip 2 dc,
DC in each of next 3 dc, Ch
1. Repeat from * across, ending with omit last Ch 1, DC
in 2nd ch of turning ch, Ch 2,
Turn.

Row 5: Skip next dc, work (DC, Ch
1, DC) in next dc, * Skip (dc,
ch 1, dc), work 5 DC under
next ch 1, Skip (dc, ch 1, dc),
work (DC, Ch 1, DC) in next
dc. Repeat from * across,
ending with Skip (dc, ch 1,
dc), work 4 DC under next ch
1, DC in 2nd ch of turning
ch, Ch 2, Turn.

Repeat Rows 2 through 5 for pattern.

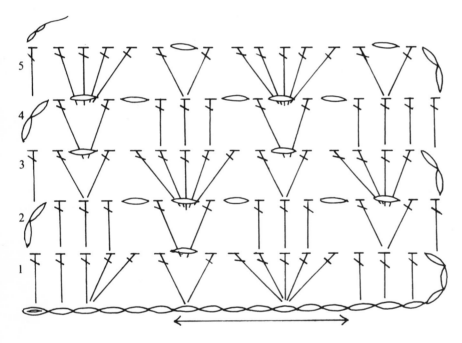

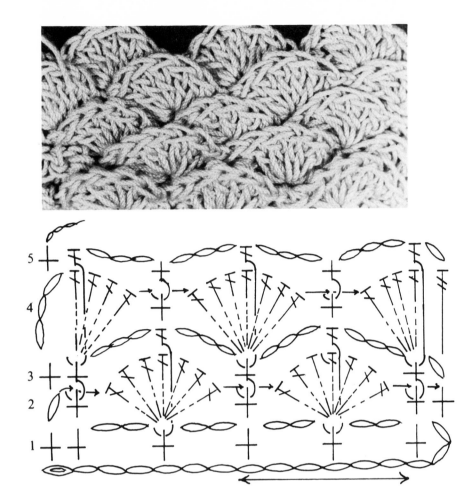

42 / Overlapping Fans
(multiple of 6 + 2 plus 2 chs)

Row 1: Working on a chain foundation, SC in 3rd ch from hook.
* Ch 2, Skip 2 chs, SC in next
ch. Repeat from * across,
ending with SC in last ch, Ch
1, Turn.

Row 2: SC in next sc (which will be
a dc on Row 6 and subse-
quent repeats of the pattern).
Work 7 Long DC (length of 3
chs) in next sc. Repeat from *
across, ending with SC in last
sc (which will be a dc on Row
6 and subsequent patterns).
SC in turning ch, Ch 1, Turn.

Row 3: * Working from the *front*, SC
around next sc, Ch 3, DC
around next sc on 2nd row
below (same sc in which 7
long dc were worked), Ch 3.
Repeat from * across, ending
with SC in turning ch, Ch 3,
Turn.

Row 4: Work 4 Long DC in next sc,
* SC in next dc, work 7 Long
DC in next sc. Repeat from *
across, ending with SC in
next dc, 4 Long DC in last sc,
TC in turning ch, Ch 1, Turn.

Row 5: DC *front around* first sc of
2nd row below (will be row 3
of first pattern), * Ch 3, work
Front DC *around* sc on 2nd
row below (same st where 7
long dc was worked). Repeat
from * across, ending with
Front DC *around* sc on 2nd
row below, SC in 3rd ch of
turning ch, Ch 1, Turn.

Repeat Rows 2 through 5 for pattern.

[EDGING: Work Rows 1 and 2.]

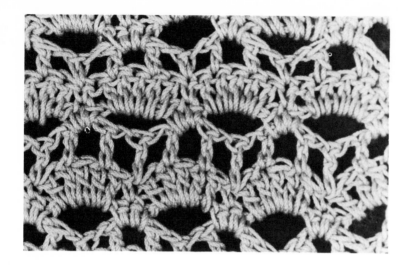

43 / May Baskets
(multiple of 6 + 1 plus 2 chs)

Row 1: Working on a chain foundation, SC in 3rd ch from hook, SC in next ch, * Ch 3, Skip 3 chs, SC in each of next 3 chs. Repeat from * across, ending with only SC in each of last 2 chs, Ch 2, Turn.

Row 2: * Work 5 DC under ch 3, Skip sc, SC in next sc. Repeat from * across, ending with SC in turning ch, Ch 1, Turn.

Row 3: SC in next sc, * Ch 1, (Skip 1 dc, DC in next dc, Ch 1) 2 times, SC in sc. Repeat from * across, ending with last SC in 2nd ch of turning ch, Ch 4, Turn.

Row 4: Skip first ch and dc, * work 3 SC under next ch. Ch 4, Skip (dc, ch 1, sc, ch 1, dc). Repeat from * across, ending with Ch 3, DC in turning ch, Ch 2, Turn.

Row 5: Work 3 DC under ch 3, * Skip sc, SC in next sc, work 5 DC under ch 4. Repeat from * across, ending with only 3 DC under turning ch, Ch 3, Turn.

Row 6: DC in next dc, * Ch 1, DC in sc, Ch 1, Skip 1 dc, DC in next dc, Ch 1, Skip 1 dc, DC in next dc. Repeat from * across, ending with last DC in 2nd ch of turning ch, Ch 1, Turn.

Row 7: Work 2 SC under first ch 1, * Ch 4, Skip (dc, ch 1, dc, ch 1, dc), work 3 SC under next ch 1. Repeat from * across, ending with only 2 SC under turning ch, Ch 2, Turn.

Row 8: * Work 5 DC under ch 4, Skip 1 sc, SC in next sc. Repeat from * across, ending with SC in turning ch, Ch 1, Turn.

Repeat Rows 3 through 8 for pattern.

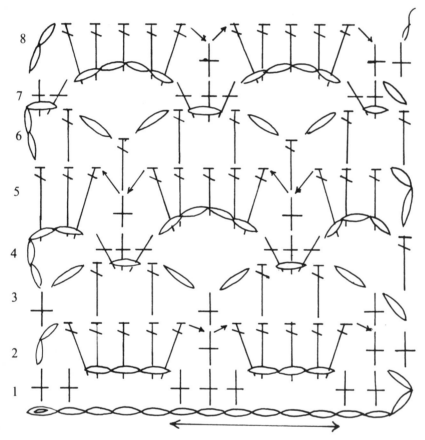

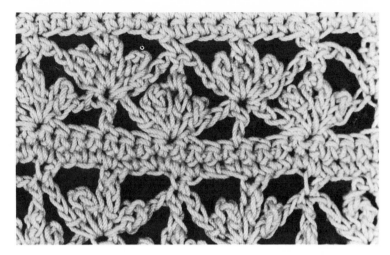

44 / Triple Crown
(multiple of 8 + 2 plus 3 chs)

Row 1: Working on a chain foundation, DC in 4th ch from hook. * Ch 2, Skip 3 chs, work (SC, Ch 4, SC, Ch 4, SC, Ch 4, SC) in next ch, Ch 2, Skip 3 chs, DC in next ch. Repeat from * across, ending with DC in last ch, Ch 3, Turn.

Row 2: TC in dc at base of turning ch, Ch 2, work (SC, Ch 4, SC) in next dc. * Ch 3, Skip (2 chs, sc, ch 4, sc), DC under next ch 4, Ch 3, work (SC, Ch 4, SC, Ch 4, SC, Ch 4, SC) in next dc. Repeat from * across, ending with only one (SC, Ch 4, SC) in last dc, Ch 3, DC in 3rd ch of turning ch, Ch 2, Turn.

Row 3: SC under first ch 3. * Ch 3, SC in next dc, Ch 3, Skip first ch 4, SC under next ch 4. Repeat from * across, ending with SC in tc and SC in 3rd ch of turning ch, Ch 1, Turn.

Row 4: SC in each (ch & sc) across, ending with last SC in 2nd ch of turning ch, Ch 1, Turn.

Row 5: SC in each sc across, ending with last SC in turning ch, Ch 2, Turn.

Row 6: * DC in next sc, Ch 2, Skip 3 sc, work (SC, Ch 4, SC, Ch 4, SC, Ch 4, SC) in next sc, Ch 2, Skip 3 sc. Repeat from * across, ending with DC in turning ch, Ch 3, Turn.

Repeat Rows 2 through 6 for pattern.

[EDGING: Work Row 1.]

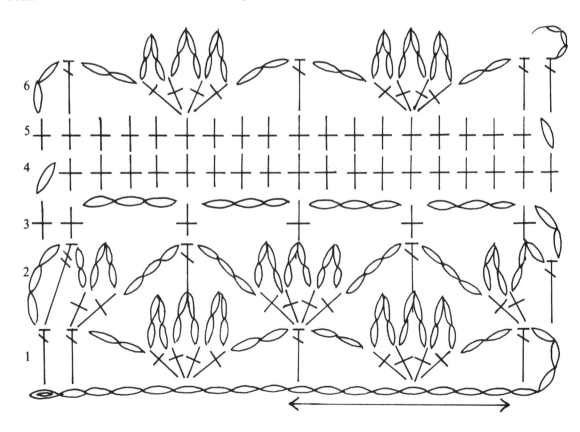

45 / Surf
(multiple of 8 + 1 plus 5 chs)

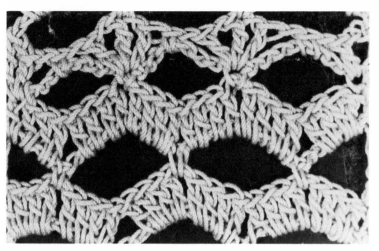

Row 1: Working on a chain foundation, work DC in 6th ch from hook, * Ch 1, Skip 3 chs, SC in next ch, Ch 1, Skip 3 chs, work a (DC, Ch 1, TC, Ch 1, DC) Shell in next ch. Repeat from * across, ending with Ch 1, Skip 3 chs, SC in next ch, Ch 1, Skip 3 chs, (DC, Ch 1, TC) in last ch, Ch 9, Turn.

Row 2: * SC in tc of next full shell, Ch 7. Repeat from * across, ending with last SC in 4th ch of turning ch, Ch 2, Turn.

Row 3: Work (4 DC, Ch 1, 4 DC) under each ch 7 across, and under turning ch, Ch 7, Turn.

Row 4: * SC under ch 1, Ch 7. Repeat from * across, ending with Ch 3 (instead of Ch 7) and DTC in 2nd ch of turning ch, Ch 2, Turn.

Row 5: Work 4 DC under ch 3, * Work (4 DC, Ch 1, 4 DC) under ch 7. Repeat from * across, ending with 4 DC under turning ch, Ch 8, Turn.

Row 6: * SC under ch 1, Ch 7. Repeat from * across, ending with SC under turning ch, Ch 5, Turn.

Row 7: DC in sc at base of ch, * Ch 1, SC under ch 7, Ch 1, work (DC, Ch 1, TC, Ch 1, DC) in next sc. Repeat from * across, ending with Ch 1, SC under ch 8, Ch 1, (DC, Ch 1, TC) in 2nd ch of ch 8, Ch 7, Turn.

Repeat Rows 2 through 7 for pattern.

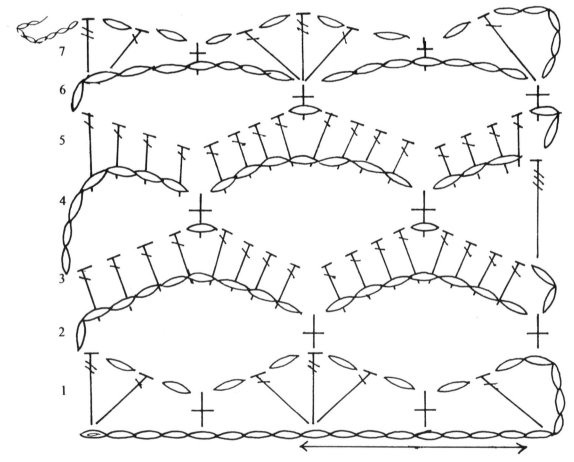

46 / Spider Web
(multiple of 15 + 1 plus 2 chs)

Row 1: Working on a chain foundation, HDC in 3rd ch from hook and in each ch across, Ch 2, Turn.

Row 2: * DC in next hdc, Ch 3, Skip 3 hdc, TC in next hdc, (Ch 1, Skip hdc, TC in next hdc) 3 times. Ch 3, Skip 3 hdc, DC in next hdc. Work from * across, ending with DC in 2nd ch of turning ch, Ch 2, Turn.

Row 3: DC in dc, * Ch 5, DC in each of next 4 tc, Ch 5, DC in each of next 2 dc. Repeat from * across, ending with last DC in 2nd ch of turning ch, Ch 2, Turn.

Row 4: DC in next dc, * Ch 5, SC in each of next 4 dc, Ch 5, DC in each of next 2 dc. Repeat from * across, working last DC in 2nd ch of turning ch, Ch 2, Turn.

Row 5: Repeat Row 4, working SC in each sc.

Row 6: DC in next dc, * Ch 3, (DC, Ch 1) in each of next 3 sc, DC in next sc, Ch 3, DC in each of next 2 dc. Repeat from * across, working last DC in turning ch, Ch 2, Turn.

Row 7: * DC in next dc, Ch 3, TC in next dc, (Ch 1, TC) in each of next 3 dc, Ch 3, DC in each of next 2 dc. Repeat from * across, working last DC in turning ch, Ch 2, Turn.

Row 8: HDC in each (dc, ch, and tc) across, ending with last HDC in turning ch, Ch 2, Turn.

Repeat Rows 2 through 8 for pattern.

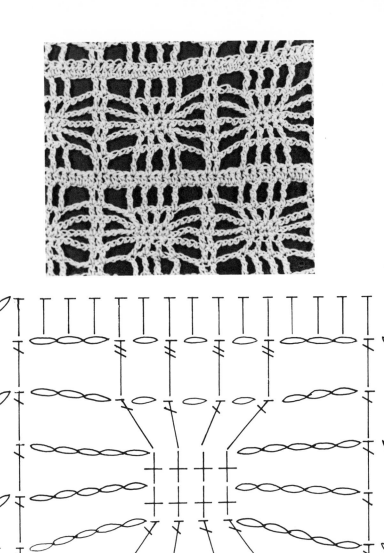

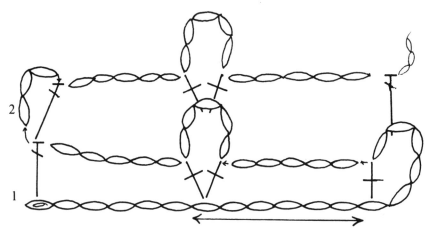

47 / String
(multiple of 6 + 1 plus 5 chs)

Row 1: Working on a *loose* chain
foundation, SC in 6th ch from
hook, * Ch 5, Skip 5 sts, work
(SC, Ch 5, SC) in next st. Repeat from * across, ending
with Ch 5, Skip 5 sts, DC in
last st, Ch 3, Turn.
Row 2: DC in dc at base of ch, Ch 5,
* Work (SC, Ch 5, SC) under
ch 5 (the one between the 2
sc), Ch 5. Repeat from *
across, ending with DC under
turning ch, Ch 3, Turn.
Repeat Row 2 for pattern.

48 / Butterfly

(multiple of 19 + 6 plus 3 chs)

Row 1: Working on a chain foundation, work 3 DC in 4th ch from hook, * Skip 6 chs, work 4 DC in next ch, Ch 5, Skip 4 chs, SC in next ch, Ch 5, Skip 6 chs, work 4 DC in next ch. Repeat from * across, ending with Skip only 4 chs, DC in last ch, Ch 2, Turn.

Row 2: Skip 3 dc, * work 4 DC in next dc, Ch 5, SC in next sc, Ch 5, work 4 DC in next dc, Skip 6 dc. Repeat from * across, ending with 4 DC in turning ch, Ch 2, Turn.

Row 3: Work 3 DC in dc at base of ch. * Skip 6 dc, work 4 DC in next dc, Ch 5, SC in sc, Ch 5, 4 DC in next dc. Repeat from * across, ending with Skip 3 dc, DC in turning ch, Ch 1, Turn.

Row 4: SC in next dc, * Ch 5, work 4 DC in 3rd ch of ch 5, work 4 DC in 3rd ch of next ch 5, Ch

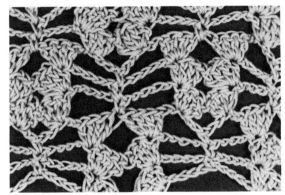

5, Skip 2 chs and 3 dcs, SC in next dc. Repeat from * across, ending with Ch 3, SC in turning ch, Ch 4, Turn.

Row 5: Skip 3 chs, * SC in next sc, Ch 5, work 4 DC in next dc, Skip 6 dc, work 4 DC in next dc, Ch 5. Repeat from * across, ending with SC, SC in turning ch, Ch 1, Turn.

Row 6: SC in next sc, * Ch 5, work 4 DC in next dc, Skip 6 dc, work 4 DC in next dc, Ch 5,

SC in next sc. Repeat from * across, ending with Ch 3, SC in first ch of turning ch, Ch 2, Turn.

Row 7: Work 3 DC in sc at base of ch, * work 4 DC in 3rd ch of next ch 5, Ch 5, work SC between 4th and 5th dcs, Ch 5, work 4 DC in 3rd ch of next ch 5. Repeat from * across, ending with Skip 2 chs and sc, DC in turning ch, Ch 2, Turn.

Repeat Rows 2 through 7 for pattern.

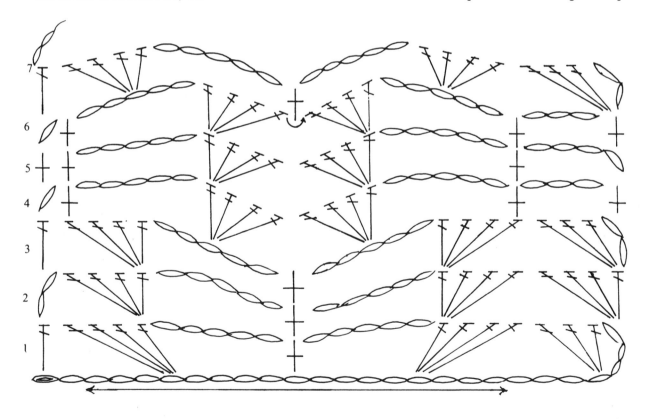

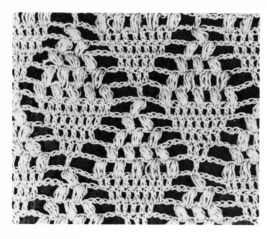

49 / Carmel Grape
(multiple of 16 + 2 plus 3 chs)

Row 1: Working on a chain foundation, DC in 4th ch from hook, * Ch 3, Skip 3 chs, work Medium Puff stitch in next ch. [*To Make Medium Puff:* (YO, Insert hook into st, Pull Up thread) 4 times in same st. YO and through all loops on hook.] (Ch 1, Skip 1 ch, Medium Puff in next ch) 4 times. Ch 3, Skip 3 chs, DC in next ch. Repeat from * across, ending with DC in last ch, Ch 2, Turn.

Row 2: * DC in next dc, DC in first ch, Ch 3, Skip 2 chs and a puff and work Medium Puff in next ch 1, Skip puff (Ch 1, work Medium Puff in next ch 1, Skip puff) 3 times. Ch 3, Skip puff and 2 chs, work DC in next ch. Repeat from * across, ending with DC in last dc and DC in turning ch, Ch 2, Turn.

Row 3: DC in next 2 dc, * DC in next ch, Ch 3, Skip 2 chs and a puff, work Medium Puff in next ch (Ch 1, Skip puff, work Medium Puff in next ch) 2 times more. Ch 3, Skip puff and 2 chs, DC in next ch, DC in each of next 3 dc. Repeat from * across, working last DC in turning ch, Ch 2, Turn.

Row 4: DC in each of next 3 dc, * DC in first ch, Ch 3, Skip 2 chs and a puff, work Medium Puff in next ch, Ch 1, Skip puff, work Medium Puff in next ch, Ch 3, Skip puff and 2 chs, DC in next ch, DC in each of next 5 dcs. Repeat from * across, ending with last DC in turning ch, Ch 2, Turn.

Row 5: DC in each of next 4 dc, * DC in first ch, Ch 3, Skip 2 chs and a puff, work Medium Puff in next ch, Ch 3, Skip a puff and 2 chs, work DC in next ch, DC in each of next 7 dc. Repeat from * across, ending with 6 DC at end of row, the last one in the turning ch, Ch 2, Turn.

Row 6: Work Puff in next dc, (Ch 1, Skip dc, work Puff in next dc) 2 times. * Ch 3, DC in next puff, Ch 3, work Puff in next dc, (Ch 1, Skip dc, work Puff in next dc) 4 times. Repeat from * across, ending with only 3 Puff, DC in turning ch. (Do not Ch between last puff and last dc), Ch 3, Turn.

Row 7: Work Puff in first ch, Ch 1, work Puff in next ch. * Ch 3, Skip puff and 2 chs, DC in next ch, DC in dc, DC in next ch, Ch 3, Skip 2 chs and puff, work Puff in next ch (Ch 1, Skip puff, work Puff in next ch) 3 times. Repeat from * across, ending with only 2 Puffs, Ch 1, DC in turning ch, Ch 2, Turn.

Row 8: Work Puff in first ch, Ch 1, work Puff in next ch. * Ch 3, Skip puff and 2 chs, work DC in next ch, DC in each of next 3 dc, DC in next ch, Ch 3, Skip 2 chs and puff, work Puff in next ch (Ch 1, work Puff in next ch) 2 times. Repeat from * across, ending with only 2 Puffs, working the last Puff in first ch of turning ch, DC in next ch of turning ch, Ch 3, Turn.

Row 9: Work Puff in first ch, * Ch 3, Skip puff and 2 chs, DC in next ch, DC in each of next 5 dc, DC in next ch, Ch 3, Skip 2 chs and puff, work Puff in next ch, Ch 1, work Puff in next ch. Repeat from * across, ending with Puff between last 2 puffs, Ch 1, DC in turning ch, Ch 2, Turn.

Row 10: Work Puff in first ch, * Ch 3, Skip puff and 2 chs, DC in next ch, DC in each of next 7 dc, DC in next ch, Ch 3, Skip 2 chs and puff, work Puff in next ch. Repeat from * across, ending with last Puff in turning ch, DC in next ch of turning ch, Ch 2, Turn.

Row 11: DC in first puff, * Ch 3, Skip 3 chs, work Puff in next dc, (Ch 1, Skip dc, work Puff in next dc) 4 times. Ch 3, work DC in next puff. Repeat from * across, ending with DC in turning ch, Ch 2, Turn.

Repeat Rows 2 through 11 for pattern.

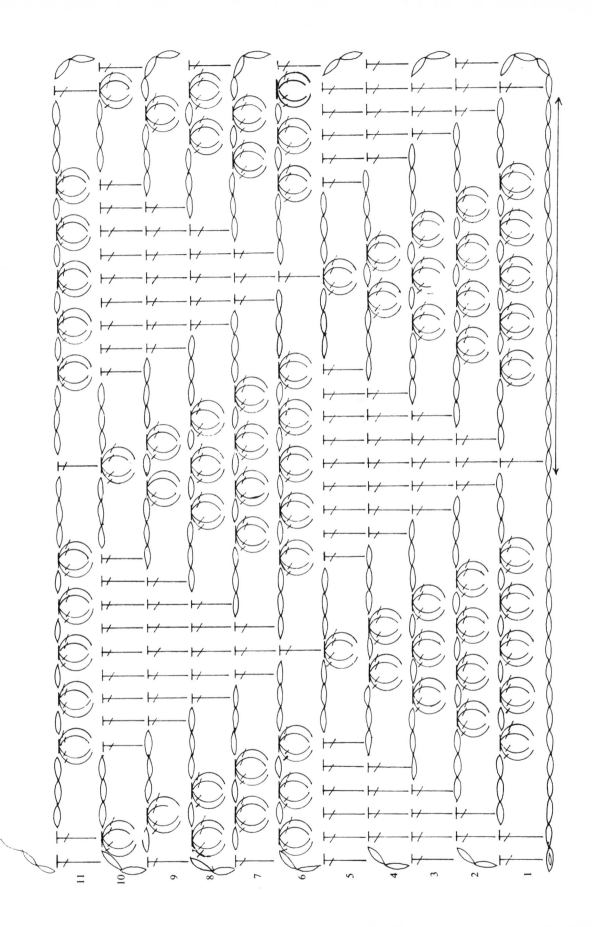

11   10   9   8   7   6   5   4   3   2   1

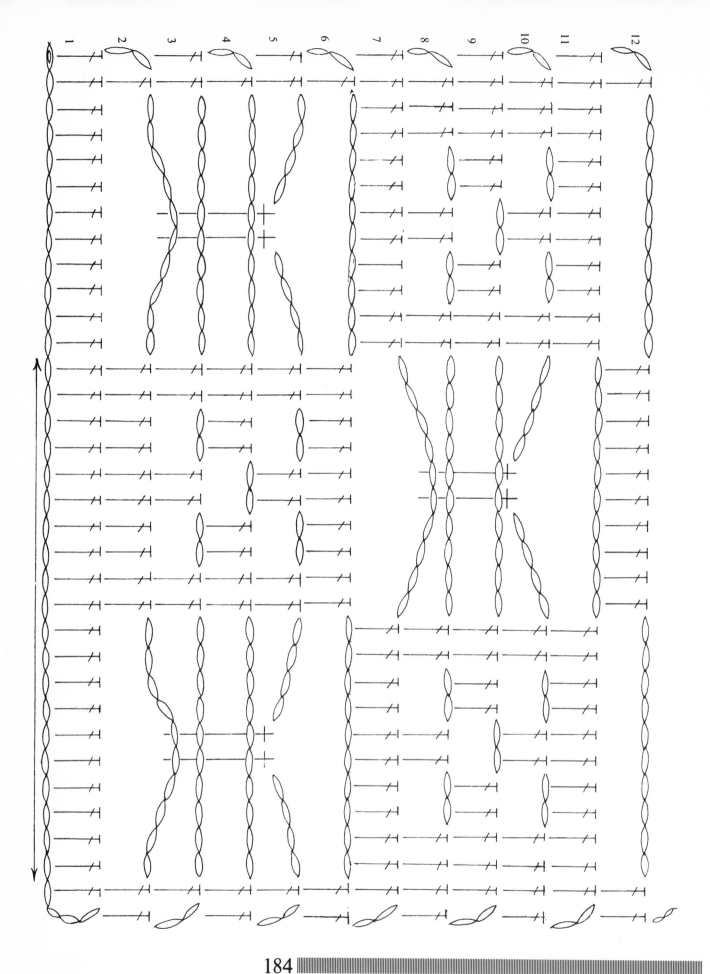

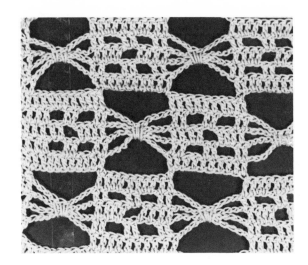

50 / Window Panes
(multiple of 20 + 13 plus 3 chs)

Row 1: Working on a chain foundation, DC in 4th ch from hook and in each ch across, Ch 2, Turn.

Row 2: DC in next dc, * Ch 10, Skip 10 dcs, DC in each of next 10 dc. Repeat from * across, ending with Ch 10, Skip 10 dcs, DC in last dc and DC in turning ch, Ch 2, Turn.

Row 3: DC in next dc, * Ch 10, DC in each of next 2 dc, Ch 2, Skip 2 dc, DC in each of next 2 dc, Ch 2, Skip 2 dc, DC in each of next 2 dc. Repeat from * across, ending with Ch 10, DC in last dc and DC in turning ch, Ch 2, Turn.

Row 4: DC in next dc, * Ch 10, DC in each of next 2 dc and 2 chs, Ch 2, Skip 2 dc, DC in each of next 2 chs and 2 dcs. Repeat from * across, ending with Ch 10, DC in last dc and DC in turning ch, Ch 2, Turn.

Row 5: DC in next dc, * Ch 4, Insert hook under 3 ch 10s, work 2 SC under ch 10s, Ch 4, DC in each of next 2 dc, Ch 2, Skip 2 dc, DC in each of next 2 chs, Ch 2, Skip 2 dcs, DC in each of next 2 dc. Repeat from * across, ending with Ch 4, 2 SC under 3 ch 10s, Ch 4, DC in last dc and DC in turning ch, Ch 2, Turn.

Row 6: DC in next dc, * Ch 10, DC in each of next 10 dcs and chs, Repeat from * across, ending with Ch 10, DC in last dc, DC in turning ch, Ch 2, Turn.

Row 7: Dc in next dc, * DC in each of next 10 chs, Ch 10, Skip 10 dc, Repeat from * across, ending with DC in each of last 10 chs, DC in dc, DC in turning ch, Ch 2, Turn.

Row 8: DC in each of next 3 dc, Ch 2, Skip 2 dc, DC in each of next 2 dc, Ch 2, Skip 2 dc, DC in each of next 2 dc. * Ch 10, DC in each of next 2 dc (Ch 2, Skip 2 dc, DC in each of next 2 dc) 2 times. Repeat from * across, ending with DC in last dc, DC in turning ch, Ch 2, Turn.

Row 9: DC in each of next 3 dc, DC in each of next 2 chs, Ch 2, Skip 2 dc, DC in each of next 2 chs and 2 dc. * Ch 10, DC in each of next 2 dc and 2 chs, Ch 2, Skip 2 dc, DC in each of next 2 chs and 2 dc.

Repeat from * across, ending with DC in last dc and DC in turning ch, Ch 2, Turn.

Row 10: DC in each of next 3 dc, Ch 2, Skip 2 dc, DC in each of next 2 chs, Ch 2, Skip 2 dc, DC in each of next 2 dc. *Ch 4, Insert hook under 3 ch 10s, and work 2 SC under chs, Ch 4, DC in each of next 2 dc, Ch 2, Skip 2 dc, DC in each of next 2 chs, Ch 2, Skip 2 dc, DC in each of next 2 dc. Repeat from * across, ending with DC in last dc, DC in turning ch, Ch 2, Turn.

Row 11: DC in each of next (3 dc, 2 chs, 2 dc, 2 chs, 2 dc). * Ch 10, DC in each of next (2 dc, 2 chs, 2 dc, 2 chs, 2 dc). Repeat from * across, ending with DC in last dc, DC in turning ch, Ch 2, Turn.

Row 12: DC in next dc, * Ch 10, Skip 10 dc, DC in each of next 10 chs. Repeat from * across, ending with Ch 10, Skip 10 dc, DC in last dc, DC in turning ch, Ch 2, Turn.

Repeat Rows 3 through 12 for pattern, ending work with either Row 6 or 11, then work 1 row DC in each dc and ch to make a firm edge.

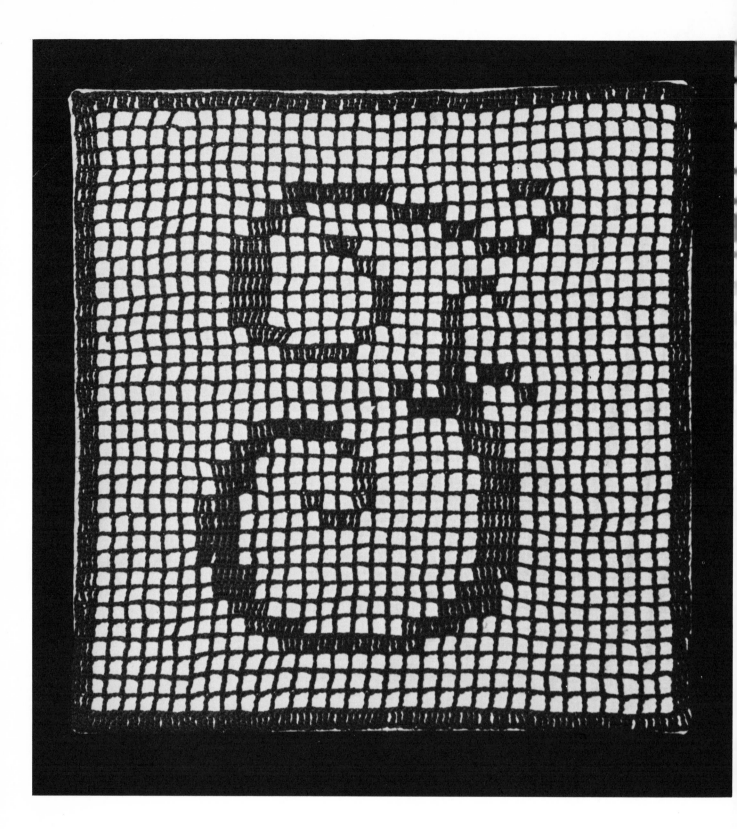

Chapter 5   Filet Crochet ▌▌▌▌▌▌▌▌▌▌▌▌▌▌▌▌▌▌▌▌▌▌▌▌▌▌▌▌▌▌▌▌

"Filet" means "net" in French. In English, the word is applied to any lace that has patterns worked in a square mesh. In crochet, the term describes a method of combining open and filled squares called spaces and blocks to form geometric patterns and pictorial designs. Some simple geometric filet pattern stitches are given at the beginning of Chapter 3.

Although many pattern books call for using a sequence of 1 DC followed by 2 Chs as the basis for working filet designs, I have found it far more satisfactory to use a progression of 1 TC followed by 2 Chs. The triple crochet method produces a truly "square" pattern—one in which the number of stitches per inch equals the number of rows per inch—and offers better pattern definition than using a double crochet stitch.

Filling the open filet space with 2 TC in place of 2 Chs makes the square a solid block. In graphed designs, this is represented by an X. Each solid block in the design consists of 3 TC. In working the filled blocks in a graphed design, think of the first line of the square as one TC, and the X as two TC. The next line is the first stitch of the next square.

Filet foundation chains ▬▬▬▬▬▬▬▬▬▬▬▬▬▬▬▬▬▬▬▬▬▬▬▬▬▬▬

When figuring the number of chains necessary for a foundation chain for filet designs, multiply the number of graphed blocks by 3 and add 4 chains. For solid areas, work the first TC in the 5th ch from the hook (2 stitches are completed). Always Ch 3 to turn. For the open spaces, work the first TC in the 8th ch from the hook (first square completed).

Filet crochet is a good way for the new crocheter to experiment with design. A few simple lines and shapes worked out on graph paper can achieve an interesting pattern. Start by adapting some of the letters given here into monograms, adding a few extra solid blocks in the corners or along the sides. The finished monogram will add an attractive personal touch to an apron pocket or a baby afghan. There are many ways filet monograms and designs can be used and a section on projects at the end of this chapter suggests some of them.

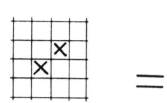

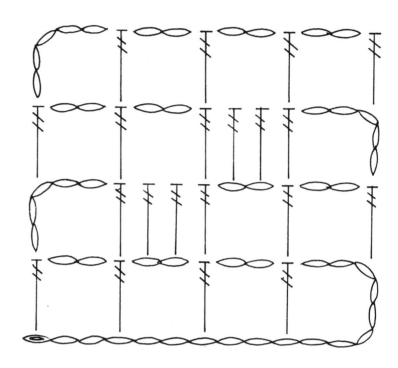

Graphed pattern and symbol diagram for a filet crochet design of two diagonally placed solid blocks surrounded by open squares. Note the part the turning chains play in working the pattern.

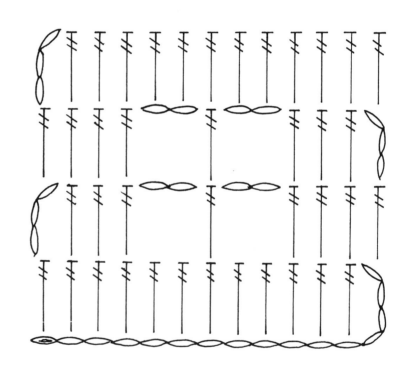

Four open squares set in a solid border. In this design, the open spaces are the motif and the solid blocks are the background.

Three different monogram alphabets are shown in the following pages. To look pleasing, a monogram should have several unfilled spaces above, below, and on either side of it, and should be visually centered. To plan a foundation chain for a monogram, count the number of squares in the letter, add the number of squares required for the background area and border, multiply by three, and add four for the turning chain.

Letters are not all the same width. Some will fill an even number of squares, and some an odd number. To be sure that your monogram will appear properly centered, plan it on a sheet of graph paper. Copy the letter first, then draw a large square around it, allowing a suitable number of squares all around for the background and border. Sketch in the border area and see how the whole thing looks. If you are satisfied with the results, count the squares and calculate the foundation chain as described above.

Centering letters can be difficult. Letters that are numerically centered may sometimes appear off balance because their design gives more visual weight to one side than the other or because they are composed of an uneven number of squares. Small dots beneath the letters in the alphabets given here show where to center them in your graph.

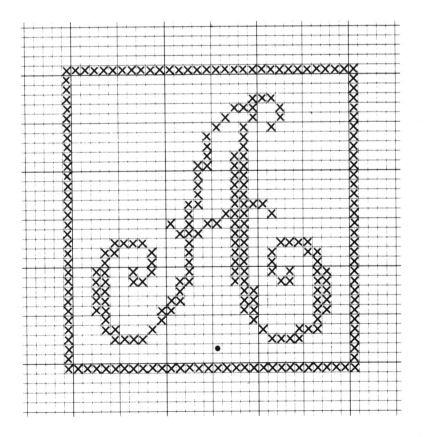

Monograms with two or more letters

For a monogram of two letters, place them a pleasing distance apart, allowing about two blank squares around the letters. Monograms with more than two letters usually have an equal number of spaces separating them but the shape of the individual letters and the amount of "white" space around them may make them appear closer together or farther apart even when the actual distance between them is the same. For example, in the letters F, G, and H in the small block alphabet the enclosed form of H makes it seem much closer to G than does the open form of F. Letters with elaborate, flowing shapes like those of the Victorian alphabet may sometimes be overlapped for a more pleasing placement. Designers often squint at their sketches to get a better total concept of a design. Let your eyes be the judge and don't hesitate to arrange things to suit your eye.

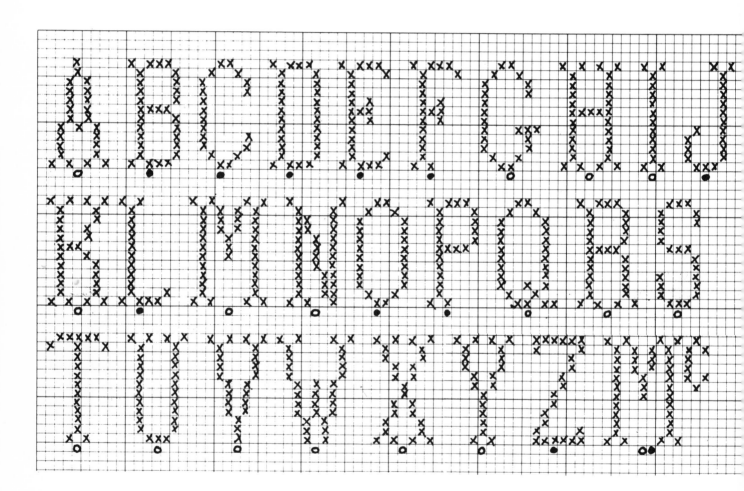

Large block letters

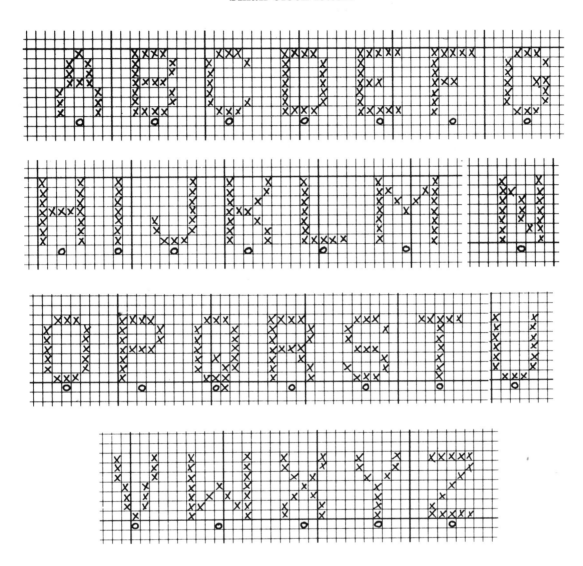

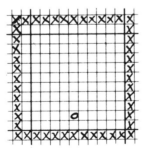

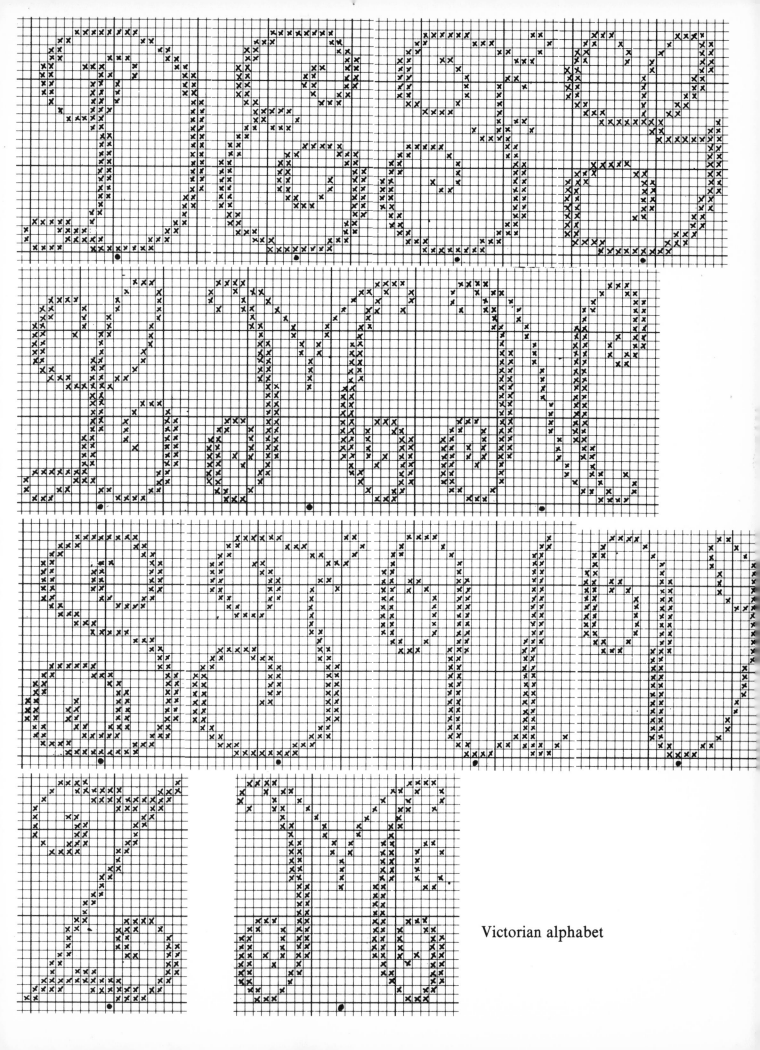

Victorian alphabet

Rose design. Make it as a centerpiece
in a linen or crocheted background or,
in fine thread, as an insert or appliqué
on a pocket or skirt. The foundation
chain is made by chaining 253. Work
the first triple crochet into the 5th
chain from the hook to complete the
first two stitches, then follow the
graph to complete the design.

Combining large and small letters

Three-letter monograms with a large center letter flanked by smaller ones can be made by taking one or two blocks out of the upper and lower sections of the uprights and centering the diminished letters on the same horizontal axis as the large one. This works easily with the large block letters. For the small letters, shorten the horizontal members as well as the uprights to preserve balance.

Work out your designs in pencil first so you can make changes and adjustments as you go along. Copy them in dark ink to make a pattern that is permanent and easy to read.

Edges for filet

To make a firm edging for filet crochet, work two stitches per row along the sides, using a single crochet or any other suitable Basic Stitch. At the corners, work the number of stitches recommended on page 29-30. For a decorative border, add a Shell pattern or simple lace stitch pattern, adding extra stitches at the corners as necessary (see page 31).

Projects

Filet monograms make welcome decorations for all kinds of things—handbags, pillows, dresses, aprons, afghans, placemats, bedspreads, or wallhangings. Crocheted in bedspread weight cotton, the letters of the Victorian alphabet make monograms of about 12″×12″ (30cm × 30cm). In #30 cotton thread, they provide squares suitable for pocket decorations.

Wallhangings: A very personal gift is a wallhanging with the recipient's initials or name in a vertical filet panel. To make the panel all in one piece rather than in separate squares, plan the letters on a piece of graph paper. Start crocheting with the bottom square. Use the top border of each square as the bottom border for the next letter. Crochet 3 extra border rows across the top to make a rod pocket. Fold it over, sew it down, and insert a rod for hanging. As a finishing touch add 1 row of Arch Pattern (Chapter 4, #1) at the bottom and attach fringe under the chains.

Nursery wallhanging: For a more colorful hanging, make each square in a different color, with 2 rows of border stitches between them, one in each of the adjoining colors.

Alphabet baby bedspread: Crochet squares using letters of the Large Block alphabet. Done in baby weight yarn with an E hook (UK 9, Int'l 3.5), this makes a square approximately 8″× 8″

(20cm × 20cm). Thirty blocks are needed for a 40″ × 48″
(100cm × 120cm) spread, so make 4 solid blocks of plain triple
crochet. (Start the block by chaining 43, TC in the 4th chain from
hook, and follow the graph.) A single crochet border around each
block will make sewing them together easier; done in another
color it will add interest. You might crochet all the blocks in one
color with white borders, or make blocks in many different colors.
Graph or sketch the color arrangement before you start to be sure
of the final effect. Or make a monogram using only the baby's initials, to be set in a background of squares of plain triple crochet.
See Chapter 1 for border suggestions.

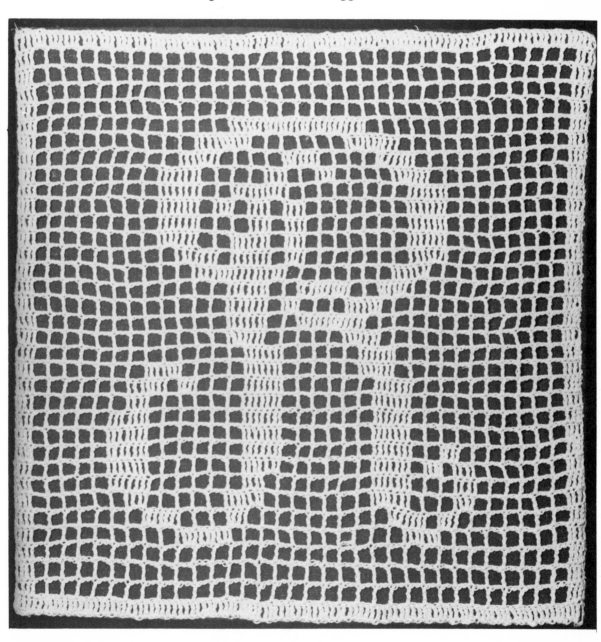

Chapter 6   Multicolored Patterns

There are various ways of creating multicolored designs in crochet. Two easy methods are to alternate colors from row to row, as shown in the examples of Ripple Stitch in Chapter 2, or from round to round, as in making afghan squares. The yarn is tied off at the end of one row or round and a second color is introduced at the beginning of the next row. Additional colors may also be introduced at intervals in a row, then dropped and picked up again on the return row, to carry the color vertically upward in the crocheting.

Another way to introduce color variation is to extend the length of stitches in an alternate color, working them not into the previous row, but down across 2, 3, or more rows into an earlier row. This is done here in the Mountains and Shadows patterns and in the Check pattern. Varying the length of the stitches and the order of the repetition makes possible many different geometric designs.

A third method is Jacquard crochet, discussed in detail later in this chapter.

Ruano (*Plate 6*)

54″ × 40″ (135cm × 100cm)
This variation of the classic poncho is a large rectangle with a lengthwise opening that reaches up the middle to a point slightly beyond the center, thus forming a divided front and solid back. The section on one side of the opening drapes over one shoulder, and the other half comes over the opposite shoulder. When belted, a ruano makes an attractive coat. Large Mountains and Shadows pattern (#2 in this chapter) was used, worked in three colors rather than the two shown in the pattern stitch sample. The ruano is worked lengthwise; the foundation chain forms the longer dimension of the rectangle, the part which comes over the wrist when the garment is worn.
Material: Four-ply yarn (knitting worsted)
   14 ounces (360 grams) each of three colors, ranging from light to dark
Hook size: H (UK 6, Int'l 5)
Gauge: 3 SC equal 1″ (2.5cm)
Make a foundation chain of 163 stitches in Color A. Work in Large Mountains and Shadows for 70 rows, alternating the colors in succession: A, B, C; A, B, C, etc. When changing colors, always

make the change on the turning chain at the end of a row (see "Changing Colors," page 24).

On the 71st row, work across in pattern, completing only 72 sts (including the turning chain). Ch 92, Turn the work, and continue working in pattern back across the chain and the 72 sts of the previous row until the row is completed. Continue working in pattern until a total of 140 rows are completed. Tie Off the yarn and block the ruano.

RUANO

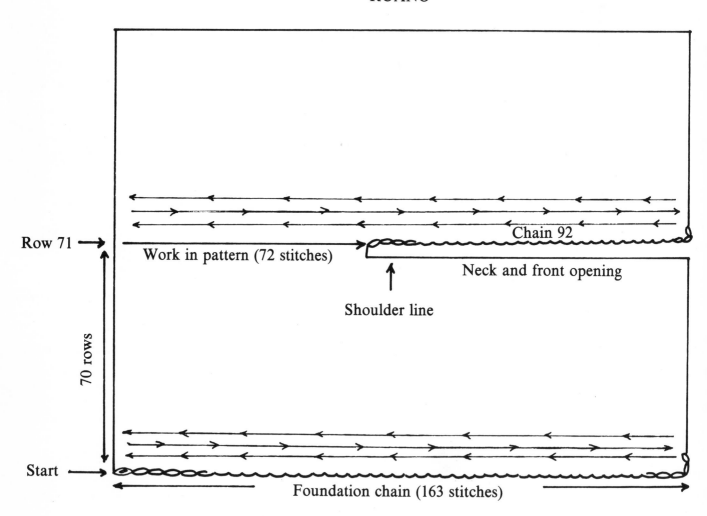

Row 71 → Work in pattern (72 stitches)

Chain 92

Neck and front opening

Shoulder line

70 rows

Start → Foundation chain (163 stitches)

Baby Afghan (*Plate 7*) ||||||||||||||||||||||||||||||||||||||||||||||||||||||||||||||||||||||||||||||||||||||||||

27″ × 48″ (68cm × 120cm)
This crib-size afghan is made with the Check pattern Pattern #3 in this chapter.
Material: One-ply (baby weight) yarn in 2 colors
   Color A: 4 ounces (120 grams)
   Color B: 6 ounces (160 grams)
   In Plate 7, Color A is blue and Color B is white
Hook size: F (UK 8, Int'l 4)
Gauge: 9 DC equal 2″ (5cm)
Using Color A, make a foundation chain of 118 stitches. Work Rows 2, 3, 4, and 5 of Check pattern 22 times for a total of 88 rows, changing colors as noted in the stitch pattern. (See also page 24.) To finish the afghan using Color B, SC around the entire piece, working 1 SC into each chain stitch across the bottom, 1 SC into each sc across the top, 3 SC into every 2 rows along the sides, and 3 SC at each corner. Tie off the yarn and block the afghan.

Basic rectangles, easily crocheted and assembled, make this smart coat. The pattern can be shortened to make sweaters or jackets, or extended to floor length for an elegant evening wrap. Plate 8 shows the coat made in Check Pattern (page 208) in four-ply yarn, but it could be done in any yarn or thread. Simply make a swatch to determine the stitch gauge and then figure the number of rows and foundation stitches required to achieve the given dimensions.

Material: Four-ply yarn (knitting worsted) in 2 colors in the amounts below

Small Color A, 20 ounces (560 grams); Color B, 24 ounces (680 grams)

Medium Color A, 24 ounces (680 grams); Color B, 28 ounces (800 grams)

Large Color A, 28 ounces (800 grams); Color B, 32 ounces (920 grams)

The alternate measurements given in the diagrams and listed for the foundation chains are for the three sizes given above.

Hook size: H (UK 6, Int'l 5)

Gauge: 3 DC equal 1″ (2.5cm)

Note: Make the foundation chain of each coat section in Color A. On the last row of each piece, do not turn at the end of the row, but continue on around the corner and work the border as described below. Work all borders in Color A.

Front sections: Make a foundation chain of 38 (42) (50) stitches and work in Check Pattern until 45″ (112cm) are completed, ending with Row 2 of pattern. Work border as described below. Make a second front section the same way.

Back: Make a foundation chain of 66 (78) (90) stitches and work in pattern until the back is the same length as the front sections. Work border around entire piece.

Sleeve: Make a foundation chain of 58 (62) (70) stitches and work in pattern until a section 18″ (48cm) long is completed, ending with Row 2 of pattern. Work border. Make another sleeve the same way.

Hood: Make a foundation chain of 62 (66) (74) stitches and work in pattern stitch until a piece 14″ (34cm) long is completed, ending with Row 2 of pattern. Work border along 3 sides.

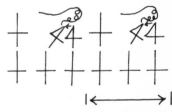

Along the top, decrease (for back fullness) as follows: SC for 4½″ (11cm), * Pull Up thread in next 2 stitches, YO and through 3 loops on hook, SC in next st. Repeat from * across until 4½″ (11cm) remain on side; SC to end, working 2 SC in last st, Sl St to beginning ch.

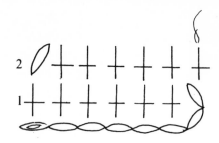

Belt: Using Color A, make a foundation chain of 8 stitches, SC in 3rd ch from hook and in each ch across. Work in rows of SC until piece measures 64″ (160cm), then Tie Off.

Pocket: Make a foundation chain of 22 (24) (28) stitches and work in pattern for 7″ (18cm), ending with Row 2 of pattern. Work border around entire piece.

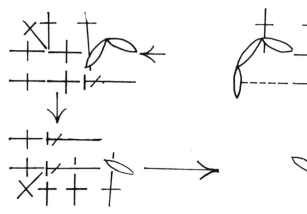

Borders: As you complete each piece, work 1 row of SC around it as follows: At end of last row: Pull Up last loop with Color A. Do not turn. Ch 1, SC along the side, working 3 SC every two rows, 3 SC at corner, SC in each ch of foundation chain, 3 SC at corner, 3 SC every two rows along side, 3 SC at corner, SC in each st of last row, 2 SC in last st at corner, Sl St into beginning ch, Tie Off.

To assemble: Be sure all the pieces show the same side of the crocheting. (You may choose which side you prefer, as this pattern stitch produces a reversible fabric.) Following the diagram, overcast the shoulder seams of the front section to the back sections between the points marked A-1 and A-2 only, using Color A. Fold the sleeves in half lengthwise and pin the top center of the sleeve to the shoulder seam. Pin the tops of the sleeves to the sides of the front and back sections, making sure the distance between shoulder seam and sleeve edge is the same on back and front and at either side of the coat. Overcast the inside seams of the sleeves and side seams of the coat. Place the pocket as shown in the drawing, with one side meeting the coat seam, and whipstitch it in place. Pin the hood to the top edges of the front and back sections. Overcast the seam, tie off the thread, and block the coat.

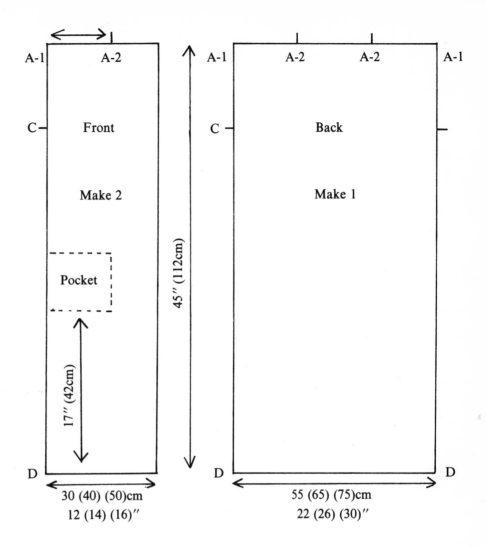

Front — Make 2

45" (112cm)

Pocket

17" (42cm)

30 (40) (50)cm
12 (14) (16)"

Back — Make 1

55 (65) (75)cm
22 (26) (30)"

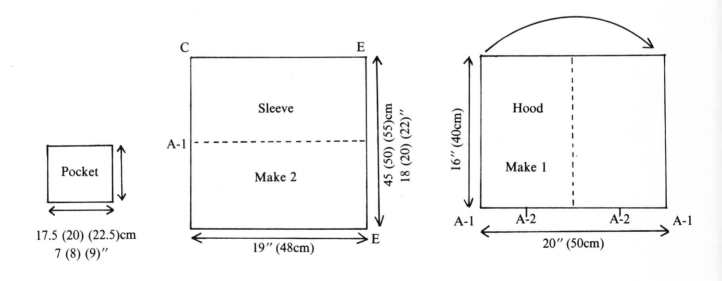

Pocket

17.5 (20) (22.5)cm
7 (8) (9)"

Sleeve — Make 2

45 (50) (55)cm
18 (20) (22)"

19" (48cm)

Hood — Make 1

16" (40cm)

20" (50cm)

1 / Small Mountains and Shadows
(multiple of 5 + 1 plus 2 chs)

Row 1: With Color A, make a chain foundation. Work SC in 3rd ch from hook and in each ch across, Ch 1, Turn.

Row 2: SC in each sc across, ending with SC in 2nd ch of turning ch, Ch 1, Turn.

Row 3: SC in each sc across, SC in turning ch, Ch 1, Turn.

Row 4: Repeat Row 3, changing colors on last YO of the final SC, Ch 1, Turn.

Row 5: SC in next sc. * SC in next sc on Row 3 (Skip sc on Row 4), SC in next sc below on Row 2 (Skip sc Rows 3 and 4), SC in next sc below on Row 3 (Skip 3 sc on Row 4), SC in each of next 2 sc on Row 4. Repeat from * across, ending with last SC in turning ch, Ch 1, Turn.

Rows 6 and 7: Repeat Row 3.

Row 8: Repeat Row 4.

Repeat Rows 5 through 8 for pattern.

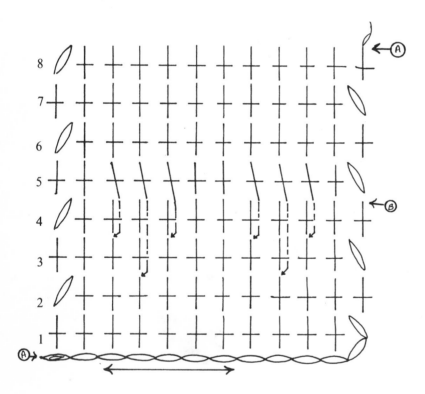

2 / Large Mountains and Shadows
(*multiple of 7 + 1 plus 2 chs*)

Row 1: With Color A, make a foundation ch. SC in 3rd ch from hook and in each ch across, Ch 1, Turn.

Row 2: SC in each sc across and SC in 2nd ch of turning ch, Ch 1, Turn.

Rows 3, 4, and 5: SC in each sc across, SC in turning ch, Ch 1, Turn.

Row 6: Repeat Row 3, changing colors on last YO of the final sc.

Row 7: SC in next sc, * SC in next sc on Row 5, SC in next sc on Row 4, SC in next sc on Row 3, SC in next sc on Row 4, SC in next sc on Row 5 (Skip 5 sc on Row 6), SC in each of next 2 sc. Repeat from * across, ending with last SC in turning ch, Ch 1, Turn.

Rows 8, 9, 10, 11, and 12: SC in each sc across, SC in turning ch, Ch 1, Turn. Change colors on last YO of Row 12.

Repeat Rows 7 through 12 for pattern.

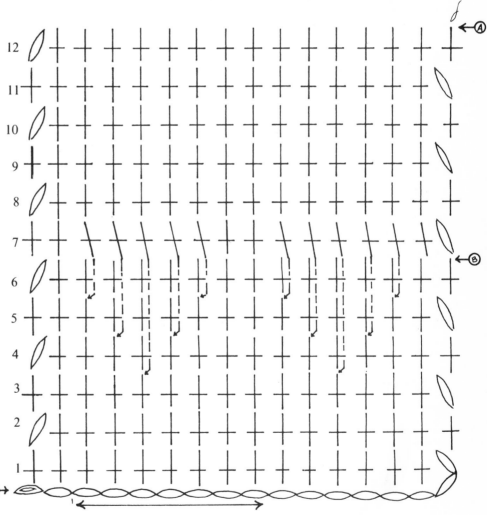

3 / Check Pattern
(multiple of 4 + 3 plus 3 chs)

Row 1: With Color A, make a foundation chain. DC in the 4th ch from hook, DC in next ch. * Ch 2, Skip 2 chs, DC in each of next 2 chs. Repeat from * across, DC in last ch, change to Color B on last YO, Ch 1, Turn.

Row 2: * SC in each of next 2 dc. Work DC into each of next 2 foundation chs, working *around* the 2 chs on last row. Repeat from * across, ending with SC in each of last 2 dc and SC into 3rd ch of turning ch, changing to Color A on last YO, Ch 4, Turn.

Row 3: Skip 2 sc, * DC into each of next 2 dc, Ch 2, Skip 2 sc. Repeat from * across, ending with DC in turning ch, change to Color B on last YO, Ch 1, Turn.

Row 4: * DC into each of next 2 sc on row 2, SC in each of next 2 dc of Row 3. Repeat from * across, ending with SC in 2nd ch of turning ch, changing colors on the last YO, Ch 2, Turn.

Row 5: DC in each of next 2 dc, * Ch 2, Skip 2 sc, DC in each of next 2 dc. Repeat from * across, ending with DC in turning ch, changing color on last YO, Ch 1, Turn.

Repeat Rows 2 through 5 for pattern, ending the piece with Row 2.

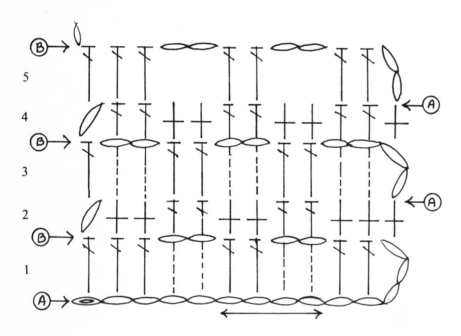

JACQUARD CROCHET

Jacquard crochet is a method of working elaborate color designs like those of Jacquard weaving of Fair Isle and Scandinavian knitting while using only one basic stitch, the Extended Single Crochet. Because this stitch yields the same number of rows per inch as stitches per inch, it is ideal for following graphed designs. Each ExSC can be regarded as the equivalent of one square in a graph. Designs for needlepoint, weaving, or knitting can thus easily be adapted for crochet, and you can invent and graph your own designs.

There are two ways to handle the multiple yarn of Jacquard crochet. One is to carry the extra yarn behind the work. (If you use this method, be sure to carry all the yarns on one side, so that the finished article will have a right and wrong side.) This should be done for sweaters and other items where thickness is not an asset.

The second method is to work over the extra yarn, concealing it within the stitches as you go along, as shown in the drawings below. This provides a heavy, woven look and is excellent for purses, placemats, rugs, and other items where thickness is desired. Choose a design that has no more than four colors, as three threads is all the ExSC can adequately cover, and too many threads will make the finished piece too stiff and bulky.

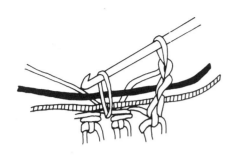

1. To insert and carry the additional colors in Jacquard crochet, hold the extra strands of yarn together and place them on top of the previous row of crocheting, leaving a 2″ tail of each color.

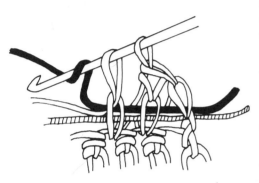

2. Work Extended Single Crochet stitches over these added strands. When you reach the last stitch in the first color, drop the yarn before the final yarn-over of the stitch, and bring up the second color instead. Working over all the other yarn, including the color just dropped, complete the stitch in the new color. (The final loop of a stitch always forms part of the next stitch.)

To determine whether a chosen design will fit within an assigned space, make a sample swatch with the yarns or thread you plan to use. Start with a foundation chain about 4″ (10cm) long. Work one row of ExSC. On the next row, work in the additional colors as shown above. Work ExSC over them. Continue this for 4 or 5 rows, being careful not to pull the carried yarns too tightly.

Count the number of stitches per inch in the swatch and multiply this by the width of the item to be made; the result is the number of squares available for the design. Count the number of squares across the design graph to see if they fall within this number.

For example, if your swatch has a gauge of 5 ExSC per inch, and the item to be made is to be 12″ square, your graphed design must have no more than 60 squares in its width or depth. If it has less than 60 squares, you can center the design and fill in around it with stitches worked in the background color, or with a multicolored border design, allowing 1 plain row for the foundation row. Mark the perimeter of your graphed design with the number of rows and foundation stitches that must be added to allow for the border or fill the background area.

If the number of squares available is too few to accommodate the design, a switch to finer yarn and a smaller hook may be the solution.

To work a design, make a foundation chain of 1 stitch more than the number of squares in the graphed pattern. Skip 2 chains and work ExSC in the next chain and in each chain across. (The turning chain represents a square on the graph.) Holding the thread as illustrated for carrying the yarn, always pull up the last loop of the stitch of the preceding color when you change to a new color. When the second stitch of the row is a color change, make the 2nd chain of the turning chain in the new color.

To adapt an ungraphed design, draw or trace the design onto the graph paper. Where the color lines go through a square, use the color that occupies the largest area of the square or the one which will give the best design line. Denote each color of the design with different marks such as dots, circles, or crosses. Mark the outside lines of the design and work as above.

Two designs for making Jacquard crochet shoulder bags are given here. Both are made from the same graphed pattern. Changing the color combinations and the placement of the design on the background makes them look quite different. In the first one, the design is shown in full on the front of the bag, and a duplicate piece is made for the back. In the other, a single rendition of the design is used, with added rows of plain color at top and bottom, so that the piece can be folded in half to make the small, tasseled, rectangular bag at the right.

·12″ × 12″ (30cm × 30cm)

The handwoven look of this over-the-shoulder bag is accomplished by working Extended Single Crochet in Jacquard Crochet technique.

Material: Rug or craft yarn; 180 yards (165M) of Color A; 60
  yards (55M) of Color B; 60 yards (55M) of Color C
  Button, toggle, or other closure

Hook size: I (UK, 5, Int'l 5.5)

Gauge: 3 ExSC equal 1″ (2.5cm)

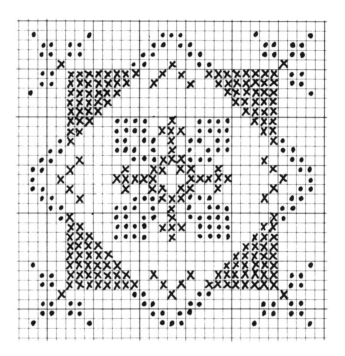

Front of the bag: Make a foundation chain of 34 stitches in Color A. Work an ExSC in the 3rd ch from the hook and in each ch across, making the last "yarn over and through . . ." of the last stitch in Color B. You will have a total of 33 stitches, including the turning chain. This is the base row. From here on continue in ExSC, following the graph for the color pattern. (When changing colors, always pull up the last loop of the stitch preceding the color change in the new color. If the color change is on the 2nd stitch of a row, make the 2nd chain of the turning chain in the new color.) Work the additional yarns into the stitches as described on page 210. Color A is represented by blank spaces, Color B by dots, and Color C by Xs. Make the last row using Color A.

Back of the bag: Make another side in the same way.

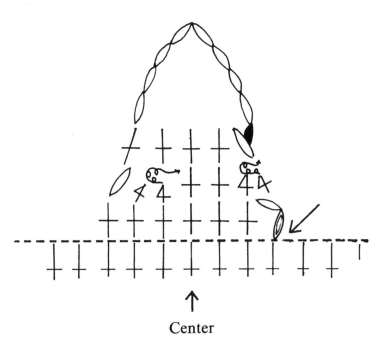

↑
Center

Flap: Count the stitches across the top of the back section to locate the center (the 17th) stitch. Attach yarn in Color A in the 5th stitch to the right of the middle stitch.

Row 1: Ch 2, work SC in each of next 6 sts, Ch 1, Turn.
Row 2: Pull Up thread in each of next 2 sts, YO and through 3 loops, SC in each of next 2 sts, Pull Up thread in each of next 2 sts, YO and through 3 loops on hook, Ch 1, Turn.
Row 3: SC in each of next 4 sts, Ch 8, Sl St in turning chain at end of row (makes closure loop), Tie Off firmly. Leave a 2″ "tail" and weave it back across last row to hide it.

Strap: The strap is a continuous piece which forms the boxed sides and bottom of .he bag. With Color A, make a loose foundation chain of 288 stitches. Work 4 rows of Single Crochet. Fold the strap in half to locate the center. Locate the bottom center of the purse front and mark it. With the right side out, pin the center points of strap and bag together, flat against each other. Fold the strap at right angles at the corners and pin in to the sides of the bag. (As it forms a boxed shape, it does not have to be eased.) With Color A, overcast the pieces together, pulling the overcasting snugly to form a corded effect, but not so tightly as to gather the pieces. Work several extra stitches at the top edge for strength. Sew the back section of the bag to the strap in the same way, making sure that the back corners meet the strap at points exactly opposite the front corners.

   Check the length of the strap, overlap the ends to the desired length, and sew them together. Fold the flap of the bag over to the front and mark it for button placement. Sew on a suitable button or other closure.

9″ × 12″ (22cm × 30cm)
The graphed design used for the box-shaped shoulder bag, done
in a different color combination and folded in half, makes an en-
velope bag with a braided strap.
Material: Rug or craft yarn: 120 yards (110M) of Color A, 60
    yards (55M) of Color B, and 60 yards (55M) of Color C.
Hook size: I (UK 5, Int'l 5.5)
Gauge: 3 ExSC equal 1″ (2.5cm)

Bag: Make a foundation chain of 34 stitches in Color A, work
ExSC in 3rd chain from the hook and in each chain across, Ch 2,
Turn. Holding the yarns of Color B and Color C together over the
completed row, work 4 more rows of ExSc around the 2 strands.
On the last row, Pull Up the last loop of the last stitch in Color B.
Continue to work, following the graph for color changes. (Al-
though the first five rows are done in only one color, Colors B and
C are worked into the stitches from Row 2 onward to give a
firmer, more even body to the bag.) In the graph, Color A is rep-
resented by blank spaces, Color B by dots, and Color C by Xs.
When the design is completed, continue to hold the strands of
Colors B and C inside the stitches, work 4 rows in Color A, drop
B and C, and make 1 more row of ExSC. Cut the yarn and weave
the ends back into the stitches.

Flap: Follow the directions for the flap of the box-shaped shoulder
bag.

Strap: Measure off the remaining yarn into 112″ (280cm) lengths.
Hold the strands together and tie an overhand knot about 4″
(10cm) from end of bundle. (The loose ends will form a tassel.)
Divide the yarn into 3 equal groups and braid them together to a
length of approximately 60″ (150cm). Tie another overhand knot,
leaving 4″ of loose ends to form another tassel before trimming
off the thread. Fold the bag in half and pin the braid along the
sides so that the knot falls just below the folded edge. Overcast the
braid to the bag catching one group of strands in each overcast
stitch, alternating between the three groups as you sew the back
and front of the bag together. Make several extra stitches at the
beginning and end for strength. Being careful not to twist the
braid, attach it to the other side in the same way. (If the braid
strap stretches with use, tie a knot in the middle to shorten it.)
Fold the flap over to the front of the bag. Mark the position of the
tassel or button and sew it on.

Braid

Chapter 7

Afghan Squares and Triangles

Symbol crochet is especially helpful in following the patterns for motifs such as the classic Granny and the popular Crusader's Cross as well as the new right-angle triangles included in this chapter. Only a few motifs are given here, for this is primarily a book of pattern stitches. Motifs are worthy of a book in themselves and indeed there have been many books about them, but a right-angle triangle that forms an integral design (rather than being just half of a square design) is an innovation and deserving of space in this book.

Most crocheters are aware of the unlimited number of design arrangements that can be achieved with the Granny by using extensive color variation and placement and employing odd bits of leftover yarn.

The Crusader's Cross, done in stained-glass colors for the centers and black for the borders, seems to glow like a cathedral window. An equally striking effect can be achieved with many two or three color combinations. Shades of blue with white produce an extremely attractive Delft effect for an afghan of four-ply yarn or a table runner made of cotton thread.

Right-angle triangles can be adapted in unlimited arrangements, especially for Indian or primitive effects. They can also be used in combination with the Granny by working the number of rows necessary to have approximately the same number of stitches along the sides of the Granny as on the long side of the triangle. For designs in Incan or Mayan styles, combine primary and secondary colors with black, or use a combination of earth colors.

A color design exercise for beginners: Take two squares of different-colored paper and fold them corner to corner twice. Unfold them and cut along the fold to make four right-angle triangles each. Arrange these triangles in as many ways as possible. Add uncut squares the same size as your original square and continue arranging and rearranging them. Cut another square into eight right-angle triangles and continue to experiment. Use these original color arrangements for anything you care to make.

While most motifs, whether they are square, round, or hexagonal, are worked from one side, in continuous *rounds,* the right-angle triangle designs given in this book are worked in *rows* and *must* be turned at the end of each row. In the symbol diagrams for each pattern, arrows indicate the direction of the row.

The functions of these motifs are many. They can be used singly, as decorations to be applied to clothing or other articles, or joined together to make placemats, runners, afghans, wall hangings, ponchos, purses, tote bags, pillows, vests, loose jackets, skirts, halters, hats, baby wear—whatever your imagination suggests.

Indian Afghan (*Plate 13*)

38″ × 78″ (97cm × 198cm)

This assembly of triangles in earth colors is inspired by the geometric designs of the Indians of the American Southwest. This right-angle triangle, a new design in Granny crochet, is worked in concentric rounds.

Material: Four-ply (knitting worsted) in four colors as follows: 4 ounces (114 grams) of Color A (rust); 8 ounces (240 grams) of Color B (off-white); 8 ounces (240 grams) of Color C (dark brown); 4 ounces (114 grams) of Color D (tan)

Hook size: H (UK 6, Int'l 5)

Gauge: 3 HDC equal 1″ (2.5cm)

1. Make 6 triangles following the pattern for the Half Double Crochet Right-Angle Triangle (Pattern #4 in this chapter) in the following sequence: Color A, 3 rows; Color B, 3 rows; Color C, 2 rows; Color D, 2 rows; Color A, 1 row.

2. Make 4 triangles, also in Pattern #4, as follows: Color C, 4 rows; Color B, 3 rows; Color A, 1 row.

Assemble the afghan as shown in the diagram, overcasting the pieces together. Attach yarn at one corner, Ch 1, and work rows of Single Crochet along the sides (but not the ends) of the afghan as follows: Color C, 3 rows; Color B, 6 rows. Ch 1 and make a SC border around the entire piece with Color C, working 1 SC in each stitch along the sides and ends and 3 SC at each corner. Sl St to the beginning ch 1, Tie Off the yarn and block the afghan.

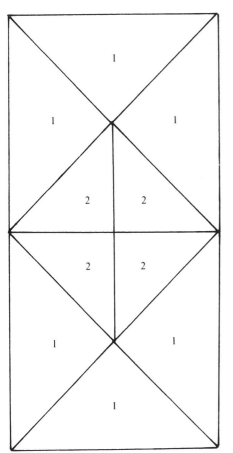

1 / Classic Granny

Ch 6, Sl St to first ch to form ring. Ch 2, and into ring work:

Round 1: 2 DC, Ch 3, 3 DC, Ch 3, 3 DC, Ch 3, 3 DC, Ch 3, Sl St to 2nd ch, Ch 2. Do not turn.

Round 2: Work (3 DC, Ch 3, 3 DC) under each ch 3 around, ending with only 2 DC, Sl St to 2nd ch. Ch 2.

Round 3: Work 2 DC between beginning ch and first dc.
* Work (3 DC, Ch 3, 3 DC) under next ch 3, work 3 DC between next groups of 3 dc. Repeat from * around ending with (3 DC, Ch 3, 3 DC) under ch 3, Sl St into 2nd ch, Ch 2.

Round 4: Work 3 DC between 2 dc, 3 dc. * Work (3 DC, Ch 3, 3 DC) under ch 3, work 3 DC between each 3 dc group across. Repeat from * across, ending with only 2 DC, Sl St to 2nd ch at beginning, Ch 2.

Repeat Rounds 3 and 4 until desired size is reached.

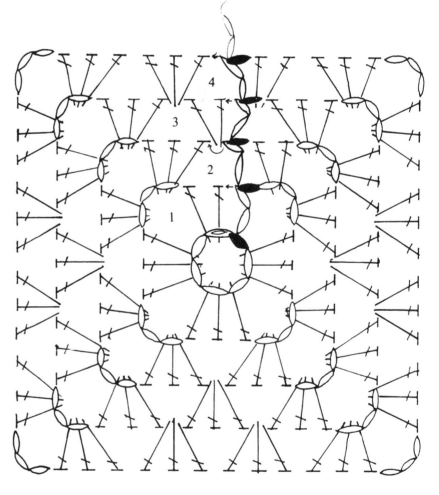

2 / Crusader's Cross

Ch 9, Sl St to first ch to form ring.

Round 1: Work 3 SC, Ch 1, 3 SC, Ch
1, 3 SC, Ch 1, 3 SC into
ring. Ch 1, Sl St in front
loop of first sc, Ch 2. Do
not turn.

In ALL the remaining stitches (SC, DC, and Chs), work in back loop of stitch.

Round 2: DC in each of next 2 sc.
* Ch 5, DC in each of next
3 sc. Repeat from * around,
Ch 5, Sl St into 2nd ch of
beginning ch, Ch 2.

Round 3: DC in each of next 2 dc, DC
in next ch, Ch 7. * Skip 3
chs, DC in each of next (ch,
3 dc and ch), Ch 7. Repeat
from * around, ending with
Skip 3 chs, DC in next ch,
Sl St to 2nd ch of beginning
ch, Ch 2.

Round 4: DC in each of next 3 dc
and next 3 chs, work (DC,
Ch 3, DC) in next ch. * DC
in each of next (3 chs, 5 dc,
3 chs), work (DC, Ch 3,
DC) in next ch. Repeat
from * around, ending with
DC in each of last 3 chs
and in dc, Sl St to 2nd ch
of beginning ch.

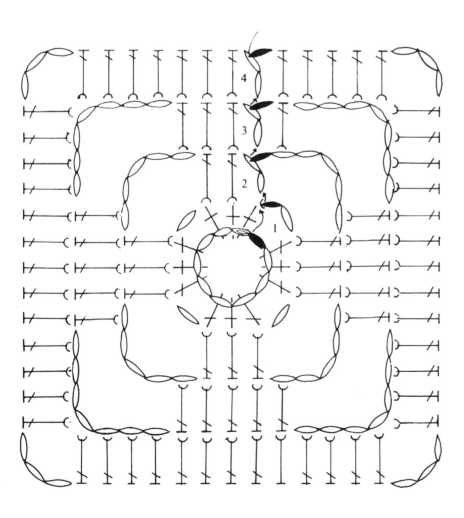

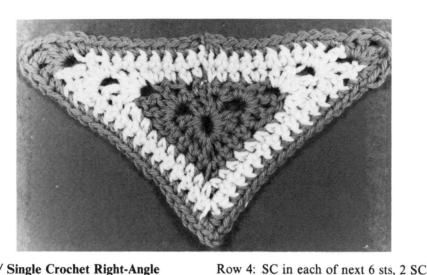

Ch 2, TC, DC) under ch 2,
(HDC, SC) in next st. SC in
each of next 15 sts, work (2
SC, Ch 2, 2 SC) under ch 2,
SC in each of next 15 sts.
Work (SC, HDC) in next st,
(DC, TC, Ch 2, DC, HDC)
under ch 2, 2 SC in next st,
SC in each of next 9 sts, Sl St
to first ch to join, Ch 1, Turn.
For a larger triangle, continue work-
ing in same manner as Rows 3, 4, and
5. On the last row, Ch 3 at corners
next to long side.

3 / Single Crochet Right-Angle Triangle

Ch 4, Sl St to first ch to form ring, Ch
1.

Row 1: Work (HDC, Ch 2, DC,
HDC, 2 SC, Ch 2, 2 SC,
HDC, DC, Ch 2, HDC) into
ring. Sl St to ch to join, Ch 1,
Turn.

Row 2: Work 2 SC in next st, (HDC,
DC, Ch 2, TC, DC) under ch
2. Work (HDC, SC) in next
st, SC in each of next 3 sts.
Work (SC, Ch 2, SC) under
ch 2, SC in each of next 3 sts.
Work (SC, HDC) in next st,
(DC, TC, Ch 2, DC, HDC)
under ch 2, 2 SC in next st, Sl
St to beginning ch to join, Ch
1, Turn.

Row 3: SC in each of next 3 sts, work
2 SC in next st, (HDC, DC,
Ch 2, TC, DC) under ch 2.
(HDC, SC) in next st, SC in
each of next 7 sts. Work (SC,
Ch 2, SC) under ch 2. SC in
each of next 7 sts, (SC, HDC)
in next st. Work (DC, TC, Ch
2, DC, HDC) under ch 2, 2
SC in next st, SC in each of
next 3 sts, Sl St to beginning
ch to join, Ch 1, Turn.

Row 4: SC in each of next 6 sts, 2 SC
in next st. Work (HDC, DC,
Ch 2, TC, DC) under ch 2,
(HDC, SC) in next st. SC in
each of next 11 sts, (SC, Ch 2,
SC) under ch 2, SC in each of
next 11 sts, (SC, HDC) in
next st. (DC, TC, Ch 2, DC,
HDC) under ch 2, 2 SC in
next st, SC in each of next 6
sts, Sl St to beginning ch to
join, Ch 1, Turn.

Row 5: SC in each of next 9 sts, 2 SC
in next st, Work (HDC, DC,

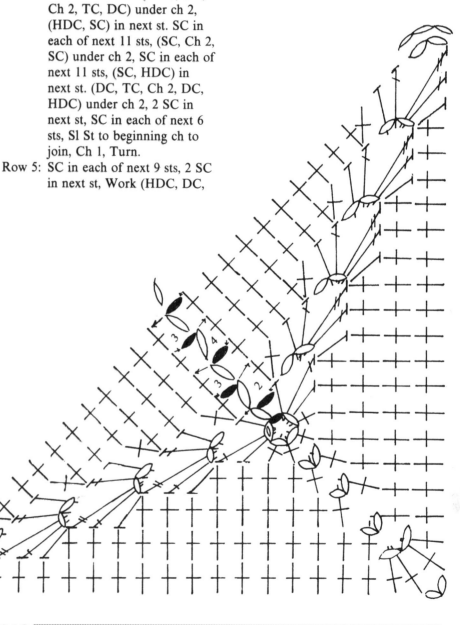

4 / Half Double Crochet Right-Angle Triangle

Ch 4, Sl St to first ch to join, Ch 2.

Row 1: Into ring, work (HDC, DC, Ch 2, TC, DC, 3 HDC, Ch 2, 3 HDC, DC, TC, Ch 2, DC, HDC). Sl St to 2nd ch to join, Ch 2, Turn.

Row 2: HDC in next st, (HDC, DC) in next st. (DC, TC, Ch 2, DTC, TC) under ch 2, 2 DC in next st, 2 HDC in next st,

HDC in next 3 sts. (HDC, Ch 2, HDC) under ch 2, HDC in next 3 sts, 2 HDC in next st, 2 DC in next st. (TC, DTC, Ch 2, TC, DC) under ch 2, (DC, HDC) in next st, HDC in next st, Sl St in 2nd ch of beginning ch to join, Ch 2. Turn.

Row 3: HDC in next 3 sts, 2 HDC in next st, (HDC, DC) in next st, work (DC, TC, Ch 2, DTC, TC) under ch 2. (DC, HDC) in next st, 2 HDC in next st,

HDC in next 8 sts. (2 HDC, Ch 2, 2 HDC) under ch 2, HDC in next 8 sts, 2 HDC in next st, (HDC, DC) in next st. Work (TC, DTC, Ch 2, TC, DC) under ch 2. (DC, HDC) in next st, 2 HDC in next st, HDC in next 3 sts. Sl St to 2nd ch of beginning ch to join, Ch 2, Turn.

Row 4: HDC in next 7 sts, 2 HDC in next st, (HDC, DC) in next st. Work (DC, TC, Ch 2, DTC, TC) under ch 2, (DC, HDC) in next st, 2 HDC in next st, HDC in next 14 sts. Work (HDC, Ch 2, HDC) under ch 2. HDC in next 14 sts, 2 HDC in next st, (HDC, DC) in next st. Work (TC, DTC, Ch 2, TC, DC) under ch 2. (DC, HDC) in next st, 2 HDC in next st, HDC in next 7 sts. Sl St to 2nd ch of beginning ch to join, Ch 2, Turn.

For a larger triangle, continue working rows in the same manner as Rows 3 and 4.

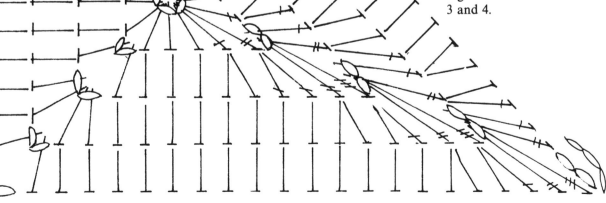

DC in each of next 10 sts, work (2 DC, Ch 1, 2 DC) under next ch, DC in each of next 10 sts, 2 DC in each of next 2 sts, (TC, DTC, TTC, Ch 2, TTC, DTC, TC) under ch 2. Work 2 DC in next st, DC in each of next 5 sts, Sl St to 2nd ch of beginning ch, Ch 2, Turn.

For a larger triangle, repeat Row 3, increasing 8 sts per row on long side and 6 sts per row on short sides. On last row, Ch 3 at corners next to long sides.

5 / Double Crochet Right-Angle Triangle

Ch 6, Sl St to first ch to form ring, Ch 2.

Row 1: Work into ring (2 DC, TC, Ch 2, TC, 4 DC, Ch 1, 4 DC, TC, Ch 2, TC, DC). Sl St to beginning ch to join, Ch 2, Turn.

Row 2: DC in next st, 2 DC in next st, work (TC, DTC, TTC, Ch 2, TTC, DTC, TC) under ch 2. Work 2 DC in each of next 2 sts, DC in each of next 3 sts, (2 DC, Ch 1, 2 DC) under next ch. Work DC in each of next 3 sts, 2 DC in each of next 2 sts, work (TC, DTC, TTC, Ch 2, TTC, DTC, TC) under ch 2. Work 2 DC in next st, DC in each of next 2 sts, Sl St to 2nd ch of beginning ch to join, Ch 2. (You will have 12 sts on the short

sides, and 14 sts, including turning chain, on the long side.)

Row 3: Work DC in each of next 6 sts, 2 DC in next st. Work (TC, DTC, TTC, Ch 2, TTC, DTC, TC) under ch 2. Work 2 DC in each of next 2 sts,

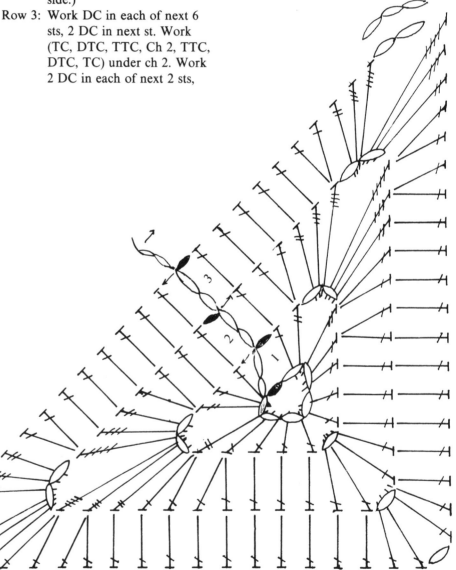

6 / Double Crochet Filet Right-Angle Triangle

Ch 6, Sl St to beginning ch to form ring, Ch 3.

Row 1: Work into ring (DC, Ch 1, TC, Ch 2, TC, Ch 1, DC, Ch 1, DC, Ch 1, DC, Ch 1, DC, Ch 1, TC, Ch 2, TC, Ch 1), Sl St under ch 3, Ch 3, Turn.

Row 2: (DC, Ch 1, DC) under next ch, Ch 1, (TC, Ch 1, DTC, Ch 2, TTC, Ch 1, DTC, Ch 1) under ch 2. (TC, Ch 1, DC) under next ch, Ch 1, DC under next ch, Ch 1, (DC, Ch 2, DC) under next ch, Ch 1, DC under next ch, Ch 1. (DC, Ch 1, TC), under next ch, Ch 1. (DTC, Ch 1, TTC, Ch 2, DTC, Ch 1, TC) under ch 2. Ch 1, DC under next ch, Ch 1, Sl St under ch 3, Ch 3, Turn.

Row 3: (DC, Ch 1) under each of next 2 chs. (DC, Ch 1, DC, Ch 1) under next ch. Work (TC, Ch 1, DTC, Ch 2, TTC, Ch 1, DTC, Ch 1) under ch 2. (TC, Ch 1, DC) under next ch, (Ch 1, DC) under each of next 4 chs, Ch 1. (DC, Ch 1, DC, Ch 1, DC, Ch 1, DC, Ch 1) under ch 2, (DC, Ch 1) under each of next 4 chs. (DC, Ch 1, TC) under next ch, Ch 1. (DTC, Ch 1, TTC, Ch 2, DTC, Ch 1, TC, Ch 1) under ch 2, (DC, Ch 1) under each of next 3 chs, Sl St under ch 3, Ch 3, Turn.

Row 4: (DC, Ch 1) under each of next 4 chs, (DC, Ch 1, DC) under next ch, Ch 1. (TC, Ch 1, DTC, Ch 2, TTC, Ch 1, DTC, Ch 1) under ch 2. (TC, Ch 1, DC) under next ch, Ch 1. (DC, Ch 1) under each of next 8 sts, (DC, Ch 2, DC) under next ch, Ch 1, (DC, Ch 1) under each of next 8 chs, (DC, Ch 1, TC) under next ch, Ch 1, (DTC, Ch 1, TTC, Ch 2, DTC, Ch 1, TC) under ch 2. Ch 1, (DC, Ch 1, DC) under next ch, Ch 1. (DC, Ch 1) under each of next 4 chs, Sl St under ch 3, Ch 3, Turn.

Continue as in Row 4, *except* work (DC, Ch 1, DC, Ch 2, DC, Ch 1, DC, Ch 1) as in Row 3, at right angle on every other row. Work 3 chs at corners on last row.

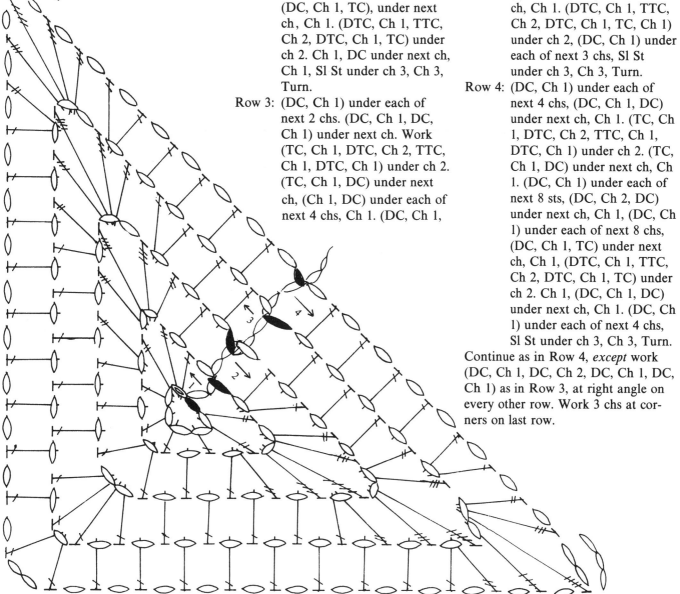

Chapter 8

Crochet (Tambour) Embroidery ▦

For centuries people have been decorating fabric with embroidery. Many techniques have been used. One of these is tambour embroidery in which a hook is used to pull loops of thread up from the back of the fabric, rather than carrying it through from the surface in the eye of a needle as is done in most other forms of embroidery. The result closely resembles the familiar chain stitch of surface embroidery. Many light cotton garments imported from the Middle East are worked in this manner. So are rugs and pillows from India, done with woolen yarns on sturdy fabrics. Early in the nineteenth century, much tambour embroidery was done in fine threads on net, imitating the patterns of handmade lace. Tambour embroidery is usually done with special hooks made for the purpose, but the same results can be achieved with a steel crochet hook. You will find that, with a little practice, crochet embroidery produces beautiful effects swiftly and easily. It can be done following a predrawn pattern or to create free-form designs directly on the fabric.

The choice of fabrics to use as a ground is wide—anything with a weave open enough to admit the passage of the hook without breaking the threads will do. Choose a hook suitable for the thread or yarn you have selected, and try working along the selvedge of the fabric to see if it can be worked. Silk organza, linen, gingham, and woolen homespun are all cloths that are possible backgrounds for crochet embroidery. All-over designs can be done on needlepoint canvas. A fabric of plain crochet could be decorated with figures or geometric designs embroidered with this crocheted chain stitch. A wedding veil or lace cloth might be given added embroidery in silk thread or fine perle cotton. Nylon net is a good fabric for crochet embroidery; illusion veiling is too thin and fragile to handle satisfactorily.

To hold the fabric firm while you are working, embroidery hoops or a tambour frame should be used. Avoid wooden hoops if possible, for any unseen rough edges will catch the threads. If you must use a wooden hoop, cut pieces of soft fabric (such as muslin or flannel) and cover both rings before inserting the embroidery fabric.

Step-by-step instructions for doing crochet embroidery follow. As you proceed, there are several important things to remember that will smooth your progress. Always use a tight embroidery hoop to hold the fabric taut. Choose the smallest hook possible that will still pull the thread through the fabric without splitting the thread. *Keep the stitches loose.* This is the most difficult part of crochet embroidery, but the problem can be solved by always pulling up a loop slightly larger than the stitch you plan to make.

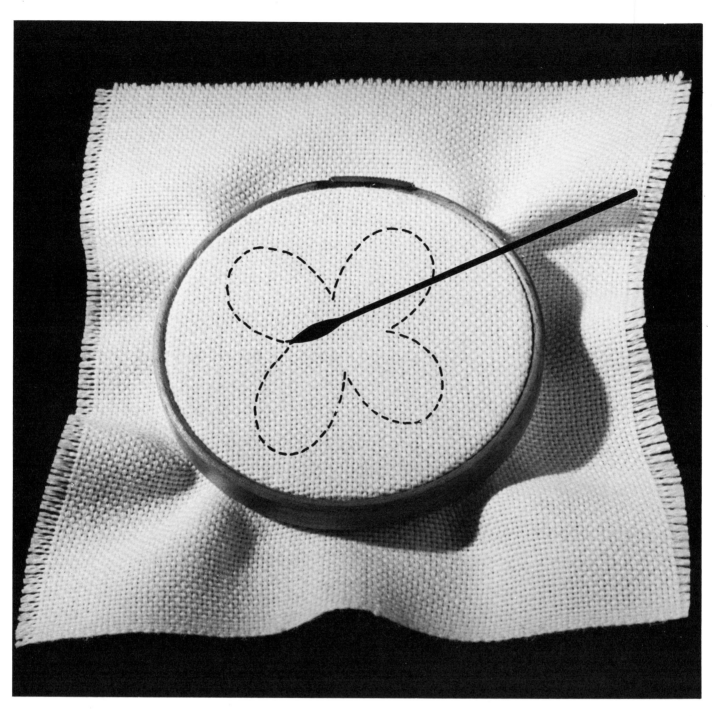

Draw the outlines of the design on the fabric. Place a section of it in the hoop.

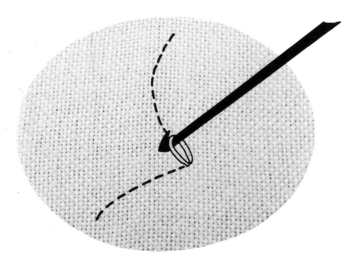

1. With the fabric held taut, start at one side of the design, inserting the hook until its widest part is reached. At the back of the fabric, loop the thread over the hook, leaving a 4″ (10cm) tail.

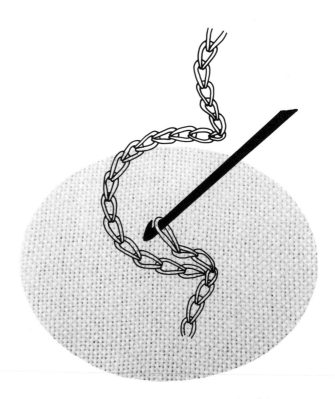

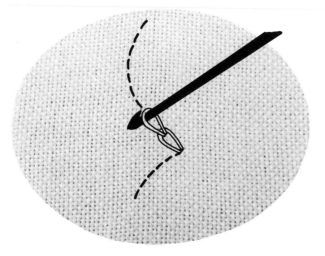

2. Pull the loop through to the front of the fabric. To avoid puckering, keep the loop slightly longer than the stitch to be made. Holding the loop on the hook, insert the hook in the fabric again. Hold the thread against the back of the fabric and engage the thread in the hook.

3. Pull the thread up through the fabric and the first loop, making a chain stitch. Continue around the outline of the design, making all the stitches approximately the same length.

4. To turn a corner in the design, make smaller stitches. To fill in a motif or make an all-over design, work rows of stitches close together.

When the design is completed, disengage the hook. Insert it through the fabric from the back and pull the last loop through to the underside. Cut off the thread, leaving a tail long enough to bring it through the loop and tie it off.

   To secure the tail of thread at the *beginning* of the work, wrap it around the hook, draw it through the back of the first stitch, and make a knot. (If you are introducing a second thread close to your original starting point, the two tails can be tied together instead.)

Crochet-Embroidered Pillow (*Plate 2*)

14″ × 14″ (35cm × 35cm)

Easily and quickly made with four-ply yarn, these pillows make elegant gifts. Both are made from the same pattern, one worked in outline only and the other with the motifs filled in.

Material—for 2 pillows: ½ yard (½ M) embroidery linen; 2 ounces (60 grams) of four-ply yarn (knitting worsted); 1 yard (1M) of fabric for the backs (corduroy, velvet, etc.). Each pillow top takes an 18″ × 18″ (45cm × 45cm) square of linen.

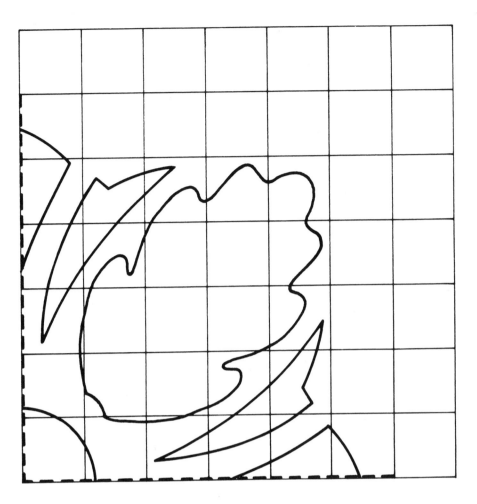

Hook size: Steel #6 (UK 2, Int'l 1.75), or the smallest size possible to draw the yarn through the linen without splitting it.

Gauge: Approximately 4 chains equal 1″ (2.5cm), with smaller chains for the corners.

Enlarge the pattern on dressmakers' graph paper with a 1″ grid. Machine stitch or tape the edges of the linen to prevent raveling. Make trial stitches on a small piece of linen or along the seam edges to find the right tension and hook size. Tight stitches will make your design look puckered. Start with the outside lines and work toward the center, going around and around without breaking the yarn. For the pillow with the design in outline only, work 2 full rows of stitches on each section of the design.

Block the embroidery by laying the piece face down on a bath towel and pressing it gently with a steam iron. Make the pillow backs. These two pillows are bound with corded piping. If you are backing both pillows with the same fabric, cut the pieces from opposite corners of the fabric, leaving a diagonal center strip that can be bias cut to make the piping.

Rainbow Skirt (*Plate 11*)

The embroidery on this skirt takes only a few hours to complete.
Material: A flared skirt made with an open-weave but firm fabric such as linen or hardanger. The skirt should be approximately 62″ wide at the bottom to accommodate the design. If a gathered skirt is preferred, draw the base line straight across instead of curved and relocate the inner half circles on the base.

Perle cotton #3 in following colors: 15 yards (14 M) each of red, orange, yellow, medium green, blue, and purple for the rainbow and flowers, 15 yards of dark green for the half circles, and 30 yards of light green for the base. See Plate 11 for the color sequence.

Hook size: Steel #7 (UK 2¼, Int'l 1.5)
Gauge: 9 chains equal 1″ (2.5cm)

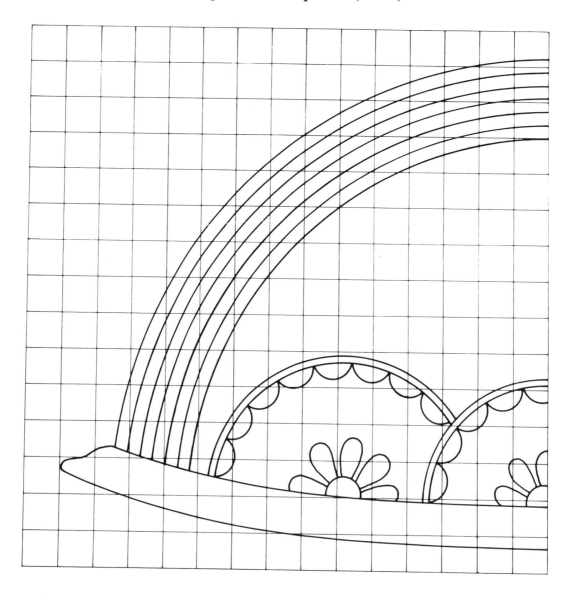

Enlarge the design on 1″ grid dressmakers' graph paper and transfer it to the skirt with dressmakers' carbon paper in the lightest color that can be easily followed. Make balls of the thread if it comes in skeins. Make test stitches on a scrap of fabric to achieve proper tension and chain length. Fill in the areas of the design solidly. Date and initial the design with embroidery stitches. Block the embroidery by placing it face down on a bath towel and steaming it with an iron. When you tire of wearing the skirt, the embroidered section will make a beautiful pillow, wallhanging, or appliquéd center for a child's quilt.

Silkmoth Shawl (*Plate 10*)

The motif for this lined shawl was worked on a separate length of the silk and then appliquéd on because embroidery hoops leave marks on sheer fabrics. If the design is worked directly onto a heavier fabric and unlined you will need only two thirds the yardage.

Material: Shawl: 3½ yards (3M) of 45″ silk chiffon

    Embroidery: Perle cotton #5 as follows: 60 yards (54M) of blue; 44 yards (40M) of light green; 35 yards (32M) of orange; 30 yards (27M) of dark pink; 40 yards (36M) of black (for outlines)

    Fringe: 600 yards (540M) of black bedspread-weight cotton

Hook size: Steel #10 (UK 4, Int'l 1)

Gauge: 5 chains equal 1″ (2.5cm)

The patterns show only one half of the shawl and of the design.

Transfer the patterns of 1″ grid dressmakers' graph paper, duplicating the outlines in reverse to make full patterns of both design and shawl. Fold the chiffon in half crosswise. Pin the selvedges together to prevent slippage. Place the shawl pattern as near as possible to the selvedge at the top and the cut edge at the side and cut out shawl and lining from the doubled fabric.

Fold the embroidery pattern in half along the dotted line and center it on the fold of the fabric, making sure there is at least 2″ of extra fabric around the design. Do *not* cut it out. Open out fabric and pattern and transfer the design to the silk with dressmakers' carbon paper. Work sample stitches on a scrap of the chiffon to attain the proper tension and chain length. Be sure your embroidery hoops have no rough edges to tear the silk. (It is wise to wrap the bottom half of wooden hoops with a strip of bias cut fabric before inserting delicate fabrics.)

If the perle cotton is in skeins, roll it into balls. Work all the black lines first, then fill in with the colors.

Place the finished embroidery face down on a bath towel. Press it gently with an iron that is as cool as possible yet still able to produce steam. Leaving 1″ around the edges of the motif, cut away extra fabric and carefully press in a hem along the black outline, clipping inside curves as necessary. Pin the embroidery onto the shawl and blind-stitch it in place. With the embroidered design inside, machine stitch the shawl and lining together, leaving 4 or 5″ of unsewn seam. Clip the neck curve every 1″, trim the corners and turn the shawl right side out. Turn in and stitch the edges of the opening. Carefully press the shawl along the edges.

Starting at the corner, work blanket stitch along the curved edge with black perle cotton, making stitches ¼″ apart. Attach crochet cotton at the corner and work Ch 2, SC under the first blanket stitch. * Ch 2, SC under the next blanket stitch. Repeat from * across around the edge of the shawl. Tie off the yarn. Take 10″ strands of bedspread cotton in groups of 6 and fold and attach them under the ch 2 of the crocheted edge to make a fringe. Add a button and loop to the neck front if desired.

If you have used a very smooth fabric to make the shawl, the heavy fringe may tend to pull it backwards off the shoulders. To hold it in place, insert small drapery weights or metal washers covered with single crochet inside the shawl, catch-stitching them to the bottom corners, or tie matching beads in the fringe at the front.

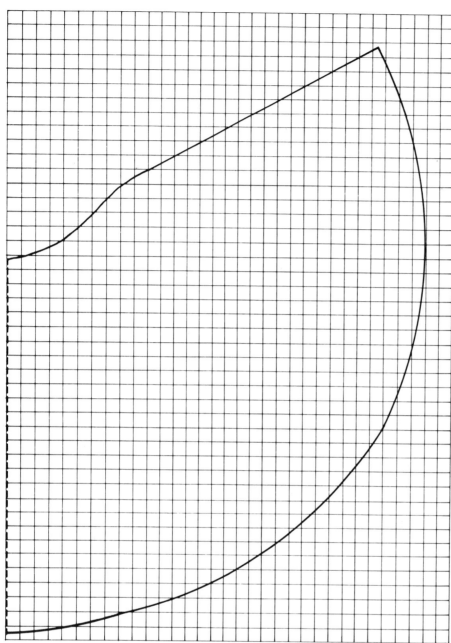

Shawl pattern. Each square = 1″ (2.5cm).

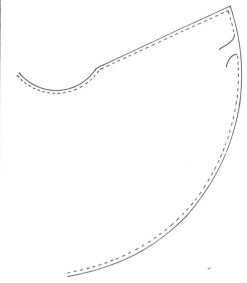

Right sides together, stitch the lining to the shawl.

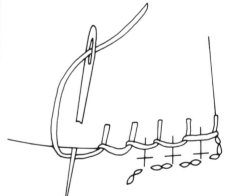

Add a border of blanket stitch and single crochet.

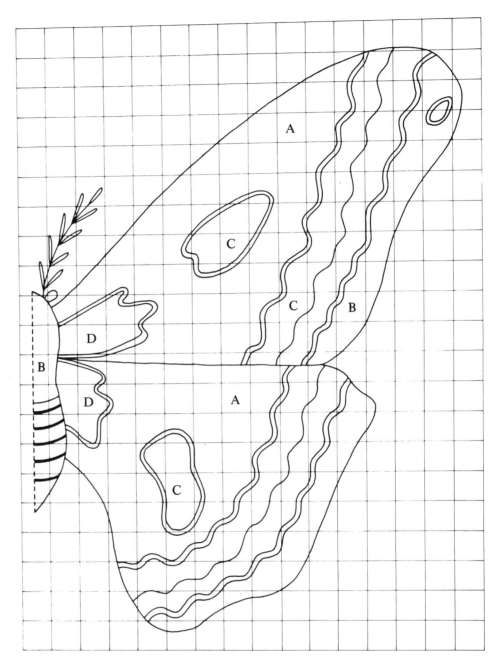

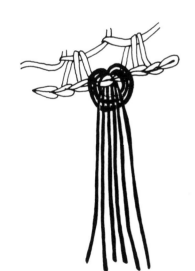

Attach fringe to the crocheted border.

Motif pattern. Each square = 1″
(2.5cm) = 5 chains.
A = blue
B = light green
C = orange
D = dark pink

Jerusalem Wall-Hanging (*Plate 12*)

A picture found in a fifteenth-century Serbian manuscript inspired this easily worked design.

Material: A rectangle 45″ × 32″ (112cm × 80cm) of embroidery
linen, hardanger, lino, or other open weave fabric. Also, crewel
wool or Persian yarn in 3-strand skeins as follows: 80 yards
(72M) *each* of A (gold), B (orange), C (turquoise), and white
(for the unmarked areas of the motif); and 60 yards (54M) of

black for all the black lines and black areas in the design. *Do not cut the yarn in lengths.* If you are using single strand skeins, triple the amounts. Finally, one 45″ × 62″ (112cm × 154cm) length of velvet (for backing) and two 45″-wide rods.

Hook size: Steel #9 (UK 3½, Int'l 10), or the smallest size hook that will not split the yarn as it is worked

Gauge: 6 chains equal 1″ (2.5cm)

Each square in the graphed pattern represents 1″ (2.5cm). With dressmakers' 1″-grid graph paper, enlarge the design and transfer it onto the fabric, placing it in the position in the assembly diagram. Be sure to line up the design with the grain of the fabric. Test the stitches on a scrap of the fabric or along the edge to achieve the proper tension.

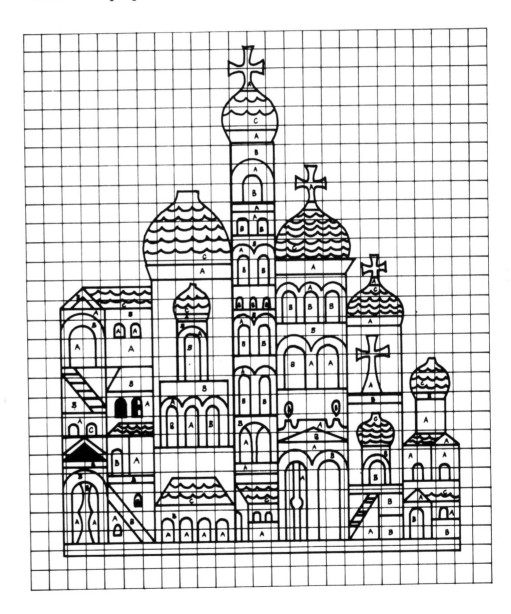

Work all the black outlines first. Fill in the colors as designated in the pattern. Or just fill in selected areas and let the background show through here and there as part of the design—you will still have a handsome wall hanging. Frame the design in a border outline of black crochet embroidery as shown in the diagram. Sign and date the piece in small crochet embroidery stitches done with a very find thread and hook, or in outline stitches made with an embroidery needle. Iron the embroidery, face down on a bath towel, steaming it well to ease the yarn and stretch out any puckering.

In the example, the velvet backing forms a broad mat around the embroidery. Blind stitch the side hems of the velvet and make rod casings at top and bottom. Turn under the edges of the embroidery along the border outline. Pin it to the velvet, blind stitch it in place, and insert rods in the casings.

If you prefer to frame the hanging or attach it to an artist's stretcher, plan the location of the border outline accordingly and work it with 2 or 3 strands of yarn.

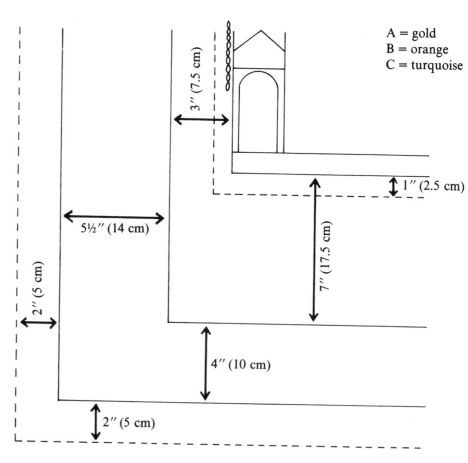

A = gold
B = orange
C = turquoise

3″ (7.5 cm)

1″ (2.5 cm)

5½″ (14 cm)

7″ (17.5 cm)

2″ (5 cm)

4″ (10 cm)

2″ (5 cm)

Each square = 1″ = 6 chains

Index